CALCULATING VISIONS

MARK STERN

Calculating Visions

Kennedy, Johnson, and Civil Rights

RUTGERS UNIVERSITY PRESS
New Brunswick, New Jersey

Library of Congress Cataloging-in-Publication Data

Stern, Mark, 1945–
    Calculating visions : Kennedy, Johnson, and civil rights / Mark
Stern.
        p.   cm. — (Perspectives on the sixties)
    Includes bibliographical references and index.
    ISBN 0-8135-1743-5 (cloth) — ISBN 0-8135-1744-3 (pbk.)
    1. Afro-Americans—Civil rights.   2. Civil rights movements—
United States—History—20th century.   3.   Kennedy, John F. (John
Fitzgerald), 1917–1963.   4. Johnson, Lyndon B. (Lyndon Baines),
1908–1973.   5. United States—Politics and government—1961–1963.
6. United States—Poltics and government—1963–1969.   I. Title.
II. Series.
E841.S75   1991
323.1′196073–dc20   91-16802
                                                                                  CIP

British Cataloging-in-Publication information available.

To Barbara, Ben, and Jeff

CONTENTS

LIST OF ILLUSTRATIONS IN THE GALLERY

PREFACE

THIS STUDY is the result of both my own efforts and the advice, criticism, and help of many other individuals. I began this project seven years ago after completing a series of papers on the growth of the southern black vote and the factors that influenced changes in congressional roll-call voting on civil rights issues. Those papers were quantitative. Yet, when I turned my attention to the question of why the major changes in civil rights legislation occurred in the 1960s, I knew that using a quantitative methodology could not help to answer the questions I was grappling with. In fact, when I examined the quantitative studies, what struck me was that they did not predict or explain the civil rights revolution of the 1960s, nor the sea change in black voter enrollment that followed from the Voting Rights Act of 1965.

My focus is on John F. Kennedy and Lyndon B. Johnson as major actors in the civil rights struggles that occurred during their presidential administrations. To anyone who studies the civil rights revolution of the post–World War II era, it is obvious that a great many individuals made contributions to the civil rights struggle, both at the local and the national levels. The civil rights movement was a mass movement: without the women of Montgomery, Alabama, who walked to work and the men who volunteered their cars to serve as taxis rather than patronize the segregated bus system, or the thousands of black citizens who put their houses up as bond for students who were arrested for participating in the movement, as well as the hundreds of thousands of others who moved the movement, it could not have happened. The major black leaders played a critical role, as did their white allies, but it took a massive outpouring of effort for it all to be effective. The term black Americans or blacks is used throughout this study, rather than African-Americans, in conformity with the usage employed in the 1960s, the era on which this study focuses. The focus of this study is on how the actions of the black and white masses, the black leaders and their white allies, and the white southern leaders and their followers moved Kennedy and Johnson, each in his own manner, to grapple with civil rights.

In the summer of 1984 I visited the John F. Kennedy Presidential Library, and I spent the following years (between teaching classes and, subsequently, directing the University Honors Program) exploring the archive collections of black and white leaders and organizations involved in the civil rights struggles. I would like to thank the staffs of the various libraries and archives I visited. They were unfailingly courteous and often went beyond the call of duty to help me understand the various cataloging systems and to retrieve materials. August Meier's NEH seminar on the history of the civil rights movement opened up to me new understandings about the black organizations and the black leadership, and it provided me with new directions for the pursuit of sources. I am pleased to know August Meier as a valued critic and friend.

Many individuals gave freely of their time in oral history interviews that helped me understand what happened during this era. In the main, the oral histories are used to fill in answers and provide a firsthand report of events only when two or more individuals involved in a given incident provided corroborative accounts. I owe a special debt of gratitude to Joseph L. Rauh, Jr., who permitted me to interview him repeatedly and who led me to other sources as new questions arose during the research process. I also wish to thank George E. Reedy and Herbert Brownell, who generously gave of their time to me. Mr. Reedy read the manuscript in its entirety and provided me with a runing commentary on the actors and events.

The University of Central Florida helped provide support for a sabbatical year during which I traveled to research collections, and the university continued its support until the project was completed. The Southern Regional Education Board repeatedly supported my travels to archives and to interviews. I also received support for this project from the National Endowment for the Humanities and the Lyndon Baines Johnson Foundation.

I have been lucky enough to have colleagues who truly meas-

ure up to the ideals of academe in terms of the time and guidance they have provided me as I worked on this study. Many of
these individuals became friends with me after reading one of
my papers, exchanging comments at a meeting, or responding
to queries. Sometimes they helped me to correct errors of fact,
and other times they posed alternative interpretations of
events. They often guided me to the next stage of the research
puzzle. All I can offer to them in return is a sincere thank-you.
Errors of fact or interpretation that remain in this book are, of
course, solely mine.

In particular, I would like to thank two of my associates at
the University of Central Florida, Joyce Lilie and Trevor Col-
bourn, each of whom read drafts of several chapters and provided both their trenchant criticism and their unswerving
support. Colleagues from other institutions whom I especially
want to thank are Robert Benedetti, Charles S. Bullock III,
Chandler Davidson, David J. Garrow, Steven F. Lawson, Frank
R. Parker, Abigail M. Thernstrom, and Stephan Thernstrom.

I was interested in having individuals who were not historians or political scientists read and critique the manuscript as
well. Larry J. Halpern, a rabbi; Joel Katzin, a physicist; and
Stanley Slater, a psychiatrist, each read major parts of the
manuscript and offered insightful comments. Minna Slater, my
intellectually curious mother-in-law, read much of the manuscript and provided me with her keen comments.

Christina Crosby, my much-valued student assistant, re-
viewed the manuscript in its entirety. Bea Prince, my office secretary, moved things along and served as the guardian of
my doorway when necessary. It was a pleasure to work with
the dedicated and highly professional staff of Rutgers University Press. Marlie Wasserman, Barbara Tischler, and Kate Har-
rie deserve special words of praise as they each edited,
consulted, and paved the way for my manuscript to emerge as a
book, which was handled with care throughout the publication
process.

My wife, Barbara, a teacher and a historian in her own right,
deserves not only a place on the dedication page, but also
a special word of note. She read draft after draft of papers, chapters, and the manuscript in its entirety, and she

commented, criticized, edited, and discussed them with me as only a partner can do.

The result is this book.

CALCULATING VISIONS

Prologue

It is the necessary nature of a political party to avoid, as
long as it can be avoided, the consideration of any question
which involves a great change.

Anthony Trollope

Plots, true or false, are necessary things, to raise up
commonwealths and ruin kings.

John Dryden

I still have a dream. It is a dream deeply rooted in the
American dream. I have a dream.

Martin Luther King, Jr.

THE USE OF POLITICAL POWER and the civil rights issue
are major themes that interweave the careers of John F. Kennedy and Lyndon B. Johnson during the 1950s and 1960s.
These two themes are central to both men's rise to the presidency and to the strategies each pursued as he counted votes,
manipulated issues, and recounted votes. When their schemes,
the usual machinations pursued by politicians to secure their
ends, were confronted by the dreams and stratagems of the
civil rights movement, the upheaval that followed reshaped the
foundations of the nation's political alignments.

The schemes of politicians often leave in their wake the hopes
of others; political power, the ability to control societal out-
comes, accrues to the successful politician. Others will bend or
be broken by the powerful. Politicians may have their private
ideals beyond that of holding public office, but those goals must
be subordinated to the exigencies of getting elected. Winning
office is their prime goal because power flows from office; and
above all else, politicians are power seekers. They deal with

issues or create policies in ways that maximize their chances of electoral success.[1] That is the crux of political strategy. A politician's public action may be consonant with a personal conception of the public interest or with a private ideal, but consuming ambition for election and reelection is the driving force behind plans and behaviors.

In democratic societies, votes count and politicians count votes. Winning office flows from winning votes, and issues are important insofar as they are tied to votes. Often, the major strategic problem for politicians is how to use an issue to win an election.

Every era has a set of issues to which political actors pay attention, and it is difficult to alter this "agenda of controversy."[2] Events, crises, and interest groups may each play a major role in changing what is on that agenda, but elections are the most predictable and the most common vehicle for its manipulation.[3] Successful politicians handle issues adroitly, thereby shaping the span and direction of the public's attention. They bring forward issues that benefit their cause and blunt or deflect those that risk putting them in harm's way.[4]

The politician in office may be reluctant to introduce new issues. Maintaining the status quo is often tantamount to sustaining a position. By contrast, candidates seeking office look for new issues that will alter the status quo. They have to challenge and redefine the current political alignment if power is to move their way. Politicians who capture top offices are often the most adept at defining critical issues in a manner that, if not wholly approved by the public, is most acceptable to the voting majority. They also know how to observe the limits of scheming and manipulation lest they be perceived as unprincipled or too manipulative. Such are the best of the political schemers.

There are also idealists, politically active individuals to whom issues or causes are most important. Idealists seek political power or access to the powerful solely as a means of achieving their vision: it is the issue that matters above all, and it cannot be traded away. Idealists are the bane of political schemers, for they are often unbending in pursuit of their cause. It is rarely their wont to consider the political necessities of the moment. Idealists and political schemers are bound to clash. The former perceives the latter as often weak compromisers or temporizers at best and at worst sellouts or betrayers of the cause in a world that needs truth and justice. The latter perceives the former as often unrealistic and unreasonable, if not irrational, in a world that moves by bargains and compromises.

Of course, this characterization is archetypical. But reality often approaches the archetypes. The political schemer is embodied in Machiavelli's prince, whose sole aim is to maintain power. Richard Nixon of Watergate is surely not far from the prince either in his drive for power or in the means he employed to maintain power. Franklin D. Roosevelt was a more democratic politician than Nixon in his respect for the constraints of power, yet even he sought to expand and redefine the powers of the presidency. For example, in the infamous court-packing plan, FDR sought to gain for presidents the power to nominate additional justices to the Supreme Court. But he had connived too much, and his stratagem ran into a firestorm of opposition. The democratic process, with its emphasis on the rights of the opposition voice, limited this drive to power.

Arthur, king of Camelot, is the prototype idealist whose guide to action is what *might be* in the most just of lands. Margaret Sanger and Eugene Debs were idealists driven to face jail sentences as they confronted the body politic with their causes. More recently, Martin Luther King, Jr., was equally willing to accept jail as he confronted both politicians and the public with his vision for racial equality and a just society. King was but one of thousands of visionaries who made the civil rights movement possible and brought the Second Reconstruction to its fruition.[5]

Civil rights were the most critical and the most durable domestic issue of the post–World War II era. The civil rights issue insistently brought into question the legitimacy of democracy in the United States. Civil rights crises, often created by the idealists, erupted time and again, pushing the nation's political leaders to confront an issue they would rather have skirted. The civil rights movement forced the national leadership and national institutions to grapple with the issue in a manner that they would have otherwise preferred to avoid.

The American dilemma, Gunnar Myrdal noted in 1944, was the contradiction between the country's constitutional commitment to democracy and the reality of second-class citizenship for blacks.[6] Crises and the movement compelled the political system to confront this contradiction. Victory over nazism, an ideology embedded in racism, focused attention on the untenable nature of black-white relations in the world's leading democracy. In addition, the lack of civil rights became a national embarrassment and a political liability for the United States in the immediate postwar years. American policy makers portrayed the United States as the defender of the free world in its battle with communism and as a friend of the predominantly nonwhite, nonindustrialized countries of the world. The status of American blacks undercut its moral claim to free world leadership.

In domestic politics, civil rights threatened the stability of the political alignment that FDR had put in place. The Democrats emerged from the New Deal with a new national majority party. The traditional base of Democratic support had always been in the South, and now the South emerged as a critically important part of the Democratic majority. The critical Democratic strategic dilemma was how to reconcile the needs of several major alliance partners who acutely disagreed over civil rights: southern whites, blacks, and the liberal allies of blacks, including the unions. The white South's attachment to the Democratic party rested on its commitment to the racial caste system of white over black.[7] Southern unity in opposition to black rights, combined with the threat of a Senate filibuster, that is, stopping the normal business of the Senate with continuous debate on the Senate floor, blocked the enactment of civil rights legislation once Reconstruction was ended. Senate Rule 22 provided that debate could be terminated by a two-thirds vote of the Senate membership, but it had never been successfully used against a civil rights filibuster. While the South maintained its veto power over civil rights, northern blacks became politically powerful in the mid-twentieth century as they moved into major, politically competitive, industrial states, and they increasingly demanded political, economic, and social equality for themselves and their southern brethren.[8]

FDR successfully finessed the civil rights issue while coping first with the depression and then with the war.[9] But the issue split the Democratic party during his successor's administration. Harry Truman directly addressed the concern with the formation of the President's Committee on Civil Rights, which issued a public report in 1947 in favor of stronger federal protection of black rights. Truman subsequently supported civil rights legislation. The South was enraged. At the 1948 Democratic National Convention the black-liberal-labor alliance wrote a strong civil rights plank into the party platform over President Truman's objections. Truman believed the South did not need to have the issue forced on it at the convention.[10] His civil rights stance was a matter of public record, and he feared a strong civil rights plank would push some leading southerners to publicly abandon the Democratic ticket. He was right. Half of the Alabama delegation and all of the Mississippi delegation walked out.[11] The ardent liberal coalition moved to force the issue on the convention floor because they believed it would give them the black votes they needed to carry state and local elections in the forthcoming campaign. They feared Truman's reelection bid would prove to be a disaster for the Democrats that fall.

Two days after Truman's nomination was in hand, dissident Southern Democrats met in Birmingham, Alabama, and chose Governor Strom Thurmond of South Carolina to head the States' Rights party ticket and Governor Fielding Wright of Mississippi to be its vice-presidential nominee. The States' Rights ticket carried Alabama, Georgia, Mississippi, and South Carolina; but Truman, with black and union help in the pivotal industrial states, carried the election. Throughout the 1950s and on into the 1960s, Dixiecrat anger towards the Democratic party grew as civil rights were increasingly injected into the national agenda of controversy.

For the Republicans, the emergence of the civil rights issue created an ongoing intraparty feud between the moderates, with their traditional commitment to black rights, and the conservatives, with their vision of a national Republican party that included a white southern wing. Although the Republican party was the party of Lincoln and union, its mid-twentieth-century ideology of a limited federal government role and economic conservatism had a growing constituency in the emerging metropolitan centers of the postwar South. Eisenhower's moderate conservatism carried the states of Florida, Texas, Tennessee, and Virginia in 1952. He added Louisiana to this group in his 1956 presidential victory. The economic conservatives of the rim South—Virginia, North Carolina, Tennessee, Texas, and Florida—found the Republicans increasingly congenial while the racial reactionaries of the Deep South were increasingly alienated from the Democrats. Republican commitment to a limited federal role was attractive across the white South.

The complexity of the civil rights movement and the events and organizations that took shape as the political system was pushed to grapple with the issue reflected both diversity and depth of support. Black leaders and their liberal allies were sometimes bystanders as events moved the issue by their own momentum. The organization of the Montgomery bus boycott, the riot at the University of Mississippi, and the heroism of James Meredith were not shaped by the major leaders of the day.

At other times, however, the major organizations and leaders of the movement did shape many of the events that maintained the issue's momentum and gave it direction. Rosa Parks prepared for her role as the obstinate Montgomery bus rider by serving as secretary to the local NAACP chapter. The student sit-in movement started quite spontaneously, but its leadership and continuity arose out of ties to black churches, black colleges, and black youth organizations.[12] Legislative maneuvering and court battles acutely reflected the presence of black leadership and resources the civil rights organizations brought to bear in the struggle. Some idealists, like the youngsters of the freedom rides and the Deep South voter registration drives, were more fervent than their older leaders. But the idealists shared a powerful vision that made the movement a political reality.

PART ONE

John F. Kennedy: Reluctant Hero of the Civil Rights Movement

There is no sense in raising hell, and then not being successful. There is no sense in putting the office of the Presidency on the line on an issue, and then being defeated.

John F. Kennedy, 1961

1

Pursuing the Presidency

ROY WILKINS, the leader of the National Association for the Advancement of Colored People (NAACP), went to Massachusetts in April of 1958 to denounce John Kennedy's courting of southern leaders. Kennedy was avidly seeking southern support for his 1960 presidential candidacy, and he was also campaigning for reelection to the Senate. JFK wrote to the NAACP leader: "I ask you in all seriousness whether you believe my civil rights record . . . warrants such an attack in my home state."[1] Wilkins replied: "You are hailed by Dixiecrat leaders of South Carolina, Georgia and Mississippi, which, with Alabama, are the 'worst' states on the Negro question." Wilkins continued, Negroes "feel uneasy over this apparent entente cordial between Kennedy of Massachusetts and Griffin, Timmerman, Talmadge, Eastland, et. al, of Dixie."[2] Kennedy shot back: "I have not asked them [the southerners] for support—I do not ask for your support. I am simply running for reelection to the Senate from Massachusetts."[3]

The senator's reply was disingenuous. He had made several presidential campaign visits to leaders throughout the South; and he had courted them and received their endorsements.[4] At the July 1958 NAACP National Convention, the Massachusetts senator was again attacked for his ties to the South. Kennedy, in exasperation, wrote to Wilkins: "I think the time has come for you and me to have a personal conversation about our future relations. I expect to be in and around Washington for a long time." Kennedy was angered. "You came to Pittsfield in the middle of my campaign for reelection to say that my record . . . did not deserve the support of Negro voters. . . . I think it is urgent that you and I have a discussion . . . on your next visit to Washington."[5]

The NAACP was a major constituency within the Democratic party, and John Kennedy needed its members' support to become president. He also needed southern support. Balancing these two major elements in the Democratic coalition was a task that had plagued the party's leadership since the days of Franklin Roosevelt. Kennedy's civil rights record was good, despite a couple of lapses during votes on the 1957 Civil Rights Act; and he was irate that the NAACP leader would attack him during his Senate election campaign. He needed a solid victory margin to impress would-be supporters for his presidential bid. He was determined to be president, and he was determined not to let the NAACP come between him and his ambition.

John Kennedy was a politician born into a family of politicians.[6] After his older brother, Joe, Jr., died, the mantle of family political ambition fell upon John Kennedy as the eldest surviving male of the younger generation. "I never would have run for office if Joe had lived," he told his longtime aide and confidant, Theodore Sorenson. "Everything seemed to point to it in 1946."[7] What pointed to it most of all was his father. Joseph Kennedy, Sr., established and financed the organizational network for John Kennedy's election to the United States House of Representatives in 1946. John Kennedy successfully ran for the Senate with the same backing in 1952. Cardinal Richard Cushing, a longtime family intimate, believed the logic of the situation was clear. "Joe Kennedy had one ambition," the cardinal recalled, "and that was to see Jack Kennedy president of the United States, and he concentrated on it."[8]

The realization of Joe Kennedy's quest began with John Kennedy's run for the United States House of Representatives when he was twenty-nine years old.[9] A war hero and the author of a well received book about prewar Britain (*Why England Slept*), John Kennedy was not sure what ideology he believed in when he ran for Congress. "Some people have their liberalism 'made' by the time they reach their twenties," he said. "I didn't. I was caught in crosscurrents and eddies."[10] As the young politician explained, "In my family we were interested not so much in the ideas of politics as in the mechanics of the whole process.

Then I found myself in Congress representing the poorest district in Massachusetts. Naturally, the interests of my constituents led me to take the liberal line."[11] His was a nonideological, bread-and-butter liberalism. As Kennedy remarked at one time in the 1950s, "I'm no liberal at all. I never joined the Americans for Democratic Action or the American Veterans Committee. I am not comfortable with those people."[12] JFK prided himself on his pragmatism and lack of ideology. The liberal ideologues, who took pride in their commitments, were uncomfortable with the pragmatic Kennedy. Throughout his career Jack Kennedy the politician would constantly be rubbing up against the devoted liberal believers.

In 1952 Kennedy successfully ran for the United States Senate seat from Massachusetts, and constituency politics conflicted directly with his constrained liberalism. Joseph McCarthy's virulent anticommunist rampage crossed the line of acceptability, and in December of 1954 the Senate voted sixty-seven to twenty to censure its Wisconsin colleague. All of the Democrats except John Kennedy voted for censure. McCarthy's censure was an issue of basic liberal beliefs and commitments. McCarthyism was a term that bespoke fear and intimidation. To the liberal Democrats and to Eleanor Roosevelt, matriarch of the liberal believers, the McCarthy issue was the litmus test of liberalism.[13] Jack Kennedy failed this test.

At the time of the McCarthy vote, Kennedy was in a hospital recuperating from a critical, but elective, back operation. Although he could not cast a roll-call vote on the McCarthy censure, he could have placed himself on the record as to how he would have voted had he been present. Yet he did not take a public position on the issue either then or later.[14] In a 1956 interview, Senator Kennedy frankly let it be known that there were two underlying reasons for his silence: opposition to McCarthy would be political suicide for a Massachusetts senator who wanted to be reelected, and his family had strong personal ties to Joseph McCarthy.[15] Robert Kennedy served as assistant counsel to Senator McCarthy's Senate Subcommittee on Investigations, and Senator McCarthy was the godfather of Robert Kennedy's firstborn child. Joseph Kennedy, Sr., not only contributed money to the Wisconsin senator's campaigns, but also invited him to family social affairs. Reelection and family were the foremost concerns of the young senator during the mid 1950s. Despite the McCarthy issue, during his first decade in public office and political campaigns, Jack Kennedy's record was generally innocuous when it came to issues. In neither house of Congress did he serve with particular distinction.[16] Justice William O. Douglas, a Kennedy family friend dating back to the New Deal years, sums up JFK's congressional record: "When he reached the House he really did nothing of importance," and "as a Senator he was as nondescript as he had been as a congressman."[17]

In the mid 1950s John Kennedy moved to tie himself to the Democratic party center. His congressional roll-call voting pattern changed from slightly conservative to more mainstream, liberal Democratic.[18] He represented a diverse, industrialized state and his constituency horizons broadened. But John Kennedy was not a political leader, and the black rights issue was not of particular interest to him. His friend and aide Theodore Sorenson recalls, "As a Senator he simply did not give much thought at all to this subject. . . . In fact, when he talked privately at all about Negroes in those days, it was usually about winning Negro votes."[19] Kennedy, the senator, was never to stray too far into the civil rights thicket. He was keenly aware of the Democratic party divisions over civil rights. White southerners wanted the federal government to stay away from this issue; in their view it was strictly a state matter. Blacks and their allies wanted federal intervention in civil rights; it was the only way to bring about change.[20] Black political power was almost negligible. The white South was a political powerhouse both on Capitol Hill and in the presidential nomination process. Federal intervention in civil rights remained off the congressional agenda.

In the 1950s Kennedy became concerned about southern votes, Democratic convention votes, and electoral college votes. While the presidency was the ultimate goal, the young senator made a brief try for the vice-presidency in 1956. To attain his objective, the South had to be wooed. John Kennedy's 1956 book, *Profiles in Courage,* won him national fame, a Pulitzer Prize, and white southern approval. The senator's account of

Reconstruction and the impeachment trial of Andrew Johnson was pointedly sympathetic to the white South. He wrote of radical Republicans who imposed a costly and onerous carpetbagger era on a prostrate South. "The Reconstruction Period," as JFK analyzed it, "was a black nightmare the South never could forget."[21] Eleanor Roosevelt commented publicly on the senator and his book after he asked for her support in the 1956 contest. "[You are] someone who understands what courage is and admires it, but has not quite the independence to have it."[22] To her, what mattered about John Kennedy was his lack of courage on the McCarthy issue. To the South, what mattered about John Kennedy was that he understood a time of southern torment. This provided a valuable entree to the white southerners who felt their cause was sorely misunderstood by most northerners.

Adlai Stevenson gave the 1956 Democratic convention the right to select his running mate in an open ballot. Kennedy had anticipated this move. Thomas P. "Tip" O'Neill, a Boston member of the House of Representatives and a Kennedy ally, was asked by JFK to appoint Robert Kennedy as a delegate to the national convention. "Tip," Jack said, "my brother Bob is the smartest politician I've ever known. He's absolutely brilliant. You know, lightning may strike at that convention, and I could end up on the ticket with Stevenson. I'd really like to have my brother on the floor as a delegate so that he could work for me." O'Neill had promised three of his seats to others but gave Bob Kennedy the seat reserved for himself. Congressman O'Neill believed that Jack Kennedy had a shot not only at the vice-presidential slot but also, eventually, at the presidential nomination.[23] The Kennedys were powerful in Massachusetts, and O'Neill believed that a favor given became a favor owed by the recipient.

In 1956 big-city organizations were anti-Kennedy. They feared a Catholic on the ticket would mean certain defeat. The southern delegations, however, were open to new facts. Estes Kefauver of Tennessee, the odds-on favorite for vice-president, was regarded by southerners as a traitor to their cause. Kefauver refused to sign the "Southern Manifesto"—a document, signed by all but three southern senators, that denounced the *Brown v. Board of Education* decision—and he openly supported the 1954 school desegregation decision.[24] It was a wide-open contest.

Kefauver eventually won the nomination, but the young New Englander made it a race by gathering southern delegate support. Kennedy's ties to the South were clear as he gathered open endorsements from its leaders. Southern votes were rounded up. Even before the convention was underway, Senator George Smathers of Florida talked to southern governors on behalf of Kennedy. At the convention, Mississippi governor J. P. Coleman helped swing Texas to Kennedy. He ran second to Senator Albert Gore of Tennessee as the South's first-ballot choice for vice-president. JFK secured 250.5 of the 332 ballots cast by the South on the second ballot.[25]

Senate Majority Leader Lyndon Johnson made a seconding speech on behalf of the "fighting sailor from Massachusetts." In the Congress following the 1956 elections, Johnson helped first-term Senator Kennedy get a seat on the coveted Foreign Relations Committee, denying the request of the more senior Estes Kefauver. "All of a sudden, Joe Kennedy bombarded me with calls, presents, and little notes telling me what a great guy I was for going with Jack during the vice-presidential fight," recounts Johnson. "But I knew all along that there was something else on his mind, and sure enough one day he came right out and pleaded with me to put Jack on the Foreign Relations Committee, telling me that if I did, he'd never forget me for the rest of his life." Joe Kennedy wanted his son to have the prestige and national exposure the Foreign Relations Committee appointment could provide for him; Lyndon Johnson was after Joe Kennedy's largess. The bargain was made because, as the Texan tells it, "I kept picturing old Joe Kennedy sitting there with all that power and wealth feeling indebted to me for the rest of his life, and I sure liked that picture."[26]

Jack Kennedy had been running for the 1960 Democratic presidential nomination even as the 1956 presidential election was underway. During the fall, he provided this assessment of his aborted try for the vice-presidential nomination to his friend David Powers: "With only about four hours of work and a handful of supporters, I came within thirty-three and a half votes of winning the Vice-Presidential nomination. If I work hard for four years, I ought to be able to pick up all the marbles."[27]

Others took positive notice of the young senator's role at the 1956 convention. He made an impressive nominating speech for Adlai Stevenson, and his brief campaign for the vice-presidency earned him kudos. Adlai Stevenson wrote to him, "[You left] a much bigger man than when you arrived. If there was a hero, it was you."[28] Governor Marvin Griffin of Georgia reflected: "While I regret you lost the nomination for Vice-President, you won respect from party leaders all over the country and can look forward to greater things in the future."[29]

It was to "greater things in the future" that Kennedy looked as he campaigned tirelessly across the country for the Stevenson-Kefauver ticket.[30] He made his first campaign foray into the South, speaking in Florida, Texas, North Carolina, Virginia, and the Deep South state of Louisiana.[31] Southern support for a Democratic presidential ticket was considered essential in the general election. Southern support, or at least acquiescence, would be necessary for Kennedy to make a run for a presidential nomination. Political alliances were undergoing change, and modifications in positions were being worked through. The young presidential aspirant was to be no stranger to the South during the remainder of the decade. In 1957 he gave talks in every southern state except Louisiana and Tennessee. In 1958 he spoke in Florida and Texas. In 1959 he added Louisiana, North Carolina, and Tennessee to his speaking tour in addition to another sojourn into Florida and Virginia.[32]

While campaigning in the South and seeking to hold on to his northern base of support, as a sitting senator, JFK also had to deal with the contending issues related to passage of the 1957 civil rights bill. This was the first federal civil rights measure to work its way into law since the end of Reconstruction. The fight over the 1957 civil rights bill placed Kennedy in opposition to black rights advocates on two crucial votes. First, he supported a southern move to have the proposed bill sent to the Judiciary Committee chaired by Senator James Eastland of Mississippi. This was opposed by nearly every proponent of the bill; it was a certainty that once the bill entered Senator Eastland's domain it would never be returned to the Senate floor.[33]

When two Boston NAACP members questioned Kennedy's vote, he explained that it was cast out of his belief in the need to follow accepted Senate procedures. He assured them of his devotion to civil rights.[34]

However, after making sure that he had legal experts to back his position, Kennedy also voted with the southerners to add a jury-trial amendment to the proposed bill. The bill, as originally written, called for contempt proceedings to be initiated by a court when an individual refused to abide by a judge's order in matters arising under the act. The senator argued that trial by jury was a basic right under the law—even though trial by jury in contempt cases was a rarity. This amendment would effectively gut attempts to apply criminal penalties to violators because it required a trial by a jury of (white) southerners, but it left civil contempt cases in the hands of judges. On the same day that the senator wrote one of his Boston NAACP constituents a letter defending this vote, he also wrote to several southern leaders to assure them that he had taken their advice on the vote.[35]

The ever-loyal Sorenson noted in a memorandum that on these votes "Northerners divided into men of reason and men of anti-southern prejudice." Kennedy, "as well as all Southern Senators and reasonable Northerners," voted correctly on both counts.[36] Of the four major 1960 Democratic presidential contenders, only Lyndon Johnson joined Kennedy in these votes; Stuart Symington of Missouri and Hubert Humphrey of Minnesota consistently supported a strong bill with most of the other "unreasonable" northerners. Even some Kennedy supporters believed JFK's 1957 civil rights votes lacked vision and courage. James MacGregor Burns, although the author of an in-house Kennedy campaign biography, refers to the senator's 1957 performance as "a profile in caution and moderation."[37]

The senator's "caution and moderation" reflected the racial dilemma of a would-be Democratic presidential nominee who needed southern support for that aspiration to be realized and a Massachusetts senator facing reelection who needed support in a liberally inclined home state. Satisfying both constituencies on the civil rights issue was almost impossible. His straddling was bound to attract a reaction from these who felt strongly about the issue. Some people would not see the reasonableness of the senator's position in light of his pursuit of the presidency, even if they understood his dilemma.

Among some civil rights advocates, the senator's performance brought forth outrage. In April of 1958 Roy Wilkins came to Massachusetts and denounced Kennedy's southern flirtation. Wilkins amplified his case in a letter to one of Kennedy's constituents.

> In our business we understand clearly the realisms and par- ✗ ticularities in politics. We know that most Democratic aspirants to the presidency feel that their strategy must be such that outright opposition to them is not generated in the Southern states, particularly prior to the nominating convention. However we must be pardoned for exhibiting some alarm at the apparent wooing of Southern support three years before the nominating convention. . . .
>
> Southern states have declared open war on Negro Americans. They cannot win this war by themselves. The only way they can make any showing at all is through the assistance they receive from outside the South. We do not believe that Senator Kennedy is committed, either intellectually or morally to the . . . Southern philosophy. We continue to hope he will disassociate himself from them in an unmistakable manner.[38]

Writing to the senator, Wilkins said, "Since the Southern record on the denial of the vote was so flagrant, and so shameful, and of so long a duration . . . [we] should have had the nonquibbling support of non-Southern [Senate] members."[39] Kennedy shot back: "I have every reason to believe that my record and views will be supported at the polls by those acquainted with them, regardless of race."[40]

The senator's reply was somewhat disingenuous. He was not "simply running for reelection to the Senate from Massachusetts." He was also running for the presidency. He needed—and wanted —a big reelection victory. On July 14 the senator wrote to a constituent of Alabama's governor, John Patterson: "I certainly appreciated the opportunity to meet with Governor Patterson. . . . Governor Patterson on his return to Alabama saw fit to make an announcement in behalf of my possible [presidential] candidacy."[41]

At the July 1958 NAACP National Convention, Clarence Mitchell, the chief lobbyist and head of the NAACP's Washington, D.C., bureau, renewed the attack on Senator Kennedy's civil rights record. As Joseph L. Rauh, Jr., a former national chairman of the liberal Americans for Democratic Action (ADA) put it, "Mitchell beat the bejesus out of Kennedy." Kennedy was exasperated with the NAACP leadership, and he wrote to Wilkins:

> I think that you would agree that it would be most unfortunate if an "iron curtain" of misunderstanding were to be erected between our two offices.
>
> It seems to me it would be important to you and your organization to lay to rest the suspicion current among many liberal Senators that I have been singled out for political reasons. Certainly the evidence supports this. You came to Pittsfield in the middle of my campaign for reelection to say that my record . . . did not deserve the support of Negro voters while, according to the local press, treating comparatively lightly the record of my Republican colleague. . . . More recently, Mr. Mitchell, whose association with Mr. Nixon is well known in Washington, "was quite outspoken against" me at the NAACP convention. . . .
>
> I can not believe that the NAACP, with whom I have had a long and friendly association, would want to be involved by two of its leaders in a partisan candidate-picking gamble of this kind at this time; and that is why I think it is urgent that you and I have a discussion, perhaps with Mr. Mitchell also, on your next visit to Washington.[42]

The NAACP leadership was hitting Kennedy where it could hurt: in his political future. It was assumed by everyone that the senator would win reelection, but the margin of victory was important to his presidential prospects as was his appearance as a liberal. While most observers assumed that the black vote leaned Democratic nationally, Vice-President Nixon would be a formidable competitor for that vote in 1960. Nixon, as presiding officer of the Senate, made several rulings that aided forces seeking to alter the Senate filibuster rules and make it easier to end debate. He also publicly fought for a strong civil rights bill during the 1957 debate. As the battle over the 1957 bill was coming to an end, Martin Luther King, Jr., wrote Nixon: "Let me say how deeply grateful we are to you for your assiduous labor and dauntless courage in seeking to make the civil rights bill a reality." The vice-president was praised by civil rights supporters for the manner in which he chaired the President's Committee on Government Contract Compliance. And he also won their praise when he sent his children to public schools in Washington, D.C., and publicly backed efforts to make the district schools a model for school desegregation. Richard Nixon was a friend of the pro–civil rights forces on the Hill and within the administration.[43] It was rumored throughout Washington that Clarence Mitchell was a "quiet" Nixon ally. Martin Luther King, Jr., also considered him a personal friend, although he was cautious in his support of Nixon:

> I was strongly opposed to Vice-President Nixon before meeting him personally. . . . I must admit that my impression has somewhat changed. I have frankly come to feel that the position and world contacts of the Vice-President have matured his person and judgement. . . .
>
> I am coming to believe that Nixon is absolutely sincere in his views [on civil rights]. His travels have revealed to him how the race problem is hurting America in international relations and it is altogether possible that he has no basic racial prejudice. . . . I also feel that Nixon would have done much more to meet the present crisis in race relations than President Eisenhower has done. . . .
>
> Finally, I should say that Nixon has a genius for convincing one that he is sincere. When you are close to him he almost disarms you with his sincerity. . . . And so I would conclude by saying that if Richard Nixon is not sincere, he is the most dangerous man in America.[44]

The presidential election and what JFK and most others believed would be the inevitable confrontation with Nixon was two years away. Of more immediate concern to the senator was the NAACP threat to his Senate victory margin. The Kennedy allies in Massachusetts with ties to the NAACP rallied to his defense and pushed for a change in Wilkins's stand.[45] In mid October Wilkins was brought around to the position of providing the senator with a carefully crafted letter of support. The letter was read at a testimonial dinner given in honor of the senator by the Massachusetts Citizens Committee for Minority Rights: "Senator Kennedy did vote for the jury trial amendment to the 1957 civil rights bill and we disagreed on this and still regret his choice." Wilkins explained, however, "The Senator's record, taken as a whole, and including his forthright and repeated support of the Supreme Court decision of May 17, 1954 [*Brown v. Board of Education*], . . . must be regarded . . . as one of the best voting records on civil rights and related issues of any Senator in the Congress."[46] Wilkins notes in his autobiography: "The headlines the next day were predictably favorable, and Kennedy's letters once again became friendly."[47]

The Wilkins letter paid off for JFK. When the count was completed, Kennedy won 73.6 percent of the total votes cast, and he carried most of the black wards by an even larger margin. Wilkins wrote the senator: "I am glad our evaluation of your civil rights record was useful."[48] Thus, the NAACP leader made the senator and other Democrats mindful that blacks and their allies had political leverage. It was limited leverage—very limited. No doubt Wilkins did not want to cut his ties to a major Democratic presidential contender, but he would not look the other way as northern contenders for the presidency worked out their expedient strategies on civil rights. Wilkins wanted to remind Kennedy and others that there were alternatives and that the game could be played out on terms not favored by the elected politicos. In this instance, Wilkins, not Kennedy, had retreated. It was a protracted, high-stakes game being played, and the participants knew that short-term victories did not necessarily presage long-term success.

John Kennedy never turned his attention from the South during this period; now that his Senate seat was again secured, the South became a central concern. But the South was increasingly caught up in a frenzied resistance to desegregation. Harry S. Ashmore, a Pulitzer Prize–winning editor of the *Arkansas Gazette* and political advisor to Adlai Stevenson, caught the texture of the region's politics when he wrote that "southern leaders have cut themselves off from the possibility of meaningful debate; they have whipped their followers into a mood where any man who yields to any degree on the segregation issue invites immediate retaliation."[49] Sorenson increasingly received mail that brought forth concern over a new southern bolt from the Democratic party.[50] The Kennedy presidential campaign, however, maintained its ties to the South's leaders. In 1959 Sorenson calculated that at least some southern first-ballot support would be needed for a successful nomination drive, and if necessary, this vote would have to be expanded to achieve a second-ballot victory.[51]

Improving relations with liberals and blacks was, on the other hand, a problem that Kennedy had yet to deal with effectively. In 1957 Marjorie Lawson, a highly respected Washington black Democratic political activist and attorney, was brought on as a Kennedy aide, but the senator kept his distance from the black rights issue and its advocates.[52] Neither John Kennedy nor Robert Kennedy, who served as his brother's campaign manager in the drive for the presidency, knew much about black America.[53] In the spring of 1959 Robert Kennedy approached Harris Wofford to work for the Kennedy campaign. Wofford's family had roots in the South. He spent his early childhood in Tennessee, but his family moved to Scarsdale, New York, when he was a teenager. He was the first white male graduate of Howard University law school and a world traveler with a deep feeling for the emerging third world nations. He developed a special devotion to Mahatma Gandhi's theories of civil disobedience and arranged a trip to India to introduce his friend Martin Luther King, Jr., to Indian followers of Gandhi. Wofford turned the Kennedy offer down. He was serving as counsel to Father Theodore Hesburgh on the Civil Rights Commission, and he had already accepted a position to help establish a center for the study of civil rights at the University of Notre Dame Law School.

In September of 1959 Father John Cavanaugh, a former president of Notre Dame, told Wofford of a "request" made by Joseph Kennedy. As Cavanaugh paraphrased the Kennedy patriarch, "Tell Hesburgh to forget the moral obligation [of Wofford to work at Notre Dame] and get that fellow on the first plane to Washington."[54] After this discussion, Wofford agreed to work part time for the Kennedy campaign during the 1959–1960 academic year. He was attracted to the charm, the intellectual stimulation, and the dynamism of the Kennedy campaign. In May of 1960 John Kennedy told Wofford that he regarded the black problem as a "political problem." The senator asked Wofford which black leaders he should talk with in order to get a better "political feel" for the matter. "Shortly after, Bob Kennedy called me and said that they concluded that they were in trouble with the Negro vote and he wanted me to come down to his office and work full-time on that subject."[55]

Robert Kennedy told him that he understood "we've been dealing outside the field of the main Negro leadership and we have to start from scratch."[56] Wofford informed his friend Martin Luther King, Jr., he was going "to join Kennedy's staff full-time for the duration of the campaign."[57] Thus, a short while before the 1960 campaign got underway, the Kennedy forces seriously turned their attention to the Negro.

The 1960 presidential political season went according to plan for JFK, although it was often a time of disappointment for the black rights advocates and their liberal allies. In Congress the South effectively filibustered a proposal to strengthen black voting rights. As a result, on May 6 President Eisenhower signed into law a weak civil rights bill, the main effect of which was to allow federal judges to appoint voting registrars under extremely limited conditions.[58] Kennedy and the other presidential aspirants in the Senate thus avoided voting on any controversial civil rights legislation in this election year. What could have been a major impediment to his nomination and a major obstacle to Democratic party unity was therefore sidestepped.

It was not civil rights, Kennedy concluded, but his Catholic religion that represented the major hurdle for him to obtain the Democratic presidential nomination. He had to convince the party leaders that his Catholicism did not make him unelectable, and he approached the issue with a directness that surprised many observers and produced remarkable results. He openly decried anti-Catholic voting as un-American religious bigotry. He also needed to soundly beat a Protestant opponent in a Protestant state. Hubert Humphrey was the liberals' presidential choice, and he was a Protestant. If Kennedy could beat Humphrey in a Protestant state, he could put an end to the belief that a Catholic was unelectable in presidential politics.

JFK took Humphrey on in the Wisconsin presidential primary election, but he did not decisively beat the Minnesotan and lost to him in many Protestant areas—reemphasizing the specter of the religious issue. In the next major contested primary state, Protestant-dominated West Virginia, Kennedy won more than 60 percent of the vote. The anti-Catholic presumption was put to rest.[59] Adlai Stevenson did not enter the primaries, and Jack Kennedy became the only viable choice for many liberals who dismissed Senators Stuart Symington of Missouri and Lyndon Johnson of Texas as too conservative.[60]

John Kennedy had strong ties to some key elements of the liberal coalition—ethnic minorities, academic intellectuals of the New Deal tradition, and AFL-CIO unions. He was the liberal supporter of the unions during the late 1950s McClellan Committee investigation into union racketeering. Kennedy's strong anti-Taft-Hartley position before union audiences swung additional support over to his side.[61] The Kennedy forces also circulated the rumor that JFK would seriously consider Hubert Humphrey as his running mate. Humphrey was the perfect bridge to the more ardent liberal-labor groups and the civil rights forces. He had almost single-handedly created the Democratic-Farmer-Labor party out of the moribund Farmer-Labor party in Minnesota. Progressivism, rural populism, and urban liberalism were tied together successfully under Humphrey's leadership.[62] Hubert Humphrey came to national prominence in 1948 as the mayor of Minneapolis and ADA firebrand who pleaded eloquently that a strong civil rights plank be added to the national Democratic platform. His liberal credentials were reinforced in the 1950s by an often vigorous leadership on behalf of unions, civil rights, and other liberal causes in the Senate.

In late April of 1960 John Bailey, a close Kennedy ally, held a discussion with Humphrey about the possibility of his coming on the ticket.[63] As he left a June 9 fund-raising lunch, John Kennedy approached Joseph L. Rauh, Jr., and asked him if they could share a taxi ride back to the Capitol to discuss mutual concerns. Rauh, a longtime Humphrey ally, expressed his hope that Humphrey would get the second slot on a Kennedy ticket. He also expressed his concern that Lyndon Johnson not be given a place on the ticket. Johnson was viewed by many liberals as the Senate leader who compromised and watered down issue after issue that they backed, especially civil rights. JFK responded, "It will be Hubert Humphrey or another Midwestern liberal." As for Johnson: "There's no need to fear." "JFK had me convinced he was going to pick Hubert," Rauh later reminisced. "There was no doubt in my mind. I just took him at his word."[64] On June 16, 1960, Schlesinger, who was now close to the Kennedy camp, wrote to his longtime friend Adlai Stevenson, Kennedy's "choice for the vice-presidency is still Hubert; and he hopes and thinks Hubert will take it."[65]

JFK's courting of the liberals started to pay off. After privately assuring a group of major liberal leaders that he would support the Supreme Court's *Brown* decision, he won their commitment to go public with a pledge of support. The liberals believed they now had a viable candidate who supported their issues. They also had a focus to use to ensure that Johnson would not take the nomination from a divided liberal camp. Lastly, they had a candidate around whom they could rally to defeat the hated Nixon. On June 17 a group of sixteen well-known Stevenson backers led by Arthur Schlesinger, Jr., issued a public letter addressed "Dear Fellow Liberals." They discussed why they had switched their support to Kennedy:

> The purpose of this letter is to urge, now that Senator Humphrey has withdrawn from the race and Mr. Stevenson continues to stand aside, that the liberals of America turn to Senator Kennedy for President. . . .
>
> We are as determined as you that the Democratic Platform of 1960 meet the issue of the day head-on. We are convinced that Senator Kennedy shares this determination. In particular some of us have discussed the question of a strong civil rights plank with him and he has assured us that he favors pledging the Democratic Party to Congressional and Executive action in support of the Supreme Court's desegregation decisions and to whatever measures may prove necessary to make voting a reality for all citizens. . . .
>
> The time has come, we suggest, to unite behind John Kennedy as the candidate of the liberal movement and to work with him to defeat Nixon in November.[66]

Harris Wofford arranged a private breakfast meeting between John Kennedy and Martin Luther King, Jr. He wanted JFK to get a "better feel" for the black perspective and perhaps heal some wounds. King was one of the most popular and visible black leaders in the United States. The two men had never met before, and King was not a Kennedy enthusiast.[67] King remembered Kennedy's 1957 civil rights votes, and he never responded to a perfunctory letter of introduction Kennedy had sent to him in November of 1959.[68] But the May meeting went well, and King wrote to Chester Bowles, a Kennedy supporter and friend of Wofford's: "I was very impressed by the forthright and honest manner in which he discussed the civil rights question. I have no doubt that he would do the right thing on this issue if he were elected President."[69] King wrote: "[I] specifically mentioned the need for strong civil rights legislation to guarantee the right to vote and to speed up school desegregation." The senator "agreed with all of these things." Perhaps, King mused, the senator's ideas were changing, for JFK told him, "Many of the developments during the sit-in movement pointed up the injustices and indignities that Negroes were facing all over the South."[70] Or perhaps the senator was telling King what he wanted to hear. Kennedy needed black support, and King was a powerful national black leader.

Soon after his discussion with King, JFK went further in his pursuit of black and liberal support. He told a New York Liberal party meeting that he did not need southern support to get the Democratic nomination and he did not want southern support if it meant compromising black Americans' rights. "Moral persuasion" by the president, he argued, was the key to ending racial discrimination. At another meeting he publicly supported the student sit-in movement by saying, "It is in the American tradition to stand up for one's rights—even if the new way is to sit down."[71] As the convention date approached, the cautious politico sounded like a moral leader.

Not all liberals or blacks were convinced by the new Kennedy rhetoric. As the July 14 Democratic National Convention got under way, John Kennedy, according to Theodore White, "was the *least* popular among Negroes of all Democratic candidates. . . ."[72] The Sunday before the convention opened, Roy Wilkins,

Martin Luther King, Jr., and A. Philip Randolph, a longtime civil rights activist who was especially known for his historic 1941 March on Washington movement, led a march of twenty-five hundred black-rights supporters to the convention site. Paul Butler, the convention chairman, met with them and was cheered when he said, "We dedicate ourselves to the elimination of all discriminatory practices at the earliest possible moment. . . . No, no. Now—not later." That evening, Humphrey, Symington, and Kennedy addressed a mass black rally at the Shrine auditorium. Only Kennedy was booed.[73]

The black rights advocates were strong enough to maneuver through the convention the boldest civil rights plank since 1948. Robert Kennedy managed the convention for his brother and gave his support to the strong civil rights plank. At almost every morning strategy meeting that took place between the key Kennedy aides and the Kennedy forces in the state delegations, RFK reminded everyone of the need for such a plank.[74] Paul Butler, skillfully using his position as convention chair, Chester Bowles, the chairman of the platform committee, and Robert Kennedy provided the leadership that enabled the convention to endorse "peaceful demonstrations for first-class citizenship which have recently taken place in many parts of this country." In addition, the platform committed the Democrats to "support whatever action is necessary to eliminate literacy tests and the payment of poll taxes as requirements for voting." The platform also committed the candidate to support legislation for a Fair Employment Practices Commission and legislation to empower and direct the attorney general "to file civil injunction suits in Federal Courts to prevent the denial of any civil right on grounds of race, creed, or color."[75]

Although the Kennedy forces believed they had the nomination in hand by the time the convention got under way, die-hard Stevenson supporters took hope at the movement of events on the convention floor. Adlai Stevenson came to Los Angeles and backed a movement that sought to give him a third try for the presidency. Eleanor Roosevelt, a devout Stevenson ally, a staunch black rights supporter, and close friend of the black leadership, as well as a determined Kennedy foe, also flew to Los Angeles in a last-ditch effort to support the Stevenson candidacy. The Stevenson forces had sentiment on their side, but they did not have the delegate strength to stop the Massachusetts senator. Kennedy won a first-ballot nomination with 806 of 1521 ballots cast. His nearest rival, Lyndon Johnson, won 409 votes, but all except 57.5 of Johnson's votes were cast by delegates from border or southern states. Adlai Stevenson only counted 79.5 votes.[76]

The nomination secured, the Kennedy team turned its attention to a running mate. A major concern was to hold the South in the Democratic column come November. In 1948 the States Rights' ticket had captured the electoral college votes of Alabama, Louisiana, Mississippi, and South Carolina. In 1952 Eisenhower had captured Florida, Tennessee, Texas, and Virginia. The popular Republican president had won these states again, plus Louisiana, in 1956. In 1960 southern delegates were again angry over the civil rights plank. As a portent of things to come, Mississippi cast its twenty-three nomination ballots for its native-son, segregationist governor Ross Barnett. Prior to the balloting, liberal forces were concerned about the possibility that Kennedy might put Johnson on the ticket to save the South for the Democrats. Robert Kennedy reassured Joseph Rauh: "It is not Johnson. You can tell them officially it is not Johnson."[77] Kenneth O'Donnell, a member of the Kennedy inner circle, recalls, "The liberals I knew would not stand still for Lyndon Johnson."[78]

Quietly, even before the convention began, John Kennedy set the stage for a Johnson vice-presidency. On June 29, 1960, Theodore Sorenson prepared a memorandum for his boss that placed Johnson at the top of a list of potential running mates. Johnson's strength with "farmers, Southerners and Texas" was the need met by putting him on the ticket.[79] Appropriate feelers were sent out during the primaries. JFK told Chester Bowles, shortly after the West Virginia victory, that Johnson would be the "wisest" choice for vice-president. He also discussed the possibility of a Johnson choice with Governor J. Lindsey Almond of Virginia.[80] On July 10, four days before the convention, John Kennedy, "seemingly idly, remarked to *Washington Post* publisher Philip Graham, that if he thought Johnson would accept the Vice-Presidency he might offer it."[81] Graham was a

Johnson confidant and, of course, repeated the Kennedy comment to the Senate leader. Two days later JFK again spoke with Graham. This time Graham brought along political insider Stewart Alsop. Kennedy told them he would offer the second position on the ticket to Johnson.[82]

The day before the balloting for the presidency was to take place, Tip O'Neill met with Speaker of the House Sam Rayburn and told him Kennedy had the nomination locked up. O'Neill told the Speaker that Johnson certainly would add strength to the ticket. Rayburn responded, "If Kennedy wants Lyndon as his running mate, Lyndon has an obligation to this convention to accept it. You tell Kennedy that if he wants me to talk to Lyndon, I'll be happy to do it." Rayburn detested Richard Nixon, and his concern was to defeat the GOP nominee-to-be. The Speaker believed that Johnson—and only Johnson—could hold the South for the Democrats and thereby carry the presidency for his party.[83] O'Neill immediately contacted Kennedy and spoke to him about the Speaker's offer. "Of course I want Lyndon," Kennedy told him, "but I'd never want to offer it and have him turn me down. Lyndon's the natural choice, and with him on the ticket, there's no way we could lose. Tell Sam Rayburn I'll call after the session tonight." Rayburn spoke with Hale Boggs, a senior congressman from Louisiana and a powerful figure on the Democratic side of the House. Although Rayburn told Boggs that he had his doubts about the wisdom of Johnson's taking the second position on the ticket, he indicated his agreement with the need for Johnson. "Lyndon's got to do it," the Speaker concluded.[84] The wheels were greased. Kennedy, assured that the Texan would accept, called Rayburn and later personally made the offer to LBJ. The ensuing convention chaos made national headlines.

Most of the Kennedy entourage was astonished at finding Johnson the nominee's choice. Some members of the Kennedy staff knew of the offer to LBJ, but they did not initially believe it was to be taken seriously. Ernest F. Hollings, a young South Carolina politician and Kennedy ally, was present when JFK announced the decision. "I was immediately convinced that John Kennedy was serious in the offer. He needed the South and Johnson was the key to the South." Robert Kennedy was stunned at the idea of Johnson as his brother's running mate. It was one of the few times John Kennedy ever caught his brother off balance in making a political decision. But JFK had made his decision, and Robert Kennedy, however reluctantly, carried out his brother's order to communicate the decision to LBJ.[85]

The black leadership, with the exception of Roy Wilkins, was appalled. "I was not only surprised, I was pained," Clarence Mitchell recalls. "I thought he [Kennedy] needed on the ticket somebody who was closely identified and would act as sort of a bridge between us and the White House. It seemed to me that [with] Mr. Johnson taking that position . . . the chance of Senator [Richard] Russell and others getting in to tell their story would be increased."[86] James Farmer, who was to become the national director of the Congress of Racial Equality (CORE) in February of 1961, regarded the Johnson nomination as "most unfortunate, probably . . . a disaster because of his southern background and voting record on civil rights."[87] Wilkins's viewpoint was not shared by his black brethren. "I felt that he was not a visceral segregationist," recalled the NAACP leader. "His behavior and votes appeared to be dictated more by Texas political considerations than by any ingrained racial hatred." Wilkins was an experienced politician. He understood that LBJ "had not often seen eye to eye with us, but he had been honest, telling us what he intended to do and keeping his word when deals were possible. He was the shrewdest legislative fox I had ever seen." As an afterthought Wilkins added, "He could provide the legislative experience Kennedy so obviously lacked."[88]

The white liberals were also up in arms over the Johnson selection. Leonard Woodcock, a vice-president in the politically powerful United Auto Workers Union, believed "Kennedy had betrayed us all. Well, I very frankly was shocked because our whole theme had been to unite behind Kennedy to stop Johnson."[89] To reassure the liberals, Johnson wrote a letter to the Michigan delegation pledging his support for the party platform; many of the Michigan liberals were still outraged. Word went out that Joe Rauh and the District of Columbia delegation would back a move by Michigan governor G. Mennen Williams to put Orville Freeman's name up for the vice-presidency. The Kennedy forces arranged with Florida Governor LeRoy Collins, the convention chairman, to have John McCormack go to the platform when the Massachusetts delegation was called on the vice-presidential roll and move that Lyndon Johnson be nominated by acclamation.[90] The Michigan delegation was never called for its vote, and the possibility of a floor fight over the vice-presidency was eliminated. The Democratic party remained intact; but the rumblings, southern and liberal, were audible.

On the other side of the partisan divide, the Republicans met in Chicago on July 25–28 to place the mantle of party leadership on heir apparent Richard Nixon. The black vote enticed Nixon. Although he was widely regarded as the candidate of the conservative wing of the GOP, Nixon wanted the support of the Republican liberals, and he went out of his way to mollify them in pursuit of a united effort for the fall campaign. The GOP included a powerful wing with a tradition of support for black rights. Liberal Republican leader Governor Nelson Rockefeller of New York threatened to conduct a convention floor fight over what he considered to be a weak civil rights plank and a weak defense commitment in the proposed party platform. Nixon went to Rockefeller's New York City residence, and the two leaders worked out a compromise. The final GOP platform contained a bold, Rockefeller-inspired, declaration: "We reaffirm the constitutional right to peaceably assembly to protest discrimination in private business establishments."[91] The result, as a *New York Times* editorial stated, was that a comparison of the two parties' positions showed the Republican's pledge as "on balance somewhat more realistic and more specific."[92] After the presidential nomination was secured, Nixon first offered the vice-presidency to Rockefeller, who turned him down, then to Henry Cabot Lodge, a well-known Massachusetts liberal, who accepted the position. The NAACP was pleased with Nixon's record and the record of his running mate.[93]

Black rights advocates were, on the whole, optimistic about the outcome of both presidential conventions. The secretary of the Leadership Conference on Civil Rights (LCCR), a coalition of black and white groups supportive of civil rights, wrote to his colleagues: "The civil rights planks that were adopted [by both parties] . . . are by all odds the strongest in history and represent a significant breakthrough on the civil rights front."[94] Roy Wilkins summed up the enviable position in which the blacks now found themselves:

> For the first time both parties have put themselves on record unequivocally as favoring the elimination of segregation and other forms of discrimination from all areas of community and national life. . . .
>
> For the Republicans, one has to admit that they went farther than anyone expected, probably due to both the Rockefeller pressure on Nixon and, I am convinced, the presence of Lyndon Johnson on the Kennedy ticket.
>
> In fact, Lyndon did better for us than he intended. His candidacy helped the Democrats adopt a strong civil rights plank because his followers could not afford to oppose the plank and still hope to recruit votes for Johnson outside the South. Then with Kennedy the winner on the first ballot and Johnson a surprise Vice-Presidential candidate pledging support of the Democratic platform, the Republicans *had* to come up with something strong on civil rights, in order to stay in the running among the Northern independents they need to add to their conservatives. They did not know at the time the South will [*sic*] feel so strong about Kennedy's religion and about the Democratic civil rights platform or they might have "sat tight" on the soft civil rights platform that the Nixon forces had outlined in advance of the Chicago convention [prior to the Nixon-Rockefeller agreement].[95]

The Republican candidate and his convention committed themselves to the pursuit of the black vote. The moderate South, the South carried by Eisenhower in 1952 and 1956 would, they hoped, again go with the GOP. Eisenhower had captured part of the northern Democratic black vote in 1956. The hope was that Nixon would cut further into this vote and swing critical competitive states of the Northeast and Midwest into his column.

However, John Kennedy would not let the Republican plan go unchallenged. Soon after the conventions were over, he talked with Harris Wofford as he drove to Capitol Hill. "Now," he said, "in five minutes tick off the ten things a President ought to do to cleanup this goddamn civil rights mess."[96]

Wofford suggested that the president could issue an executive order banning discrimination in federally assisted housing. In addition, Wofford told the nominee he should move quickly to exercise executive action on the programs mentioned in the Democratic platform. On August 8 Kennedy issued a statement in which he urged that "by the stroke of a presidential pen" the president could sign an executive order on the equal opportunity in housing bill. He added: "I have supported this proposal. . . . A new Democratic administration will carry it out, but there is no need to wait another six months. I urge the President to act now."[97]

The words sounded right, but they were not ardent enough for the strong liberals. They were profoundly disappointed by the Johnson nomination. Kennedy had made promises to the contrary, and the turnabout left liberals with feelings of distrust and concern. A measure of the intensity of these feelings was given by Arthur Schlesinger, Jr., in two long letters he wrote to Kennedy at the end of August. The first letter stated: "The campaign thus far has failed to elicit the all-out support of the kind of people who have traditionally provided the spark in Democratic campaigns. These people," he noted, "are the liberals, the reformers, the intellectuals. . . . They care deeply about issues and principles." Schlesinger went on: "The number directly involved may be small. But these are the kinetic people and their participation or non-participation profoundly affects the atmosphere and drive of a Democratic campaign." These Democrats, Schlesinger warned, need to be enthused. "To develop enthusiasm we have no choice but to give the enthusiasts something to believe in."[98] That was a key element missing in the Kennedy campaign.

After he returned from the Americans for Democratic Action National Board meeting, Schlesinger sent his second letter to Kennedy. The Harvard professor told the presidential nominee that the tone of the discussion at the meeting was, "as someone put it, 'We don't trust Kennedy and we don't like Johnson; but Nixon is so terrible that we have to endorse the Democrats.'" The ADA fiercely debated the possibility of endorsing only Kennedy. In the end, the Kennedy-Johnson ticket was endorsed, but not before the following sentence was eliminated from the proposed statement: "In the critical fields of human concern—foreign affairs, economic and social policy, civil rights—he has shown himself the aggressive champion of creative liberalism." The majority of the board "simply refused to believe these things about you." As sharply as he could, Schlesinger told the young candidate to move quickly and pointedly to reassert himself with the liberals.

On September 1 Kennedy officially kicked off his campaign with a speech that included a call for Senator Joseph Clark of Pennsylvania and Congressman Emanuel Celler of New York to "prepare a comprehensive civil rights bill, embodying our platform commitments, for introduction at the beginning of the next session" of Congress.[99] In mid September he again met with King. King believed that Kennedy had a better grasp of civil rights than at their earlier meeting. Kennedy wanted a joint public appearance with King as well as his support. King pointed out that the Southern Christian Leadership Conference (SCLC) was a nonpartisan organization, and as its leader he could not endorse any candidate for partisan office. Discussions about a possible joint appearance foundered over King's insistence that he had to invite Vice-President Nixon to any public appearance he would make with the Massachusetts senator. Kennedy would not agree to this condition.[100] At the end of the meeting, King recalled: "I said, 'but something dramatic must be done to convince the Negroes that you are committed on civil rights.' I did not feel at that time that there was much difference between Kennedy and Nixon."[101]

In the first televised presidential debate, Kennedy had mentioned the need for executive action, noting that a "stroke of a pen" could right many civil wrongs. But the civil rights issue remained on the sidelines throughout much of the campaign. Then, on October 19, Martin Luther King, Jr., was arrested for picketing an Atlanta department store, and the subsequent series of events probably changed the outcome of the election. On October 22, through the intervention of Atlanta's Mayor Bill Hartsfield, King was released from jail. He was immediately rearrested for violation of a parole agreement stemming from a conviction of driving with an Alabama license while a resident of Georgia. King was sent to a rural Georgia prison for a four-month term at hard labor. Coretta King panicked. She called Wofford and cried, "They're going to kill him." I know they are going to kill him."[102] Wofford called Sargent Shriver, who was in Chicago campaigning with JFK. He told Shriver of the pregnant Mrs. King's near hysteria.

Shriver, a Kennedy in-law, was head of the Catholic Inter-racial Council of Chicago. During the Montgomery bus boycott, he had introduced King to his first mass audience in Chicago. Shriver was the active liberal Kennedy clan member. Wofford told Shriver, "The trouble with your beautiful, passionate Kennedys is that they never show their passion. They don't understand symbolic action." Shriver listened and agreed to rush over to Chicago's O'Hare Airport, where JFK was waiting for a plane, and talk with him about calling Mrs. King. Shriver would try to speak with the candidate alone. The campaign staff, Shriver and Wofford agreed, could get bogged down in a discussion of whether or not to allow the telephone call to be made. Perhaps they would demand the candidate not make the call; it was risky, given the possibility of a Southern white backlash vote.

Shriver went to O'Hare Airport and, when the candidate was alone with him in a room, told him of King's arrest and Mrs. King's condition. "Why don't you telephone Mrs. King and give her your sympathy," Shriver recalls telling JFK. And then he made his case: "Negroes don't expect everything will change tomorrow no matter who's elected. But they do want to know whether you care. If you telephone Mrs. King they will know you understand and will help. You will reach their hearts and give support to a pregnant woman who is afraid her husband will be killed." Kennedy's spur-of-the-moment response to Shriver was, "That's a damn good idea. Get her on the phone."[103]

No advisor discussed the matter or intervened with the candidate between the time Shriver made the suggestion and the moment the call was made. The conversation between Kennedy and Mrs. King was brief. As Coretta King recalls, John Kennedy said, "I want to express to you my concern about your husband. I know this must be very hard for you. I understand that you are expecting a baby, and I just want you to know that

I was thinking about you and Dr. King." He closed the conversation by indicating, "If there is anything I can do to help please feel free to call on me."[104]

Soon afterward, Louis Martin, the editor of a major black newspaper, the *Chicago Defender*, and a member of the Democratic National Committee, called Bob Kennedy and told him, "You know, Jackie Robinson [a Nixon supporter, corporate executive, and former baseball star] . . . is trying to get Nixon to call a press conference, and they're going to blame the jailing of King on the Democrats because that judiciary [committee] and everybody down there are Democrats, and I think you've got to do something about it." At three o'clock the next morning, Bob Kennedy called Louis Martin back: "I just called the judge and I told him to get him [King] out of there [jail] or I'll take care of him and I gave him hell."[105] King was soon released from jail.[106]

There was concern within the leadership of both parties as to how this King-Kennedy episode was going to affect the election outcome. "Suddenly," recalls John Siegenthaler, Robert Kennedy's administrative assistant during the campaign, "civil rights was a crucial part of that 1960 campaign and we were flooded in the campaign headquarters with calls from governors and state party leaders from all across the South." They were concerned that the Kennedy actions would hurt them or the party. The Kennedy camp tried to smooth over white southern concerns and downplayed the affair in the public press. Robert Kennedy, as campaign manager, ordered the civil rights campaign group—Shriver, Wofford, and Martin—to close up shop. Henceforth, there was to be no more civil rights promotional activity in the Kennedy campaign.[107] He believed that the loss of southern white votes resulting from the Kennedy intervention would more than likely offset any gain in black votes.[108] He hoped that the incident would quickly move off the front pages. In fact, the *New York Times* initially gave scant space to the story of JFK's call to Mrs. King.

Nixon would not get openly involved in the affair. It was clear to many observers that Nixon's strategy had shifted as his campaign progressed. An early campaign swing through Greensboro, Atlanta, and Birmingham demonstrated to the candidate that there were large numbers of southern white voters willing to support him if the right appeal could be made. Nixon told newsman Theodore H. White, "I think it is time for the Republican candidate to quit conceding the South to the Democratic candidates."[109] But Henry Cabot Lodge inadvertently created consternation in the Nixon camp. He was still pursuing black votes while the signals at campaign headquarters had changed to a southern strategy. On October 12 in Harlem, the Massachusetts liberal stated, "There should be a Negro in the Cabinet. . . . It is part of our program and it is offered as a pledge." The next day, on orders from Nixon, he publicly withdrew his pledge.[110]

When King was arrested and the vice-president was asked about his reaction, he responded, "No comment." The Republican nominee wanted the White House to release a statement in support of King. Eisenhower refused—this was Nixon's campaign. Over the objections of the campaign staff, E. Frederic Morrow, the only black traveling with the Nixon campaign, implored the candidate to contact Mrs. King and to offer "to use his good offices to ameliorate the situation with the mayor or governor." Other black Republicans outside of the campaign staff, most notably Jackie Robinson, also asked the vice-president to intervene on behalf of the jailed minister. "The Negroes were waiting in the wings waiting to see which one of the candidates was going to make some specific pronouncements," recalls Morrow. "Mr. Kennedy did an excellent job and did the very thing that I suggested to Mr. Nixon." Morrow's advice was not taken. Nixon remained silent, and Morrow left the campaign train.[111]

But the issue would not be left in silence. Martin Luther King, Jr., released a public statement on the matter: "I want to make it patently clear that I am deeply grateful to Senator Kennedy for the genuine concern he expressed in my arrest." He continued: "Senator Kennedy exhibited moral courage of a high order."[112] King, Sr., a registered Republican and a prominent Atlanta leader and minister, expressed his gratitude for the Kennedy intervention. Coretta King also offered her profuse and public appreciation to the Kennedys for their support.

Harris Wofford and Sargent Shriver were genuinely concerned about Mrs. King, and that was the reason they had wanted the candidate to call her. They also believed that neither the candidate nor the rest of the campaign staff understood the depth of concern of black voters over King's well-being. While they understood that there might be a loss of southern white votes, they believed that this could be more than offset by a gain of black votes if the Kennedy camp acted quickly and smartly. The civil rights campaign group—Shriver, Wofford, and Martin—was determined to use this affair to pursue the black vote despite Bob Kennedy's admonition to close up shop. Wofford and Martin told Shriver that they had to get the message to the black voters. "They don't read the *New York Times* or the *Atlanta Constitution*," Martin commented. Shriver agreed. "Okay. We've got to use these wonderful quotations of Mrs. King, Martin Luther King. Jr., and his father. That's not propaganda, it's just reporting what has been said. Bobby couldn't object to that." As Wofford recalls, "We now had the ammunition and we were going to use it. That was precisely what we weren't supposed to do at all according to Bobby."

They sent their message directly to local black communities across the nation. Nearly two million pamphlets were eventually distributed by a Democratic front organization, the Freedom Crusade Committee. Harris Wofford and Louis Martin wrote the text of this political propaganda piece, "The Case of Martin Luther King, Jr.," with one bold captioned phrase on the cover page: "'No Comment' Nixon versus a Candidate with a Heart, Senator Kennedy." Between October 29 and November 1, they inundated the black community with the message. Robert Kennedy never objected to this propaganda barrage by the civil rights group. Later he remarked, "Louie Martin was the best; he had the best judgement."[113]

Arthur Schlesinger, Jr., wrote to John Kennedy that now even Eleanor Roosevelt "expressed herself with absolutely unprecedented enthusiasm about you." He also wrote that Mrs. Roosevelt said: "'I don't think anyone in our politics since Franklin [Roosevelt] has had the same vital relationship with crowds. . . . His intelligence and courage elicit emotions from his crowds which flow back to him and sustain and strengthen him.'"[114] Now there was enthusiasm and movement in the liberal camp.

King, who had maintained his neutrality despite repeated entreaties from the Kennedy camp, was furious. "Nixon just decided he would say nothing. . . . It indicated the direction this Presidency, this man, would take if he became President." King seethed. "He had been supposedly close to me, and he would call me frequently about things, getting, seeking my advice. And yet, when this moment came it was like he never heard of me, you see. So this is why I really considered him a moral coward."[115] The Nixon campaign moved on with its southern strategy.

The South and black civil rights became the hammer and anvil of the 1960 election. John Kennedy's decision was to strike a precarious balance between the two antagonists. Johnson of Texas was his draw to the South, and Johnson waged an effective campaign throughout the region. A strong civil rights plank and, more especially, his actions in the King episode were Kennedy's draw to the blacks and their liberal allies. The decision to call Coretta King was bold.

Nixon moved in a different direction. At the GOP convention he put together a northern-based alliance with a strong civil rights platform and a liberal vice-presidential nominee; but then he endorsed a southern partnership after his repudiation of Lodge's pledge and his silence during the King affair. His silence was deliberate; he, too, was gambling. But his gamble did not pay off. His southern gains were limited, and they did not offset his damage in the North.

The 1960 election was extremely close. Kennedy won by a margin of less than one percent of the popular vote. He was elected by only a plurality of the vote, and his opponent received 4 percent more of the total white vote. In the South, only Florida, Tennessee, and Virginia went Republican. Six Alabama electors and one Oklahoma elector joined all of the Mississippi electors to cast their electoral college votes for the States' Rights candidate, Harry F. Byrd of Virginia. Economic conservatism, anti-Catholicism, and racial reaction formed the basis for the southern defection from the Democratic party.[116]

On the other hand, 70 percent of the black vote went into the Democratic column—9 percent more than in 1956. The black vote was a major factor in Kennedy's victory in such key states as Illinois, Michigan, New Jersey, New York, Pennsylvania, South Carolina, and Texas.[117] More blacks than ever moved into the ranks of regular Democratic voters.[118] Civil rights were not a critical issue as the 1960 election got under way, but they became a major issue as the election moved to its conclusion. And John Kennedy did well for himself as he and his team advanced the issue.

2

An Intimidated President

JOHN KENNEDY'S CONCERNS moved from election to governance, and on a more distant horizon, to reelection. He moved to avoid civil rights battles, believing that his narrow election victory combined with the powerful presence of the southern congressional delegation limited his options on the legislative agenda. Of the twenty standing committees of the House, ten were chaired by southerners; nine of the sixteen standing committees of the Senate were chaired by southerners. According to James M. Burns, a Kennedy ally and biographer, southern congressional power "haunted" the president well into the second year of his administration.[1]

Furthermore, according to Wofford, the president was "intimidated by Congress."[2] Early in his administration, JFK wryly told a press conference, "The fact is the Congress looks more powerful sitting here than it did when I was there in Congress, particularly the bloc action, and it is a substantial power."[3] Larry O'Brien, head of the White House legislative liaison office, knew how to do his job, but he needed a president who could handle the Congress. He needed a president who could skillfully maneuver congressmen with the right personal touch, or the right bargain, or the right kind of political persuasion. "Kennedy," O'Brien recalls, "rarely asked a member [of Congress] for his vote on a specific piece of legislation."[4] He was uncomfortable in that role. He was never a Senate insider. Generally considered to be distant from his congressional colleagues, he did not seek nor did he become a member of the Senate's inner club. Kennedy was too busy running for the next office to bother to master either the members or the rules and manners of the Senate.[5] "He didn't really know what was possible and what wasn't in Congress," Roy Wilkins later wrote. "He was always hesitating, weighing what he could and could not do. I don't believe he ever understood the South [or Congress]."[6]

The fight to wrest control of the House Rules Committee from its chairman, Judge Howard W. Smith, dramatized the struggle for power both within Congress and between Congress and the young president.[7] The House Rules Committee controlled legislative access to the floor of the House, and the Rules Committee was controlled by Judge Smith with the support of a conservative Republican–southern Democratic voting bloc. In the August 1960 post-convention session of Congress, Judge Smith's committee blocked consideration of three critical pieces of legislation that the Kennedy-Johnson forces wanted to enact as a showpiece of the forthcoming campaign: federal aid to education, an increased minimum wage, and an expanded housing program.[8] Now the Kennedy administration had to wrest control of the Rules Committee from Judge Smith if it was going to move on its agenda.

To create a more compliant Rules Committee, Speaker Sam Rayburn suggested adding three new members to the committee, two Democrats and one Republican, thus providing the administration with a working majority of its membership. The Speaker went all out in support of the president. In an unusual move, he left the rostrum and, as an ordinary House member, pleaded with his colleagues to provide the leadership of the House and the president with a working majority on the committee. "The issue is very simple," the Speaker stated. "Shall the elected leadership of the House run its affairs, or shall the chairman of one committee run them?"[9] By a vote of 217 to 212, with 64, mainly southern, Democrats opposed, the House voted to support the Speaker and the president.

Rayburn saw the vote, in part, as an indication of Kennedy's poor standing with the Congress. The president had made telephone calls to House members in an attempt to persuade them to vote for the plan. But "he didn't change a vote," said the Speaker privately.[10] The president, on the other hand, interpreted the vote as another indicator of the South's power. "With all that going for us, with Speaker Rayburn's own reputation at stake, with all the pressures and appeals a new President could make, we won by five votes. That shows you what we are up against."[11]

The decision to delay civil rights legislation specifically was made before Kennedy took the oath of office. "Within ten days of his election," recalls Wilkins, "came word that he was not going to advocate any new civil rights legislation because he did not want to split the party."[12] The administration would pursue executive orders and other routes to black equality but not the legislative route.[13] As one White House aide said, "We knew that there were several Senators who might hold our [legislative] program hostage, and that was our primary consideration in delaying the bill." Another aide summarized the administration position: "We believed that civil rights had to wait until we could strengthen our hold in Congress."[14] At the opening of the Eighty-seventh Congress, the administration did not support the perennial liberal battle to ease the Senate filibuster rule. In fact, some liberals suspected that the president's forces weighed in against the change.[15] "There was great pressure from the liberal wing of the party on civil rights, and other areas," recalls Larry O'Brien, "but civil rights was the pressure point. They didn't realize what we had to overcome and this could only be done on a personal basis." O'Brien explains that personal efforts were being undertaken to win over the conservatives. "As time went on we were beginning to make progress. But it was to take time. The southerners and some of the other conservatives came to like John Kennedy and they began to work with us. They just didn't know John Kennedy when he was on the Hill with his absentee record and all of that."[16] As a newly elected president, Kennedy traded off any hopes for a civil rights bill for the time he needed to build up his relationship with the Congress.

In his first State of the Union Address to the Congress, the president included only one innocuous sentence on civil rights: "The denial of constitutional rights to some of our fellow Americans on account of race—at the ballot box and elsewhere—disturbs the national conscience and subjects us to the charge of world opinion that our democracy is not equal to the high promise of our heritage."[17] That was the sum and substance of his civil rights position. The administration did not publicly disavow civil rights legislation, but the abandonment of the legislative route was now a matter of Washington rumor. In early February Joseph Rauh, accompanied by Harvard political scientist Samuel Beer, columnist Robert Nathan, and liberal business executive Marvin Rosenberg, met with the president to discuss economic measures and civil rights proposals. JFK argued with the group jovially that they should "go out and make me" support legislation to help the unemployed and the poor. As Rauh recalls, "Then I started talking about civil rights and the President's whole demeanor changed. All he said is that the Attorney General was going to bring some voting rights suits." Rauh countered that the nation needed civil rights legislation. JFK's mood changed to anger. "He was perfectly happy to be pressured on the economic issues, but he was very unhappy to be pressured on civil rights."[18]

Some black rights advocates believed that the executive order strategy could work to secure a good share of the civil rights agenda. John Hannah, the chairman of the Civil Rights Commission and Roy Wilkins, on behalf of the NAACP and the LCCR, gave the White House a list of areas in which they wanted the immediate issuance of an executive order. Martin Luther King, Jr., wrote in the *Nation*: "It is no exaggeration to say that the President could give segregation its death blow through a stroke of a pen."[19] There were great hopes for the executive order route. There was also hope among the pro-rights activists that the president would eventually support, or at least not oppose, civil rights legislation.

On February 6 Sorenson met with several black leaders to discuss administration civil rights strategy. Sorenson told the black rights leaders that there would be no civil rights legislation but that the administration would pursue the executive order route. The next day Wilkins wrote to Sorenson: "Already there are grumblings, not only from Negro citizens but from independents and liberal Democrats, at the delay of indicating more than run-of-the-mill action in this area. The risks are there whether the Administration does much or little: the opposition is opposed, period. . . . [It is] surely too late for the Kennedy Administration to offer warmed-over, slightly revised, or piecemeal civil rights proposals which might have been daring in 1948 or 1953, but are mild as milk and toast today."[20] In mid February JFK informed a White House aide, "I don't want statements issued that we have withdrawn our support of this matter."[21]

Did the president withdraw support, or was he still thinking it over? His private comments on the issue revealed ambivalence. And, when pushed to take a public stand, he remained ambivalent. On March 8, 1961, he was asked at a news conference, "Do you feel that there is a need now for legislation in this area?" His response: "When I feel that there is a necessity for a congressional action, with a chance of getting that congressional action, then I will recommend that to the Congress."[22] Kennedy privately told Arthur Schlesinger, Jr., "There is no sense in raising hell, and then not being successful. There is no sense in putting the office of the Presidency on the line on an issue, and then being defeated."[23]

Civil rights were not an issue with which Kennedy had ever felt particularly comfortable. This did not change when he became president. As Arthur Schlesinger, Jr., wrote:

> He had at this point [in early 1961], I think, a terrible ambivalence about civil rights. While he did not doubt the depth of injustice or the need for remedy, he . . . concluded that there was no possible chance of passing a civil rights bill. Moreover . . . a fight for civil rights would alienate southern support he needed for other purposes. . . . And he feared that the inevitable defeat of a civil rights bill after debate and filibuster would heighten Negro resentment, drive the civil rights revolution to more drastic resorts and place a perhaps intolerable strain on the already fragile social fabric.[24]

Schlesinger recounts how the president wanted "to keep control over the demand for civil rights and this . . . might well, if stimulated, get out of hand." That was the great administration fear, and the fear would later become a reality. But for now, institutional politics, controllable politics, was the situation at stage center.

The pro–civil rights Republicans took advantage of the situation when the new president refused to follow up on his campaign rhetoric. In early May, Republican senator Kenneth Keating of New York remarked on the Senate floor, "[I] wonder, as to how so many who criticized President Eisenhower for not going far enough in this field can sit by silently accepting every excuse for this administration's failure to move forward one inch toward the goal of fair treatment for all Americans."[25] On May 10, 1961, Senator Clark and Congressman Celler introduced the civil rights bill called for by candidate Kennedy the previous summer. The White House responded: "The President has made it clear that he does not think it necessary at this time to enact civil rights legislation."[26]

The perspective of the liberals outside of the Oval Office differed from the perspective of those within. "It had been too much, perhaps, to expect that the Administration would press for the far-reaching, hard-hitting [civil rights] bill," stated one ADA report. "It was not unrealistic to hope that the White House might be benevolently neutral. Its blunt statement of disassociation . . . struck Clark and Celler like a dash of cold water."[27] The NAACP's Roy Wilkins publicly blasted the administration. He termed JFK's call for executive action rather than support for legislation "an offering of a cactus bouquet to Negro parents and their children."[28] Privately, Wilkins wrote: "A key phrase in the [New York Times] dispatch noted that there had been 'very little pressure' for new civil rights legislation." The implication, Wilkins inferred, was that "we shall obtain no more in the way of badly needed new legislation [than w]hat we elicit by the breadth and strength of our indicated interest."[29] This was not an auspicious debut for a pro–black rights administration.

It was also not an auspicious debut for an administration wedded to a liberal program. Eventually, Kennedy's tax program, the reduction of corporate taxes to increase productivity, was enacted into legislation. A watered-down minimum wage bill was also signed into law. However, the administration's priority liberal legislation in education, housing, and medical care, all "as familiar to Congress as Sam Rayburn's bald head," according to New York Times correspondent Tom Wicker, never went anywhere."Between his apparent paucity of ideas, and his obvious conciliation of the South," Wicker continues, "Kennedy was diluting the enthusiastic loyalty he needed from the urban liberals."[30] The administration's legislative record declined even further as the years went by, despite the presence of additional liberal Democrats in the next Congress. In 1961 48.4 percent the president's legislative requests were approved by the Congress. In 1962 congressional approval declined to 44.6 percent. By 1963 it had declined to 27.2 percent—the lowest approval rating ever recorded by Congressional Quarterly, a nonpartisan research service.[31]

With the legislative approach foreclosed, the civil rights forces still believed they could turn to the courts as an avenue of appeal. The courts had been the major vehicle by which blacks had pursued their rights. The *Brown* decision mandated desegregation of schools, and the Montgomery bus boycott was judicially resolved in favor of the blacks. Martin Luther King, Jr., after his experience with the Montgomery boycott, wrote in 1958:

> It was a great relief to be in a federal court. Here the atmosphere of justice prevailed. No one can understand the feeling that came to a Southern Negro on entering a federal court unless he sees with his own eyes and feels with his own soul the tragic sabotage of justice in the city and state courts of the South. The Negro goes into these courts knowing the cards are stacked against him. Here he is virtually certain to face a prejudiced jury or a biased judge, and is openly robbed with little hope of redress. But the Southern Negro goes into the federal court with the feeling that he has an honest chance of justice before the law.[32]

The Kennedy administration's pursuit of the southern Democrats altered the composition of some key federal district courts in the South, so that they all too often came to resemble the "stacked" state and county courts. In what Louis Martin believes was a deal worked out between the Kennedys and Eastland, John Kennedy appointed five segregationist judges to the federal bench in the South and five black judges elsewhere.[33] The ubiquitous southern problem was put forward by the Kennedys as the basis for these appointments. The Senate Judiciary Committee was chaired by Mississippi's Senator James Eastland, an absolute segregationist. Naturally, the senator from Mississippi was going to oppose the appointment of liberal judges to the southern federal bench. But the Kennedys believed that they needed Eastland's support or acquiescence for the confirmation of any federal judicial appointments. In return, Eastland needed the Kennedys' nominating powers to be used on behalf of his friends and his interests. The Kennedys, of course, believed that the costs of the modus vivendi were worth the benefits, but the costs were high.[34]

The original Kennedy hope was that the federal courts would continue to be a major focus for black rights. The Kennedy appointments cut deeply into the realization of this hope. The NAACP had taken the legal approach as the strategic route for securing black rights. Black citizens looked to the federal court system as their steadfast ally. With the reliability of the courts in question, blacks were going to have to reconsider their strategic options; but the administration was determined to use court appointments as a bargaining chip with the South.

Burke Marshall, the assistant attorney general for civil rights, found that "Senator Eastland was not hard to deal with on judicial appointments." And Robert Kennedy opined that Eastland "never . . . caused us any troubles." This was a matter of judgment. When JFK asked Justice William O. Douglas for a recommendation to fill a Supreme Court vacancy, the justice recommended Circuit Judge J. Skelly Wright of New Orleans. Wright was an avowed defender of the Supreme Court's constitutional position on desegregation. It was Judge Wright's order that began the desegregation process in New Orleans. Kennedy said he could not get Eastland to accept Wright. "It would be a terrific battle," he told Douglas. "But that is the kind of battle to pick—and you would win," the justice countered. JFK disagreed. Instead he sent Wright's name up for an appointment to the Fifth Circuit Court of Appeals in the South. Even this was not to be. "In the end, Bobby told me they were sending up the name of J. Skelly Wright to fill a vacancy on the Court of Appeals for the District of Columbia," Douglas writes. "It was a bitter pill for me to swallow because the South needed a Skelly Wright on one of its courts and the Supreme Court needed a Skelly Wright on it, for on racial problems our Court was much more fragile than the appearances indicated."[35] The administration would not challenge Eastland and the southerners on their home turf if a challenge could be avoided. Thus, it was not hard to deal with Eastland on judicial appointments.

The first Kennedy judicial appointment to the southern bench was William Howard Cox, a lifelong Mississippi friend of Senator Eastland.[36] The chairman of the American Bar Association's Judicial Selection Review Committee, Bernard Siegal, was disturbed by Cox's racial views, and he recommended to the attorney general that he personally interview the candidate. Cox flew to Washington. "We sat on my couch, in my own office, and I talked to him," recalled RFK. "I said the great reservation I had was the question of whether he'd enforce the law and whether he'd live up to . . . the interpretation of the Constitution by the Supreme Court. He assured me that he would."[37] Roy Wilkins assured the attorney general of quite the opposite: "The consensus that William Howard Cox is considered a conservative by his fellow Mississippians bodes ill for any litigation not keyed to the mores of 1861. For 986,000 Negro Mississippians," the black leader added, "Judge Cox will be another strand in their barbed wire fence.[38]

Judge Cox became notorious for his outrageously bigoted remarks from the bench, for his unconscionable delay of pending civil rights litigation, and for his absolute refusal to adhere to Supreme Court civil rights rulings. In open court he called black voting applicants "a bunch of niggers . . . acting like a bunch of chimpanzees."[39] When John Doar, a Justice Department attorney, asked for a trial date for a pending case, Judge Cox called him "stupid" and wrote: "I spend most of my time fooling with the lousy cases brought before me by your department in the Civil Rights field."[40] Judge Cox had more civil rights cases reversed on appeal than did any other federal judge. In Alabama, Georgia, Louisiana, and South Carolina, this pattern was repeated. Kennedy's deputy attorney general, Nicholas deB Katzenbach, later said of the poor Kennedy appointments, "The trouble is that none of the politicians really understand what a high price it is to appoint bad judges."[41]

The Kennedy administration also mixed electoral politics into its dealings with the courts. Time and again civil rights litigation was delayed at the insistence of the attorney general, so that southern political allies would not be embarrassed or defeated in election campaigns. The United States Civil Rights Commission hearings were repeatedly postponed in Louisiana and Mississippi at the insistence of the president and his brother so that they would not interfere with pending litigation or cause undue hardship to the reelection efforts of other southern allies. For example, in the spring of 1961, as commission hearings were about to get under way in Louisiana, RFK called Berl Bernhard, the staff director of the commission. "Do you know what you're doing?" the attorney general yelled. "If you continue with your hearing and make race a big issue, DeLessups Morrison will lose the primary election for mayor and you will have destroyed one of the truly moderate politicians in the South. I want it called off— now!" The hearings were called off.[42]

In December of 1962 Robert Kennedy wrote to Civil Rights Commission chairman John Hannah: "It is my judgement that the work of the Department of Justice might be severely hampered by hearings held by the Commission in Mississippi at this time. As the Commission knows, we are engaged in very far-reaching and important litigation against the state and public officials of Mississippi."[43] This judgment remained constant throughout the Kennedy presidential years, and Civil Rights Commission hearings did not take place in Mississippi until 1965. Although federal litigation was still in process, the hearings had no tangible impact on the outcome of any case.

In March of 1963 the attorney general reiterated his opposition to newly proposed commission hearings in Mississippi. "In my view," Robert Kennedy argued, "the reasons against such a step which are set forth in my letter of December 15 [1962] to you on this subject are still valid."[44] "Two or three times we decided to hold . . . hearing[s] in Mississippi," recounts Father Theodore Hesburgh, a commission member, "and [they] were called off because of political considerations. . . . And this would generally come from the Attorney General or from, in one case I think, the President. . . . I had the impression all along that political expediency was a very strong force in this whole administration."[45]

The Civil Rights Commission was never the Kennedy administration's favorite government agency. In the early months of the administration, Robert Kennedy told a meeting of the commissioners, "You're second guessers. I am the one who has to get the job done." When commission members argued that litigation alone would not get southern blacks registered to vote but that it would take legislation striking down literacy tests and the creation of federal voting registrars, the attorney general responded, "I can do it, and will do it, in my way, and you're making it more difficult."[46]

In the summer of 1961 the administration backed legislation to provide for a two-year extension of the commission. But as Roy Wilkins noted, "The Democratic party platform . . . promised 'the new Democratic Administration will broaden the scope and strengthen the present Commission and make it permanent.' Now, today, August 30, the Senate is voting on a proposal to extend the CRC *for only two years*. Nothing about 'broadening the scope.' Nothing about permanence." With indignation Wilkins pointed out, "It is voting this way because the Senate Majority Leader Mike Mansfield has turned his back upon the platform pledge. . . . It is reported that Senator Mansfield's action has been endorsed by very high Administration leaders and that a conference at the White House agreed upon the two-year limitation."[47] To Clarence Mitchell, the chief NAACP lobbyist, the bargains being struck were beginning to make the Kennedy administration look "suspiciously like a dude ranch with Senator James O. Eastland [of Mississippi and the Judiciary Committee] the general manager and Howard Smith [of Virginia and the Rules Committee] the foreman."[48]

These machinations not withstanding, the president did provide his black allies with some rewards. Yet even these actions were often equivocal.[49] Military reserve units were desegregated, but state National Guard units were permitted to remain segregated. State employment agencies were ordered to stop filling discriminatory employment orders, but federal funds were not cut off if the orders were disobeyed. Administration support for school desegregation became stronger than it ever had been during the Eisenhower years. Through 1960, only 17 school districts in the South were desegregated; by 1963, 166 schools districts were desegregated. Yet, in Mississippi and Alabama there were no desegregated schools until 1963, and only one percent of the black children living in all of the former Confederate states went to school with white children.[50]

To civil rights advocates, probably the most irritating inaction by JFK involved the promised order to end racial discrimination in federally assisted housing. This was the one commitment the president could carry out on his own, and he had repeated this pledge throughout the campaign, even using it during his debate with Nixon. Yet nothing had come of his personal pledge. Civil rights supporters sent thousands of pens to JFK to remind him of his "stroke of the pen" pledge, and black leaders repeatedly contacted the president about his pledge to issue the order. In December of 1961, for example, Roy Wilkins telegraphed: "Current reports suggest that the long-awaited Executive Order banning discrimination in federally aided housing may be pigeonholed indefinitely for fear it will irritate Southern congressmen and thus endanger the Administration's legislative program in the forthcoming session of Congress." The NAACP leader reminded the president: "The same argument was used to justify the Administration's lack of support for vitally needed civil rights bills in this year's session. We were told that Executive Orders were the better strategy because they would arouse less opposition from the South."[51]

The White House maintained its view of the matter. In October of 1961 the Office of Legal Counsel in the Justice Department drafted an order to ban the use of federal loans for segregated housing.[52] It was a restrictive order, with the president telling Sorenson to "make the order as broad as we were certain our writ would run and no further."[53] As Wilkins feared, even this limited order was delayed. Lee White, one of JFK's key civil rights advisors, argued that in the North and in the South "there were an awful lot of people running for reelection who let it be known that, if the President signs that Order [prior to the 1962 elections], tell him he'd better plan on someone else representing my district."[54] Some business and banking officials feared that the order might harm the construction industry.

A major justification put forward by the administration for

the delay of the housing order was that it wanted to create a Department of Urban Affairs. Robert C. Weaver, the black chairman of the Housing and Home Finance Agency, was in line to head the proposed department. The signing of the order, it was feared, would jeopardize the appointment of Weaver to this cabinet post when—or if—it was created. The chairmen of the committees dealing with this legislation were Senator John Sparkman and Congressman Albert Rains, both of Alabama. As Lee White noted in a November 1961 memo to his chief: "[Both] are, of course, strongly opposed to any independent housing order. And quite clearly the bill to create [a] Dept. [of] Urban Affairs would be lost if [the] order [is] issued—it is already in trouble, however, and on the civil rights issue."[55] Weaver made it clear to White that he preferred the order be signed even if it meant his losing the chance to join the cabinet.[56]

In the end, during a Thanksgiving weekend news conference, sandwiched between an announcement of the Soviet withdrawal of bombers from Cuba and the easing of the Sino-India border conflict, the president acknowledged that he had issued an executive order banning discrimination in housing built with federally aided loans.[57] The promised "simple stroke of a pen" took almost two years to be accomplished and affected only 20 percent of new housing. The announcement was deliberately downplayed, and the order was so limited in impact that the *Pittsburgh Courier*, a leading black newspaper, editorially commented: "Negroes are getting very weary of tokenism hailed as victories."[58]

The Kennedy administration, yielding to pressure, did provide blacks with some very real victories. The administration established the Committee on Equal Employment Opportunity and appointed the vice-president to head it. Kennedy appointed more blacks to federal judgeships and executive positions than any previous president. Not only were several outstanding blacks given highly visible administrative posts, but in many departments the systematic recruitment of blacks into middle-level management posts was undertaken with great success. Louis Martin prepared a list of 750 "superblacks," blacks with

Ph.D.s; he constantly prodded the administration to fill vacancies with names from his list.[59] And the administration provided symbolic rewards to blacks through rhetorical support of black rights and visible Presidential contact with black leaders.[60] Eisenhower met but once in the White House with a group of black leaders. John Kennedy regularly invited groups of black leaders to the national mansion. In the period after Little Rock, the Eisenhower administration provided little leadership to the nation in its handling of civil rights.[61] The outrage with which southern leaders reacted to the Little Rock Central High School desegregation episode, in which the president sent in federal troops to uphold the desegregation order of the federal courts, was not soon forgotten. More concerned with maintaining continuity in civil rights policy than with striving for change, the Kennedy administration provided equivocal leadership: there clearly were some substantive and symbolic victories for blacks, but they had expected more.

Eisenhower was gone. The Camelot administration raised expectations. To most black leaders the payoffs received from the Kennedy White House did not match the promises that had been made. Equal treatment was expected but not given. Wilkins's plaintive words to Harris Wofford in April of 1961 reflected the increasing frustration of the black leadership with the Kennedy approach to politics, blacks, and the Democratic coalition.

> It may be that the Administration has proceeded in other fields as it did in civil rights, but I would be inclined to doubt it. . . . I may be in error, but not once were the responsible Negro leaders called in and told formally what the Administration planned to do. . . .
>
> Obviously if such a sharp departure as planning no legislative action were in the plans, the civil rights leaders not only were entitled to be told, but to be told, in more or less precise terms, what substitute action on what levels, the government planned. . . .
>
> The Kennedy Administration has done with Negro citizens what it has done with a vast number of Americans: it has charmed them. It has intrigued them. Every seventy-two hours

it has delighted them. On the Negro question it has smoothed Unguentine on a sting burn. . . .

It is plain why the civil rights legislation was abandoned, but nothing was accomplished by the maneuver. It did not save the Minimum Wage Bill from gutting and it did not save other legislation. The Southerners and their Northern satellites . . . function whether a civil rights bill is proposed or withheld. An Administration gets as much by whacking them as by wooing them. JFK might as well have had a civil rights bill in the hopper.[62]

The president's summer 1961 meeting at the White House with NAACP national and state leaders illustrates some of the problems as Wilkins saw them. JFK personally arranged the chairs for his guests. Jackie Kennedy put in a gracious appearance, talking about the Lincoln china. The NAACP leaders pressed for a commitment to civil rights legislation while the president listened attentively and respectfully. When the presentation ended, he said no. He then gave several of the NAACP leaders a delightful tour of the White House. Much to Wilkins chagrin, "just about everyone left the White House feeling charmed by the man."[63] John Kennedy was a gentleman, but he was implacable in his opposition to civil rights legislation. His assessment remained: the issue had to be finessed. It was simply too politically important to be left to the believers.

Robert Kennedy, the family political genius, was placed at the head of the Justice Department to handle the most politically sensitive issues faced by the administration, including civil rights.[64] It was a high-risk decision to appoint Bob Kennedy the attorney general of the United States; it openly tied the president to the Department of Justice. But civil rights would be under the watchful eye of the president's most trusted surrogate.

Robert Kennedy was unequivocal about how he and his brother viewed his position: "It was just understood by us, which has always been understood, that I have my area of responsibility and I'd do it."[65] Wofford, who was a White House civil rights advisor during the first half of the administration, noted that "most of his [JFK's] key decisions, anything that was really cutting in civil rights, were made alone with Bob Kennedy, and you really didn't know what happened."[66] The closeness of the two brothers in this area was taken for granted by the black leaders. "Whenever I talked with the Attorney General," said King, "I always felt I was talking with the President. . . . And I felt that when he said something to me, he was speaking for the President. So I always interpreted our conversations . . . as he was really articulating the convictions of the President. This was true in all our dealings."[67] As Wilkins succinctly put it, "I think we were able to say 'the Kennedys' because I don't think there was any difference between Robert and Jack."[68] What ever Justice did or what ever it did not do, it was the president's department.

Robert Kennedy staffed the Justice Department with some of the best attorneys in the land. They were mostly Harvard and Yale men. They were able, cautious, committed to procedural due process under the law, and imbued with the idea of dispassionate justice.[69] The Kennedy concept of the Justice Department is evident in the basis of the decision not to hire Wofford as the assistant attorney general for civil rights. "The major one [appointment] I worried over was the head of the Civil Rights Division," Bob Kennedy recalled in 1964. "The fellow that naturally should have been appointed was Harris Wofford, who worked for us on civil rights during the campaign. I was reluctant to appoint him because he was so committed to civil rights emotionally and what I wanted was a tough lawyer who could look at things—matters, objectively, and give advice and handle things properly. That's why I finally settled on Burke Marshall and didn't have Harris Wofford."[70]

Wofford picks up the thread of the story. "Robert Kennedy called to explain to me that he had decided upon Burke Marshall. He emphasized the problem of dealing with the Chairman of the Senate Judiciary Committee, Senator Eastland of Mississippi. . . . Identification with the civil rights movement would be a great liability for the Assistant Attorney General." Wofford understood what was also left unsaid. "I realized the liability he mentioned extended to my relationship with him and [Deputy Attorney General Byron] White. If they viewed me as a crusader, and did not think I could be committed and critical at the same time, they would regularly discount my judgement."[71]

Soon after taking office, the administration decided that black enfranchisement was the major civil rights activity to be pursued by the Justice Department. John Kennedy was convinced, Sorenson writes, "that enfranchising the Negroes in the South—where less than ten percent were registered in many counties . . . could in time dramatically alter the intransigence of Southern political leaders on all civil rights measures, shift the balance of political power [in a liberal direction] in several states, and immunize Southern politics from the demagogues."[72] "I felt," said Robert Kennedy, "nobody could really oppose voting. . . . [And] from the vote, from participation in the elections flow all other rights far, far more easily." It was natural to go after voting. "[This] was the area in which we had the greatest authority. . . . And we could do something here."[73] A two-pronged strategy was developed: aggressive litigation in the courts and an active program of support for black voter registration in the South.[74]

What appeared to be a safe and viable solution to two important and interrelated problems had been worked out. Southern blacks would be enfranchised and hence get their civil rights through voting pressures on southern politicians; southern politicians would become more liberal and therefore more politically compatible with their northern Democratic colleagues. The Kennedys did not consider that the white southerners also understood this line of reasoning and that they were not about to easily yield to its logic. Then again, most Americans believed that voting was sacred, and overt interference with the ballot would be unacceptable even in the South. This was the premise held by the Eisenhower administration and by Lyndon Johnson, as well as by many liberals when they passed the 1957 Civil Rights Act.

But the 1950s civil rights legislation had proved to be ineffective against an intractable South. Not a single black voter had been added to the voting lists by litigation carried out under the Eisenhower Justice Department.[75] Eisenhower's Justice Department filed only eight voting-rights suits and had only six cases brought to trial from 1958 through 1960. Kennedy's Justice Department filed fifty voting-rights suits and tried thirty-three from 1961 through 1963.[76] Yet there was a flaw in this part of the strategy in addition to the judicial appointments problem. William L. Taylor, an attorney on the Civil Rights Commission staff and later director of the commission, notes that the commission "had come to the conclusion in 1959, after investigating voting denials, that you just couldn't get at this problem in a real way by bringing case by case litigation."[77] It was simply impossible to go at this matter piecemeal and make a significant dent in the problem. The Civil Rights Commission joined the black rights advocates in their position: only legislation was going to solve the problem.

Black voter registration, under pressure from ever tougher registration requirements and massive disfranchisement, as well as hostile white voting registrars, actually declined in many areas of the South during the 1950s. Just over a quarter of all age-eligible southern blacks were registered to vote in 1960, and in the Deep South there were many counties with almost no black registrants.[78] In 1959 the Civil Rights Commission recommended that a system of federally appointed registrars be established by Congress to permit blacks to register when local authorities refused to act.[79] But the Kennedy administration was determined to pursue its litigation strategy. The Justice Department pursued "legal suits that took a lot of manpower and a lot of time and [it was] very difficult to get results," recounts Assistant Attorney General Katzenbach. "In fact," he continues, "in my judgement, they never did get any results until the 1965 Voting Rights Act was passed. You could not deal with it by lawsuits."[80] But the strategy was in place and was not revisited by the Kennedys. The possible alternative approaches were simply precluded by administration leaders, given their priorities and their assessment of the political landscape.

The legal strategy was time-consuming, and the black revolution was not waiting patiently for it to unfold. A burgeoning activism by young southern blacks, usually backed by respected black leaders and the black community, was getting out of control. The repertoire of black tactics expanded from sit-ins to pickets and boycotts. The black rights activists often confronted white hostility and violence.[81] Covertly, and often overtly, members of state and local law enforcement agencies frequently sanctioned the white violence. "What makes the South so dangerous," Virginia Durr, a southern white liberal, wrote to Burke Marshall, "is that the law itself has become lawless."[82] The lawlessness of the South would occasionally be exposed to the North when a particularly infamous lynching or miscarriage of justice took place. But by and large, the South was not perceived to be a lawless region.

A group of seven black and six white freedom riders left Washington D.C., on May 4, 1961, the seventh anniversary of the *Brown* decision, and headed for New Orleans, resolved to test a 1960 Supreme Court ruling, *Virginia v. Boynton*, which ended legal racial segregation of interstate travel. Across the South, interstate facilities—restrooms, cafeterias, lodging—still remained segregated, and the interstate buses still moved with blacks to the rear and whites up front. On May 14 an integrated freedom ride bus was burned in Anniston, Alabama; as its passengers fled, they were attacked by a white mob. When another freedom ride bus reached Birmingham, its occupants were brutally beaten by a white mob. A paid informant told the FBI in advance that the Birmingham public safety commissioner, Eugene "Bull" Connor, was going to give local Ku Klux Klan members fifteen to twenty minutes to beat the riders until "it looked like a bulldog got ahold of them." Afterwards, the riders would be arrested. All went according to Chief Connor's plan. The FBI director, J. Edgar Hoover, was informed in advance of the matter but watched the events unfold and never notified the attorney general of the planned attack.[83]

The freedom rider strategy created a crisis for the nation and the administration because it brought into public display the lawlessness of the South and the lack of control of the situation—by the administration. The riders were determined to bring the conscience of the nation into confrontation with the reality of segregation.[84] The momentum of the movement was now taking on an irreversible life of its own. The freedom rides created a stir that confronted the administration's fears that things might well "get out of hand."[85]

The freedom ride episode convinced the Kennedys they had

to move to halt the black demonstrations—the blacks were creating a crisis. They were acting as provocateurs, and the white reaction was embarrassing to the administration. It all had politically dangerous repercussions both nationally and internationally. Robert Kennedy was surprised and angry that the bus rides took place. He called Wofford, now the White House assistant for civil rights, and told him, "Stop them! Get your friends off those buses."[86] He telephoned King and asked him to stop the freedom riders, because they would "alienate a lot of support" and "embarrass" the president at his upcoming meeting in Vienna with Premier Khrushchev.[87] The attorney general called for a "cooling off" period.[88] James Farmer, the national director of CORE replied, "We have been cooling off for 350 years. If we cool off any more, we will be in a deep freeze."[89]

The original CORE-recruited group, their ranks decimated by beatings, was augmented by volunteers from the Student Nonviolent Coordinating Committee (SNCC). The scenes of bloody attacks continued to go out over the airwaves. On May 20, when the riders reached Montgomery, they were again attacked by a white mob with the connivance of local police; this time the FBI agents watched on the sidelines, taking photographs and making notes.[90] RFK could not understand what the riders were doing: "They had made their point. What was the purpose of continuing with it?"[91]

The administration moved to protect the riders and to get them out of immediate danger. Federal marshals were sent in to observe events and keep order. The marshals protected King and Farmer as they held a meeting in a Montgomery church, surrounded by an armed mob of whites determined to wreak vengeance upon them. Things were so far out of hand that the attorney general persuaded Governor Patterson of Alabama to send in the Alabama National Guard to keep the peace.[92] When Greyhound bus drivers refused to drive the buses after the violence and rioting, the attorney general called the Greyhound management and hectored them into providing a driver for the group. He wanted the riders out of Alabama.

The determination of the riders to go from Alabama into Mississippi shocked the attorney general. "Oh my God," he said, when Fred Shuttlesworth, a black rights leader in Alabama, told him of the plans, "not through Mississippi!" Shuttlesworth responded, "You yourself said you can't tell people where to travel on the highways."[93] To the freedom ride sponsors Mississippi was a perfect place to go. King chaired an SCLC meeting that concluded: "[The need is] to intensify the freedom ride so that national public attention can be brought to examine the denial of legal rights of interstate travel . . . in the hard-core Southern states."[94]

The attorney general may not have understood what King was up to, but he did understand that he needed to get the situation under control. He had to come up with a strategy to stop the mayhem that was inevitably going to come in Mississippi if the riders and the white mobs were allowed to pursue their independent courses of action. The attorney general explored the situation with Senator Eastland, talking to him "seven, eight, or twelve times each day about what was going to happen when [the riders] got to Mississippi and what needed to be done."[95] An agreement was reached between the attorney general, Governor Ross Barnet, and former governor James P. Coleman. In return for the state of Mississippi making sure that no mobs would attack them, the riders would be summarily arrested when they arrived in Jackson. On May 21 the riders left Montgomery, rode through Mississippi under National Guard protection, and were arrested when they arrived in Jackson. Of course, as Burke Marshall later stated, the arrests "were unconstitutional . . . without any question."[96]

Robert Kennedy spoke with Martin Luther King, Jr., who was in Jackson with the freedom riders. Kennedy asked King to halt the rides, and in return he would arrange for everyone arrested to be released on bail. King said he could not agree to the arrangement. "It's a matter of conscience and morality," said the minister. "They must use their lives and their bodies to right a wrong." RFK replied, "This is not going to have the slightest effect on what the government is going to do in this field or any other. The fact that they stay in jail is not going to have the slightest effect on me." King said that perhaps if thousands of students came down that might help. The attorney general countered, "The country belongs to you as much as me.

Don't make statements that sound like a threat. That's not the way to deal with us." King replied, "You must understand that we have made no gains without pressure, and I hope that pressure can always be moral, legal, and peaceful." The attorney general shot back, "[Only] strong federal action" will solve the problem. At the end of this conversation, King told RFK, "I'm deeply appreciative of what the administration is doing. I see a ray of hope, but I am different than my father, I feel the need of being free now!" Subsequently, King told his fellow activists, "You know, they [the administration] don't understand the social revolution going on in the world, and therefore they don't understand what we're doing." The attorney general was perplexed. He told Harris Wofford, "This is too much. I wonder whether they have the best interests of their country at heart."[97]

The freedom ride episode was over. By June some of the riders were headed back north. Most of the riders would not be out of jail until CORE posted a five-hundred-dollar bond forty days after they were arrested. Burke Marshall joined Harris Wofford in asking the president to say "a few stout words" of support for the riders when they returned to Washington.[98] The CORE leadership and King's Southern Christian Leadership Conference also requested that the president see the riders. These requests were turned down.[99] On May 29 the administration asked the Interstate Commerce Commission (ICC) to ban segregation in interstate bus terminals. JFK told a July 19, 1961, press conference, "In my judgement, there's no question of the legal rights of the freedom travelers—Freedom Riders, to move in interstate commerce. And these rights . . . stand provided they are exercised in a peaceful way."[100] The riders were peaceful, and they were peacefully arrested with the foreknowledge of the attorney general and the president. Two days before the president's press conference, Father Hesburgh wrote to Harris Wofford that he was concerned about "the Administration's stance on civil rights progress versus practical politics."[101] On September 22, 1961, the ICC banned racially segregated interstate transportation facilities.[102] The immediate objective of the freedom rides was met. In addition, the nation was again paying attention to black grievances.

The freedom ride episode had several long-term consequences for the black rights movement and for the Kennedys.
"We were successful; we created a crisis situation. It was world-
wide news and headlines and everybody was watching it—
people all over the world," said James Farmer. "The Attorney
General had to act; and he did. He called upon the ICC to issue
an order—a ruling with teeth in it which he could enforce."[103]
Wilkins believes the rides "began to bend the Administration or
at least to convince the Administration that perhaps the attack
[on segregation] agreed upon was not adequate."[104] Thurgood
Marshall, the head of the NAACP legal team, recalled that "the
Freedom Rides upset everybody's charts and tables—including
our time table at the NAACP. . . . Everybody was pushed to
move faster than they had moved before."[105]

3

A Reluctant Participant

THE KENNEDYS HESITATED to make more of a commitment to civil rights. The administration's fear of southern defections on the Hill and in the electorate was still more potent than its fear of more civil rights crises. But the administration could not avoid being drawn deeper into the civil rights battle. John Lewis of SNCC noted that for the black activists this was a conscious decision. "We tried to use the federal government as a referee, and as a sympathetic referee."[1] The last thing the administration was interested in was being a referee between the black rights movement and the white South. This was a no-win situation from its perspective. As a referee the administration would have to make decisions that could alienate either the white South or the blacks and their liberal allies from the Democratic party. The White House hoped to find a way to ameliorate the conflict between the two increasingly antagonistic alliance partners while appearing to be above the fray.

Frederick Dutton, a liberal Kennedy aide, wrote a memo to Harris Wofford and Louis Martin, two of the strongest black rights advocates with access to the president, and summed up the general state of political realities: "The dynamics both here and abroad compelling desegregation in this country are accelerating. How to provide leadership for those forces and to moderate Southern difficulties without destroying the [Democratic] Congressional coalition at mid-term is the nub of the problem."[2]

The Voter Education Project (VEP) became the administration vehicle for dealing with this problem. The Kennedys concluded that a Southern black voter-registration program with widespread black-based participation would get blacks on

the voting list, usefully channel the fervent energy of the movement, and at the same time, limit the antagonism of the white
South toward blacks and the administration.[3] The immediate
administration goal was to move blacks from participation in
dangerous and unpredictable demonstrations to participation
in safe and controllable voter-registration projects.[4]

The specifics of the VEP arrangement developed out of a
series of talks during the spring of 1961 among Burke Marshall; Harold Fleming, the director of the Southern Regional
Council (SRC), an established southern biracial organization
that promoted interracial understanding; and Stephen Currier, a millionaire and founder, underwriter, and president of
the Taconic Foundation, an organization founded to promote
racial harmony and economic opportunity.[5] Fleming had a personal relationship with Burke Marshall and personal contacts
with both of the Kennedy brothers.[6] "Freedom Rides and the
sit-ins made life difficult for the Kennedys," Fleming points
out, "and they were looking for some way to channel it all."
Fleming viewed the origin of the VEP as emerging out of discussions between himself and Burke Marshall. 'I first talked to
Stephen Currier. I told him about Burke's interest, etc. . . . One
thing was certain, nothing could happen without the money
and the tax exemption." After the initial Marshall-Fleming conversations, "Bobby Kennedy met with some groups at Justice."[7]

On May 15, 1961, the day after the burning of the freedom
ride bus in Anniston, Alabama, Roy Wilkins met with Robert
Kennedy and Burke Marshall to discuss a voter-registration
drive. On June 16 Burke Marshall and several key Justice Department officials met with leaders of the NAACP, CORE,
SCLC, SNCC, and the NSA (National Student Association, a
nationwide college-based group of student activists). Leaders of
the National Urban League were to attend future meetings and
join the project, but the NSA dropped out of the project. The
assistant attorney general told the group that voter registration
would be far more useful to the black rights movement than
freedom rides or other demonstrations.

Currier-planned VEP meetings followed on July 11, July 28,
and August 23. It was agreed that the SRC would serve as the
umbrella organization under which the VEP would operate.

The five black groups would receive funds from the VEP to register voters in the South.[8] Foundation funds would be located to aid the project, and the Justice Department would cooperate in any way possible to ensure the success of the VEP.[9]

The administration played an active role in pulling the final pieces of the project together. Wiley Branton, an attorney who represented the children in the Little Rock school crisis, became executive director of the project after Burke Marshall and Bobby Kennedy directly approached him to take the job—"Twisting my arm a little bit," he said.[10] The last major impediment to the creation of the VEP was the need for the program to have tax-exempt status. Everyone involved understood that this was imperative for major contributions to be obtained. First, Fleming and others wrote up an application for a federal tax exemption that described the VEP as an educational endeavor, that is, the VEP would pursue research on the causes and consequences of black disfranchisement.[11] Then Robert Kennedy worked with the director of the Internal Revenue Service, and they agreed that the IRS would grant the project tax-exempt status.[12] Things were going according to plan, and the Kennedys hoped it would continue that way.

Generally, the mainstream civil rights leaders backed the administration–Southern Regional Council plan, but the more activist groups refused to give up the tactic of mass demonstrations. Martin Luther King told the attorney general, "Well, we realize the importance of this [voter registration drive], but I think demonstrations are very important to bring the issue of discrimination and segregation . . . out in the open."[13] Farmer emphasized the position that direct action and voter registration were "not mutually exclusive."[14] SNCC had a fierce internal debate over the issue of voter-registration efforts versus other activities. As a consequence, SNCC established two separate wings, one for voter registration and one for other activist pursuits.[15] Thus, early on, the administration was aware that the voting-rights drive as a tactic to control black activism would have only limited success.

In March 1962 the Voter Education Project was officially launched. The major black organizations all participated in the effort. The administration was kept abreast of project developments as they occurred.[16] As the project got underway, Burke Marshall wrote to Leslie Dunbar, the SRC executive secretary: "I have no doubt there are going to be a lot of problems, and I urge you to feel absolutely free to call me at any time that you think we can be of assistance in any official fashion."[17] The Taconic Foundation, the Edgar Stern Family Fund, and the Field Foundation provided almost 90 percent of the $885,000 VEP budget expended through November 1964. Over six hundred thousand new voters were registered directly under VEP auspices, and the VEP directly intervened to prevent "more than fifty thousand voters being purged from the rolls."[18] Almost half of the total increase in Southern black voter registration from 1962 through 1964 is accounted for by project efforts.[19]

The downside of the VEP is perhaps as appalling as its upside is triumphant. The rights activists became embittered and angered at what they considered to be the administration's perfidy. They believed they had been promised protection and direct aid by the administration. They never received either.

From the outset of the project some of the younger activists mistrusted the administration. A three-week seminar starting on July 30, 1961, paid for by the New World Foundation, was to expose the students to "Understanding the Nature of Social Change." Movement leaders, scholars, and justice officials discussed the student role and the government commitment to changing the situation in the South.[20] Throughout the VEP organizational discussion meetings, administration officials and leaders from the more established organizations stressed the need to work in the urban south where black voter registrations would quickly add up. The students countered that voter-registration work was most important in the rural South. King, Wilkins, Whitney Young of the Urban League, Fleming, and Marshall all argued that going into the cities would not only get more votes but would be much safer. The rural South was just too dangerous to touch.

According to Chuck McDew, the SNCC chairman during the early 1960s, the students understood.

> To disrupt the power in the South of the United States we would have to work in the rural areas. Most of the people who

were powerful in the U.S. House and Senate came out of the rural counties in the South. They were elected from counties with high black populations—50–60 percent, some as high as 90 percent, and black people didn't vote. . . . If we get rid of any old racist and he's replaced by a new racist, it's okay as he is no longer senior in these important [congressional] committees. . . .

The administration wanted . . . to use us to sort of muster the troops, be the door-bell ringers and do the canvassing, and on the other hand it would sort of blunt what we were involved in. On a third level it would not give a true sort of picture of what was really happening when people tried to vote in the South. . . .

After the first meeting Burke Marshall said, "You go out there and there's nothing we can do." We said, fine. That's our decision. You will be in rural Mississippi. Maybe not now, but you will be in rural Mississippi.[21]

The administration could not control the students. They went into the rural, Deep South, and turmoil ensued.

The VEP initially funded student voter-registration projects in rural Mississippi. In 1964, as the violence and intimidation of the voter-registration effort in Mississippi became too brutal for the VEP to bear and the actual number of registrants stayed abysmally low, the VEP withdrew its support from this project. But other sponsors, particularly a group of prominent entertainers brought together by singer Harry Belafonte, stepped in to help with the minimal financing needed to sustain the Mississippi project.[22]

The violence and intimidation faced by the students and the black Mississippians they worked with devastated both them and the nation. The more the administration learned of the situation, the more it protested it could not move federal law officers into the area to alleviate the problem. Burke Marshall was convinced that the federal government had no right to use its police forces to enter this situation. Despite protestations from civil rights sympathizers to the contrary, his argument carried the day in the Justice Department and administration.[23]

One Mississippi case reflects the usual cycle of events. On September 26, 1962, Herbert Lee of Amite County, Mississippi, was murdered. Lee was the first black person to register to vote in Amite since the end of World War II and only the second black in the county to be registered in the twentieth century. He was murdered for the effort. E. H. Hurst, a white Mississippi state representative, claimed self-defense in the killing and was cleared by a coroner's jury. McDew recalls how he telephoned Robert Kennedy, "saying that 'people were willing to testify that they saw Herbert Lee murdered . . . and they wanted to testify but were scared. Can you provide them with police protection?'" The nation's chief law officer replied, "Well, look Chuck, what do you expect us to do, put guards around them for 24-hour protection for the rest of their lives? We can't do that. They should be willing to come forth and testify as good American citizens." The nonviolent SNCC chairman's response to the attorney general was vivid. "I remember calling Bobby Kennedy a bunch of names and saying, 'You guys have lied to us. You don't intend to do shit and you're not going to protect the rights of Negro voters as you promised.' . . . We understood that clearly we were out there by ourselves."[24]

Bob Moses, a SNCC project director in Mississippi, called the Justice Department for protection of a black witness to the Lee shooting and was told, "There was no way possible to provide protection for such a witness at such a hearing and probably, in any case it didn't matter what he testified to [because Hurst] would be found innocent." The FBI let the sheriff's office know the witness's name; he was subsequently beaten badly by a local deputy sheriff.[25] A few years later, an unknown assailant murdered him near his home.

The young activists believed they had been betrayed by the administration. Timothy Jenkins, a black voter registration worker in Mississippi, explains one small yet important betrayal:

> Burke Marshall had agreed, that the SNCC people in the South could call collect to the Justice Department. . . . When certain key congressmen found out that Justice was receiving [these calls] they raised hell about it and they [Justice] stopped receiving collect calls, which was a wipeout. Because here you have these guys with the expectation that at least that one call was going to get them salvation, and they make that one call collect, and it's refused. . . . on technical grounds that the fed-

eral government can't receive a collect call. Shit. Tell me that's
not a recanting of our original commitment. I don't know what
is.[26]

Leslie Dunbar ruefully recalls how the administration dealt
with the project once it was underway.

> The Department of Justice almost entirely abandoned the
> commitments which all of us *at the time* believed it had made. To
> be specific, all of us at the time believed that the Department
> was telling us that it would (a) share information with us closely
> and (b) would diligently provide enforcement of the rights of
> voter registration workers. It never did the former; in fact,
> V.E.P. had difficulty getting even routine mailings from the De-
> partment, although a fair bit of telephone and person-to-person
> communication at our initiative took place. The Department
> never provided the kind of enforcement protection which we all
> expected.[27]

Those individuals in the movement who were more sympathetic to the Kennedys' problems could understand how it all
happened, but still had trouble reconciling understanding with
forgiveness. Harold Fleming states his feelings with eloquence,
"Nobody [in the movement] would ever forgive the Kennedys
for playing politics, because they weren't supposed to on this
front. The very fact that there was a sense of partnership had
much to do with it. We all thought we were *part* of the administration—which is absurd. We were not on the payroll. We were
not forced to grapple with the Administration's priorities."[28]

The priorities of the administration, the rights activists, and
the southern politicians differed. The Kennedys had hoped
they could resolve the conflict without a confrontation. As Dunbar put it, there was "a great reluctance to accept the fact that
you had to be on somebody's side in the South."[29]

It was the impetuousness of youth and the obstinacy of a
racist tradition that upset the Kennedys' plans. The Kennedys
wanted progress for blacks, acceptance of black rights by the
South, and the preservation of the Democratic coalition they
had inherited. Mutual accommodation and control of the

situation were the processes by which they sought to achieve their goals. The rights activists were not interested in accommodation, the maintenance of the Democratic coalition, or administration control of the situation. They wanted the South to comply with the law of the land and its black citizenry to be treated with dignity, even if it took unprecedented action to achieve these ends. The southern politicians were determined to keep their way of life safe from federal intrusion, even if it took unparalleled actions on their part. The Democratic party was historically important to the South and a continuing source of southern power, but white southerners would not countenance those who proposed black equality. "The Kennedys," as Arthur Fleming sees it, "underestimated the depths of Southern racism. They did not anticipate the kind of things that went on in Mississippi. They honestly did not believe the kind of things that people wanted to do to turn back the civil rights initiatives."[30]

Early in the administration, Governor Ross Barnett of Mississippi helped make the Kennedys believers in doing more for blacks. On January 21, 1961, James H. Meredith, a black air force veteran, wrote to the University of Mississippi requesting an admissions application. The University of Mississippi would not knowingly let a black man enter its student body and refused Meredith's request for admission. On May 31, 1961, the NAACP Legal Defense Fund filed suit in the District Court of Southern Mississippi, asking that Meredith be admitted to the university. The suit was dismissed. The Fifth Circuit Court of Appeals reversed the ruling in June 1962, finding that Meredith had been denied admission "solely because he was a Negro."[31]

On September 13, 1962, the district court issued an order for Meredith's admission. That night, Governor Barnett broadcast a televised speech heard throughout Mississippi. The governor spoke of the federal policy of "racial genocide" and cited the 1832 South Carolina Act of Nullification, which declared any federal law that violated state law to be null and void, as the basis for his refusal to allow Meredith to enter the University of Mississippi. On September 15 Robert Kennedy contacted the governor and was assured that there would be no violence. But the governor personally denied Meredith entry to the university when he attempted to register on September 20. Mississippi highway patrolmen escorted Meredith, several U.S. marshals, and Justice Department attorneys off the campus amidst a crowd of jeering, rock-throwing students.[32] The stage was set for the worst confrontation between the federal government and a state government since the desegregation of Little Rock's Central High School.

Governor Barnett repeatedly refused to honor a court of appeals order to admit Meredith to the university. On September 28 the governor was found guilty of contempt of court and ordered by the court of appeals to purge himself or face arrest and a ten-thousand-dollar-a-day fine. That night, amidst the roar of a wildly approving crowd, the governor asked for support and shouted, "I love Mississippi. I love our people. I love our customs."[33]

The president decided that he had to take action and uphold the law. On September 30, shortly after midnight, having spoken fruitlessly with the governor several times during the day, President Kennedy federalized the Mississippi National Guard. He issued a proclamation calling on the governor and the citizens of Mississippi to "cease and desist" their obstruction of the court order and to "disperse and retire peaceably forthwith." That evening, Meredith was taken to the campus by Deputy Attorney General Katzenbach, three hundred federal marshals wearing riot gear, and a large contingent of state troopers.

Aware of the impending federal action, Governor Barnett went on television to urge Mississippians "to preserve peace and to avoid violence in any form." He went on, "Surrounded on all sides by the armed forces and oppressive power of the United States of America, my courage and my convictions do not waver. My heart still says 'Never,' but my calm judgement abhors the bloodshed that would follow."[34]

The president addressed the nation as Meredith went on to the university campus. He began by saying, "The orders of the court in the case of *Meredith versus Fair* are beginning to be carried out. . . . Our Nation is founded on the principle that the eternal safeguard of liberty and defiance of the law is the surest road to tyranny." He continued, "Americans are free, in short, to disagree with the law, but not to disobey it. For in a government of laws and not of men, no man . . . is entitled to defy a court of law." He emphasized that

> The United States Government was until recently not involved. Mr. Meredith brought a private suit in Federal court against those who were excluding him from the University. A series of Federal courts all the way to the Supreme Court repeatedly ordered Mr. Meredith's admission to the University. When those orders were defied . . . the enforcement of its order became an obligation of the United States Government. Even though this government had not originally been a party to the case, my responsibility as President was therefore inescapable. I accept it. My obligation under the Constitution was and is to implement the orders of the Court with whatever means are necessary, and with as little force and civil disorder as possible.[35]

While the president spoke to the nation, a riot broke out at the university. As the rioters were getting up steam, the governor pulled the state troopers off the campus. Mayhem ensued. When it was over, one-third of the U.S. marshals had been injured, twenty-eight by gunfire; two civilians were killed; more than three hundred persons were taken into federal custody; almost five thousand federal troops, including a federalized Mississippi unit, were called to the campus; and James Meredith was registered for classes.

Back in March of 1961, Robert Kennedy had told a *Look* magazine reporter, "I don't think we would ever come to the point of sending troops [into a state]. . . . I cannot conceive of this administration's letting such a situation deteriorate to that level."[36] That was the same position voiced by Eisenhower in the months preceding the federal intervention in Little Rock. "We had to send the troops in," recounts Katzenbach, "and that was regarded by both President Kennedy and Bobby Kennedy as a great failure. They both, and particularly the President, had a real conviction that it was wrong to send troops in. . . . [The president] felt that Little Rock was a great failure in the Eisenhower administration . . . because they sent in troops."[37] The use of troops was an admission that the federal relationship had failed. JFK had hoped to avoid this admission.

Still, Kennedy's Ole Miss speech reiterated the Eisenhower theme that troops were sent to enforce the law, and it was his duty to send in the troops whether or not he agreed with the law. Thurgood Marshall points out, "when the chips were down and the state of Mississippi stood out against the federal government, the President of the United States used every weapon in his arsenal to protect the federal government."[38] The protection of the federal government, not the protection of civil rights, was the issue for Eisenhower at Little Rock, and it was also the issue for Kennedy at the University of Mississippi. Both presidents viewed the abrogation of black rights as a sidelight to the main issue at hand: federal government rights. Neither the presidential position nor the southern white position had changed since 1957.[39]

John Kennedy continued to avoid the heart of the matter, the necessity for a legislative approach to the issue.[40] In 1961 the administration had refused to deal legislatively with the issue, and in January of 1962 the *New York Times* reported that the president "has let it be known that he will put forward no major civil rights legislation."[41] In his State of the Union Address, however, the president mentioned that "the right to vote, for example, should no longer be denied through such arbitrary devices . . . as literacy tests and poll taxes."[42] In February of 1962 the administration submitted legislation to ban the poll tax in federal elections. A proposed constitutional amendment was speedily sent to the Hill as a substitute measure when southerners questioned the legality of a statute in this area.[43] Only five states—Alabama, Arkansas, Mississippi, Texas, and Virginia—still had a poll tax for federal elections, and the proposed amendment was sponsored by a conservative southerner, Spessard Holland of Florida. By September of 1962 it had passed the House by a vote of 294 to 86 and the Senate by 77 to 16. Within two years it was ratified as the Twenty-fourth Amendment to the Constitution.

From the administration perspective the poll tax ban was a splendid piece of civil rights legislation. It was not contentious; even many Southerners could support it. And it was directly productive for the Kennedys. Sorenson noted, "The number of Negroes and less affluent whites enabled to vote by that measure alone, the President believed, could make a difference in his 1964 re-election race in Texas and Virginia."[44]

In response to liberal pressure for more effective federal action to deal with black disfranchisement, on January 25, 1962, Senate majority leader Mike Mansfield introduced a bill that permitted evidence of a sixth-grade education to be used in lieu of a literacy test wherever such tests were required for federal election registration. While the liberals pressed for the proposed legislation to cover state and federal elections, the attorney general supported the bill as proposed by Mansfield.

Roy Wilkins, while pleased that the administration finally offered some civil rights legislation, called the bill a "token offering." Joseph Rauh of the ADA argued that the only solution to "Negro registration in any State is direct Federal administration of elections."[45] In March, Hubert Humphrey, Paul Douglas, Philip Hart, and Joseph Clark, all longtime Senate advocates of civil rights, agreed that they favored stronger legislation; but they would not publicly criticize the administration.[46]

On March 28 the Republicans came forward with a proposed legislative package. Joseph Rauh called it "the most complete answer to segregation and discrimination yet offered in Congress."[47] One of the Republican legislators commented with obvious partisan relish, "If the President will not assume the leadership in getting through Congress urgently needed civil rights measures, then Congress must take the initiative."[48] In April, twenty-two liberal congressional Democrats, including Humphrey, Douglas, and Hart, brought forward extensive voting-rights bills. Wilkins was downcast at the turn of events because the administration remained aloof from a real commitment to civil rights and the black organizations were quarreling among themselves as they defined their programs of action.[49]

The South, on the other hand, was not about to accept the administration's meager legislative proposal. Senator Sam Ervin, chairman of the Senate subcommittee in charge of hearings on this legislation, believed that the proposed legislation was unconstitutional because it did not deal with an abridgement of the right to vote under the Fifteenth Amendment to the Constitution, but rather with "a Federal standard or substitute for all the State literacy tests."[50] The bill was immediately stalled in committee.

On April 25 Senator Mansfield and Republican minority leader Everett Dirksen decided to bring the literacy-test proposal to the floor of the Senate as an amendment to a private bill. A "decorous and genteel [southern] filibuster ensued," as one analyst described the situation, "while the Senate maintained its customary time schedule."[51] On May 9 the president publicly backed the bill at a press conference and argued that literacy tests, as administered, "don't make any sense."[52] That same day, thirty northern Democrats and thirteen Republicans voted for cloture, while thirty southern and western Democrats, joined by twenty-three Republicans, voted against cloture. This was far short of the required two-thirds majority.

To keep the ball in play and to allow the northern Democrats and Republicans who wanted to go on record in favor of civil rights to do so, Mansfield moved to have the bill tabled. This time four western Democrats, three border-state Democrats, and fourteen Republicans voted to keep the bill on the floor. On May 14 a motion for cloture was again considered, but was defeated by a vote of forty-three to fifty-two.[53] It was all very desultory, and the bill never did come to a straight up or down vote on the Senate floor. *Time* magazine reported that the episode "had all the conviction of a professional wrestling match: everybody played his role for the crowds, but nobody got hurt. . . . Almost as if the whole thing were merely to make propaganda in the North, Kennedy aides made no real effort to push the bill."[54]

The literacy-test fiasco reinforced JFK's belief that substantial civil rights legislation could not be achieved. "In view of Solid Southern Democratic intransigence," wrote Sorenson, "greater Republican and Western Democratic support was required, and with no broad public interest in such legislation outside of the various civil rights organizations, that support was not obtainable."[55]

Roy Wilkins was concerned about not only the liberals' lack of backbone on the issue, but also the Republicans' apparent move southward in pursuit of votes. In June, Wilkins wrote to William Miller, the chairman of the Republican National Committee: "I know there is a disposition on the part of many influential Republicans to 'write off' the Negro vote as one irrevocably in the possession of the Democrats. They have the curious notion they can replace the vanished Negro support with Southern white gains. If they hope to do this by competing with the race-baiting school of Southern Democrats," warned Wilkins, "then they will be doing nothing more than further riveting Negro support to the Democratic Party in the non-Southern urban centers." Wilkins offered a more positive view to the Republican chairman: "It is the belief of many observers that the Republican Party could win back many scores of thousands of Negro voters with a well-planned program." The black leader reminded Miller: "The Republicans adopted a good civil rights plank in their 1960 platform, but instead of showing up the Kennedy Administration by pushing for it at strategic times in the Congress and forcing the Administration to come along or to oppose, the GOP chose to show up the Administration by opposing its proposals and helping to defeat them."[56]

The year 1962 was not good for civil rights supporters. Not only was there little legislative progress, but the activists suffered one of their most bitter defeats in Albany, Georgia. From the winter of 1961 through the summer of 1962, King led a series of peaceful demonstrations to protest the segregated way of life in Albany, Georgia. The protests were met by resolute and legal white law enforcement. Chief of Police Laurie Prichett studied King's tactics and writings, and he concluded that police restraint was the best way to defeat the black leadership.[57] Blacks were jailed but not beaten. It was all done in an orderly, quiet, and efficient manner. The black leadership ran out of bail money, out of bodies for the jails, and out of spirit before the white leadership met their demands.

When King left Albany, the city was as segregated as when he had arrived. "We ran out of people," one SNCC demonstrator points out, "before [Chief Pritchett] ran out of jails."[58] "The white church, the white community let us down," recalls a black minister. "The white community was without a heart, without a conscience. My sole reason for demonstrating was to reach the better people—who hadn't thought about injustice before. I don't know what happened. We were depending on the white community. We had faith."[59]

For King, Albany was a painful defeat. "My schedule for the Fall [of 1962] has been extremely heavy," wrote King to another black leader, "and it has been necessary to attempt to re-coup some of the losses to our program incurred by the Albany situation."[60] King and the black leadership were going to have to rethink the strategy and tactics of nonviolence. Demonstrations in Birmingham were to be the result of this rethinking.

In the midst of the Albany struggle, with no commitment of legislative or other support from the administration, King wrote: "The chilling prospect emerge[s] of a general administration retreat" on civil rights.[61] In September of 1962 the title of an article in the *Nation*, "The Leaderless Liberals," summed up the liberal view of the state of political leadership in the nation's capital.[62] After meeting with President Kennedy in the fall, King wrote of a man who "vacillated." King believed JFK was unsure of himself; he was "trying to sense the direction his leadership could travel while retaining and building support for his administration."[63]

What was vacillation to King was fine-tuned political balancing to Kennedy. The public—in the North and in the South—generally approved of Kennedy's presidential performance. The Gallup Poll showed him with a 65 percent approval rating in the South and a 68 percent approval rating in the North.[64] In the November 1962 mid-term elections, the Democrats had a net gain of four seats in the Senate and a net loss of only two seats in the House. In the South, however, the Republicans picked up five seats and narrowly missed defeating Lister Hill, a Kennedy loyalist. Lou Harris, the president's pollster, argued that the reason for the Republican gains in the South "is that the entire Democratic Party of the South is changing rapidly into a far more moderate and liberal party." And, he predicted, the Republicans would make more inroads in this region in 1964 and 1966, but with right-wing candidates.[65]

4

A Reluctant Commitment

THE KENNEDY TIGHTROPE act on civil rights continued into 1963. In his State of the Union Address, the president made it clear that "tax reform overshadows all other domestic problems in Congress." As for civil rights: "I wish that all qualified Americans permitted to vote were willing to vote, but surely in this centennial year of the Emancipation all of those who are willing to vote should always be permitted."[1] In January of 1963 the president spoke with King and told him that "if he presented civil rights legislation, it would arouse the anger of the South . . . they would set out to block his whole legislative program."[2]

But others disagreed with the president. On January 24 Robert Kennedy privately informed his brother, "Additional legislation is necessary to insure prompt relief . . . where the facts indicate that substantial numbers of Negroes are being deprived of the right to register and vote because of race."[3] The Leadership Conference on Civil Rights (LCCR), a biracial organization representing the major civil rights organizations as well as religious and union groups, had delegates from every state in the union lobby their congressmen for civil rights legislation.[4] NAACP chief lobbyist Clarence Mitchell was so angry with the president over his lack of fortitude on civil rights that he refused to attend a Lincoln's Day dinner given at the White House. More than eight hundred black leaders attended the affair. Mrs. Mitchell attended without her husband. "While I could understand his [Mr. Mitchell's] viewpoint," she recounts, "I could also understand how everyone wanted to go to a White

House affair, and I chose to go."[5] Symbolism again took precedence over substance.

The Republicans, however, moved on substance. It was perhaps a move designed more to embarrass the Democrats than to accomplish anything of substance, but move they did. In mid February, the Republican House leadership introduced a group of broad civil rights bills.[6] The president then allowed his staff to come forward with a narrow voting-rights bill. The administration bill contained a proposal to permit temporary voting referees to register voters if less than 15 percent of the black population was registered and if the attorney general filed a complaint.

Civil Rights Commission chairman Berl I. Bernhard and the commission staff director, William L. Taylor, commented on the administration proposal:

a. *It is difficult to pass a bill that nobody favors.*
b. *It is difficult to pass a bill that nobody understands.*
c. *It is difficult to pass a bill when you can't state publicly the real reason you want it.* This bill is needed for only one reason: there are federal judges . . . who are so racially prejudiced that . . . some method is being sought in Congress to compel them to act.[7]

On February 28, 1963, the president sent his first civil rights message to Congress. JFK wanted as little as possible to do with this legislation. The follow-up recommendations to the Congress were not completed until May of 1963. When the proposals were sent over to the Hill, the president, half in jest, called Burke Marshall and said, "What's this bill of yours and Bobby's?"[8] The president was expected to be the legislative leader of the administration, but on civil rights there was no such leadership coming out of the Oval Office.

Liberals on the Hill and in the civil rights organizations were disheartened by the administration bill.[9] "If tokenism were our goal," wrote King, "this administration has adroitly moved us toward its accomplishment."[10] It seemed that when it came to civil rights, the administration lagged behind the country. "Clearly, the force of the new mood abroad in the land," argued a liberal analyst, "was not reflected in this narrow bill."[11]

"Well, the legislation just never had any chance of passing," recalls Robert Kennedy. "Nobody was interested in it." At least nobody within the immediate sight of the administration was interested in it. Martin Luther King, Jr. changed that. Birmingham was the turning point. "What aroused people generally in the country," Bob Kennedy explained, "was the Birmingham riots in May of 1963. Prior to that, when I testified on voting, people forgot even that I went up and testified on it."[12] The Birmingham demonstrations involved a new strategy that evolved out of the bitter defeat in Albany, Georgia, and verged on nonviolent provocation rather than peaceful persuasion. If the adults were all going to be jailed, then the children would march in their place. The nation was going to have to confront the moral crisis of segregation. King was willing to risk everything on this encounter. The great crusade began on April 3, 1963. King set out to "break the back of segregation all over the nation."[13] He believed that if he could defeat the segregationist tradition in Birmingham, it would symbolize to the South and the nation that racism could be defeated everywhere.

Before the spring of 1963, King had given up on the courts as the major arena for achieving a solution to the black rights issue.[14] He was confronting the president and the legislative arena. The previous week, in an article he wrote for the *Nation*, he told the administration that it was at "a historic crossroad" and now it was going to have to face "its moral commitment and with it, its political fortunes."[15] Several times the administration asked him to wait before demonstrating—wait until a new, more moderate city administration would came into office. King rejected this advice.[16] He wanted confrontation.

On Good Friday, April 12, King marched for the conscience of the nation. He had always worn a jacket and tie when he joined demonstrations; this time he wore blue denim work clothes. He was one with the people, and again he was going to be arrested with the people. When clergymen and other leaders argued about his decision to demonstrate and go to jail, he wrote his famous "Letter from a Birmingham Jail."[17] The marches continued, and he remained in jail. When the jails were filled with black adults, the black leaders turned to the black children to march.[18] The children marching, the dogs attacking, the fire hoses being turned on with fury caught the attention of the nation and the world and created a sense of conscience-stricken outrage at what was happening in Alabama.

While King was proceeding in Alabama, violence against the voting-rights workers in Mississippi continued apace. The Civil Rights Commission openly prodded the administration to be bolder in defense of black rights.[19] On April 16, 1963, the chairman of the Civil Rights Commission sent a letter to the president with an "Interim Report." The commission decried the lawlessness of Mississippi, where citizens were continually "terrorized because they sought to vote. . . . The Commission has concluded unanimously that only further steps by the Federal Government can arrest the subversion of the Constitution in Mississippi." The most important step recommended by the commission was "that the President explore the legal authority he possesses as Chief Executive to withhold Federal funds from the State of Mississippi, until the State of Mississippi demonstrates its compliance with the Constitution of the United States."[20]

John Kennedy was unhappy with the report. "I still don't like it," he told Arthur Schlesinger, Jr. "If the Commissioners have made up their mind, I presume they will issue the report anyway. . . . It [the commission] is independent, has a right to be heard, but I do wish you could get them to reconsider."[21] "They say things are not going fast enough [in Mississippi] and maybe they're right," Katzenbach commented. "But it's a difficult process to speed up."[22] When asked about the commission recommendation at his April 24 news conference, the president responded, "We shall . . . continue not to spend federal funds in such a way as to encourage discrimination. What they were suggesting was something different, which was a blanket withdrawal of Federal expenditures from a State." The president then made his point: "I said that I didn't have the power to do so, and I do not think the President should be given that power, because it could be used in other ways differently."[23] The president was not looking for a confrontation with the South.

The Birmingham demonstrations continued, and the president's hand was being forced on the issue. On May 4 John Kennedy met with a group of ADA leaders and told them the attacks on the children in Birmingham made him "sick." That same day Burke Marshall arrived in Birmingham to mediate the situation.[24] On May 8, with Birmingham still in the midst of chaos and congressional hearings on civil rights legislation about to begin, JFK was asked at a news conference what could be done. He responded: "In the absence of such violation [of federal law] or any other federal jurisdiction our efforts have been focused on getting both sides together to settle in a peaceful fashion the very real abuses too long inflicted on the Negro citizens of that community."[25]

"I talked to King and asked him what he was after," Burke Marshall recounts. "He really didn't know. . . . In fact the complaint was over service in the lunch counters. That was the principal complaint, and it was not a complaint that could be solved under law in any way at that time." Marshall returned to Washington and went to a White House meeting with Katzenbach, Sorenson, Robert Kennedy, and the president. "And they thought [about] what to do for four or five hours," recalls Marshall, "and they ended up with nothing. I mean there was nothing to do."[26]

Marshall and the administration missed the point of King's demonstration. King was not demanding a new law here or a change there. He was demanding that the soul of the nation be inflamed. He wanted a national mobilization on behalf of the political rights and the moral rights of its black citizens. He wanted commitment; he wanted major legislation, not a piecemeal offering. That was what the administration did not hear— or could not hear.

The administration helped arrange an agreement between the city and the demonstrators and persuaded Walter Reuther, the head of the United Auto Workers Union and a civil rights supporter, and Joseph Rauh to raise $160,000 in bail money as part of the peace agreement. On May 10 the demonstrators were bailed out of jail.[27] On the same day, Dr. King and the Reverend Fred L. Shuttlesworth, the Birmingham leader of the black demonstrations, announced that they had reached an agreement with the white Birmingham leadership on a desegregation plan. The Kennedy administration was interested in the restoration of civil peace and believed they had calmed things down.

The night after the announcement of the agreement, two bombs exploded in Birmingham—one at the hotel used by the black leadership and one at Martin Luther King's brother's house. Twenty-five hundred Birmingham blacks rioted in reaction.[28] "Events in Birmingham in the last few days have seemed to electrify the Negro concern over civil rights all across the country. As this is written, demonstrations and marches are underway or being planned in a number of major cities." Louis Martin continued his May 13 report to Bobby Kennedy: "The accelerated tempo of Negro restiveness and the rivalry of some leaders for top billing, coupled with the resistance of segregationists, may soon create the most critical state of race relations since the Civil War."[29] The outburst of black demonstrations across the nation frightened the public and perplexed the administration. The Kennedys wanted to help but grew increasingly anxious as they saw the demonstrations hurting rather than helping the black cause.[30]

On May 14, as if to add emphasis to Martin's warning, the Executive Council of the AFL-CIO issued a sweeping statement: "The racial disturbances in Birmingham have been shocking by any standard. They should not have happened; they must not continue; they must never occur again anywhere in America." The union leaders called for legislation to create equal opportunity in employment, voting rights, education rights, and job rights.[31] The president called for calm. In a May 18 speech at Vanderbilt University, he argued that the black demonstrators were acting "in the highest tradition of American freedom."[32] The administration threatened to send federal troops into Birmingham if the governor did not restore order.[33] "The essence of Kennedy's civil rights strategy," writes Sorenson, "had been to keep at all times at least one step ahead of the evolving pressures, never to be caught dead in the water."[34] But events and the push of the movement on events outpaced the administration's efforts to stay on top of things.

Now the administration was ready to act. Within a few days of his return from Birmingham, Marshall spoke with JFK.

"The President became convinced," Marshall recalls, that he "had to deal with what was clearly an explosion in the racial problem that could not, would not go away." Norbert A. Schlei, head of the Office of Legal Counsel, recalls that in mid May, after the Birmingham demonstrations ceased, the attorney general called a meeting of the top Department of Justice staff in his office. According to Schlei, Robert Kennedy told the group, "It seemed apparent major civil rights legislation ought to be proposed, and I sensed from him also that he now had the conviction that it could be enacted." Schlei understood Kennedy "believed that as a result of this Birmingham thing, the people of the country have really gotten an inkling of what it was like to be a Negro in the South . . . and they were prepared to support something important in the field of civil rights." Schlei was told to form a team "and get out a draft of a proposed bill by the close of business on Monday. This was Saturday night."[35] On May 22 John F. Kennedy announced that the administration was considering major new civil rights legislation.[36]

But Robert Kennedy still was not sure exactly what the black demonstrators wanted. On May 23 he met with black author James Baldwin. They agreed to meet again at the Kennedys' New York City residence with a group of black leaders to discuss the range of black concerns.[37] The New York meeting produced three hours of chaos. The blacks vented their rage at the Kennedys, at whites, at the country. Kenneth Clark, a noted black psychologist and confidant of the black political leadership, recalls, "It became one of the most violent, emotional verbal assaults . . . that I had ever witnessed before or since." Clark summarized the situation: "Our considered judgement, was that the whole thing was hopeless; that there was no chance that Bobby heard anything that we said. . . . Kennedy was not unimpressive. He didn't minimize or condescend. But he just didn't seem to get it."[38]

On his return to Washington, Kennedy told Arthur Schlesinger, Jr., "They don't know what the laws are—they don't know what the facts are—they don't know what we've been doing or what we're trying to do. You can't talk to them the way you can talk to Martin Luther King or Roy Wilkins. They didn't want to talk that way. It was all emotion, hysteria."[39] But RFK soon rethought his position. He came to believe that something had to be done to calm the turmoil and to confront the national crisis of civil rights.

At the end of May, John Kennedy told a news conference that he was considering a legislative package "which would provide a legal outlet for a desire for a remedy other than having to engage in demonstrations which bring them [blacks] into conflict with the forces of law and order in the community."[40] On June 1 the president, the vice-president, and the attorney general met with the top administration officials concerned with civil rights. Robert Kennedy argued for a comprehensive administration bill to deal with racial discrimination. He wanted a public-accommodations section included in the legislation, as well as a Title III section, giving the attorney general the power to initiate enforcement litigation—but only in school desegregation cases. The staff opposed the attorney general, arguing that Congress would not accept the proposals. The president ordered the drafting of legislation.

On June 3 the vice-president spoke with Theodore Sorenson about the administration's civil rights strategy. Aside from the May discussion, Johnson had not contributed very much to the administration's civil rights strategy. He had not seen the draft of the proposed legislative package; he was outside of the administration's civil rights planning prior to this point. It was a deliberate omission that was partly the result of the vice-president's submergence under the president and partly a reflection of his own reluctance to get into the issue more aggressively.[41] Now Johnson was asked for his advice on the issue, and he gave it forcefully.

Johnson told the president's advisor that "the President has to go in there [into the South] without cussing at anybody or fussing at anybody . . . and be the leader of the nation and make a moral commitment to them [the Negroes]." LBJ continued, "You see, this fellow Baldwin, he says, 'I don't want to marry your daughter, I want to get you off my back,' and that's what these Negroes want. They want that moral commitment." The president "should stick to the moral issue and he should do it without equivocation. . . . I know the risks are great and it might cost us the South, but those sorts of states may be lost anyway."

The vice-president talked of political costs and benefits. "I think the Southern whites and the Negro share one point of view that's identical. They're not certain that the government is on the side of the Negroes." LBJ continued, "The whites think we're just playing politics to carry New York. The Negroes feel . . . we're just doing what we got to do. Until that's laid to rest I don't feel that you're going to have much of a solution. I don't think the Negroes' goals are going to be achieved through legislation. . . . What Negroes are really seeking is moral force."

Finally LBJ went back to explaining political strategy as he saw it. "The President is the cannon. You let him be on all the TV networks just speaking from his conscience, not at a rally in Harlem, but at a place in Mississippi or Texas or Louisiana and just have the honor guard there with a few Negroes in it. Then let him reach over and point and say, 'I have to order these boys into battle, in the foxholes carrying that flag. I don't ask them what their name is, whether it's Gomez or Smith, or what color they got, what religion. If I can order them into battle I've got to make it possible for them to eat and sleep in this country.'"

The mood of the country was changing. On May 28 Walter Lippman, the dean of American columnists, wrote: "The cause of desegregation must cease to be a Negro movement, blessed by white politicians from Northern states. It must become a national movement to enforce national laws, led and directed by the National Government."[42] On June 5 the Republican congressional leadership met for five and one-half hours and arrived at a consensus that new civil rights legislation was needed.[43] Civil rights legislation now became the subject of discussions between the congressional leaders of the two major parties.[44] On June 6, John P. Roche, national ADA chairman, wrote the president: "We earnestly urge you to propose to the Congress civil rights measures that meet the needs of the epoch."[45]

There is considerable evidence that public opinion outside the South now strongly supported black civil rights, although the public opposed demonstrations. On balance, the president had a net gain in public opinion support because of his civil rights stance.[46] Congressional constituency surveys showed a public strongly backing legislative initiatives in the area.[47]

Martin Luther King, Jr., was still concerned about what the administration was going to do. On June 10 the *New York Times* carried a major story in which King stated that the president "has not furnished the expected leadership and has not kept his campaign promises."[48] But unbeknownst to the black leader, the president and the attorney general were now busily trying to round up support for an administration civil rights bill before it was sent up to the Hill.[49] On June 10 Robert Kennedy met with all of the Republican members of the Senate to discuss the pending civil rights proposals. JFK wrote to Eisenhower asking him to endorse the proposed legislation, but the former president believed that a "whole bunch of laws" were not the answer to the problem and turned the president down.[50] The next day the president met with the Republican congressional leadership to discuss his legislative proposals.[51] Bobby Kennedy briefed the southern Democrats on the administration's civil rights proposals. Senator Russell's public comment on the matter was, "We had a complete meeting of the minds. We agreed to disagree."[52]

The vice-president wrote to Sorenson: "There would be a tremendous value to the President taking the lead in defining the issues. The best way to do this," he suggested, "would be to call in the Negro leadership and strive for an agreement for a statement of principles desired by the Negro community and accepted by the President."[53] It was critical for the president and the black leadership to define the agenda, and it was also critical that the president get some more time to work with the Republicans before he submitted the legislation to the congress.

The administration had little time to maneuver on the issue. On June 11, for the first time in history, two young blacks attempted to enroll at the University of Alabama. Governor George Wallace of Alabama personally blocked their entry. After making a well-choreographed show of confrontation with Deputy Attorney General Katzenbach, the governor permitted the students to enter the university. The president federalized the National Guard, and violence was avoided.[54]

Governor Wallace provided the immediate opportunity for

the president to address the nation on the subject of civil rights; but "Birmingham and the Negroes themselves," as Schlesinger put it, "had given [the president] the nation's ear."[55] The president seized the opportunity; in a nationwide television broadcast, he discussed the issue in a manner that differed profoundly from how he or any other president had dealt with it. He started with a discussion of Birmingham: "I hope that every American, regardless of where he lives will stop and examine his conscience about this and other related incidents." He subsequently discussed the mistreatment of blacks with respect to educational opportunity, service in public facilities, and the right to vote. "It ought to be possible, in short," he argued, "for every American to enjoy the privileges of being American without regard to his race or color. . . . But this is not the case." The president than set forth his conclusions:

> It is better to settle these matters in the Courts than on the streets, but new laws are needed at every level. But law alone cannot make men see right. We are confronted primarily with a moral issue. . . .
> We face . . . a moral crisis as a country and as a people. It cannot be met by repressive police action. It cannot be left to increased demonstrations in the streets. It cannot be guided by token moves or talk. It is time to act in Congress.[56]

The speech was warmly endorsed by civil rights leaders. Roy Wilkins sent a telegram to the president: "Your speech last night to the nation on the civil rights crisis was a clear, resolute exposition of basic Americanism and a call to all our citizens to rally in support of the high traditions of our nation's dedication to human rights."[57] King called it "one of the most eloquent, profound and unequivocal pleas for justice . . . made by any president."[58] The tone of the speech was unlike any other made by John Kennedy. He appeared to have made an absolute commitment to the issue in starkly moral terms. The president was now part of the move to have the national political institutions come to grips with the issue. As Larry O'Brien put it, "With this civil rights proposal we were in the most serious domestic political battle we ever had. Everything was at stake."[59]

Within hours of the president's speech, Medgar Evers, the NAACP Mississippi field secretary, was assassinated in Jackson. A presidential speech was not going to change some things in a timely enough manner. Evers was buried in Arlington National Cemetery, with Robert Kennedy in attendance. And the president, in a gesture that was the kind of thing he did so well, had the Evers family stay at the White House for the several days they were in Washington to attend the funeral.[60]

On June 12 JFK felt the first sting of retribution by the South for his support of civil rights legislation. The administration's area redevelopment bill was defeated by a vote of 209 to 208 in the House. Eighteen southern Democrats and twenty Republicans switched their votes of previous support for the bill. That same day, seventeen southern Democratic senators and Republican John Tower of Texas emerged from a joint caucus with Senator Richard Russell of Georgia leading a denunciation of the administration's stand on the civil rights struggle.[61] In early July Russell said, "I don't think there will be an all-out war against the Kennedy program just because he proposed civil rights legislation, but it can't possibly help."[62]

Passage of the president's major tax-reform legislation was also linked to the civil rights bill. The president was asked at his July 17 news conference, "Would you want the Congress to dispose of the civil rights proposals before they begin concentrating on a tax bill?" He responded, "I think the tax bill and the civil rights bill are both very important and also they are very complex pieces of legislation, and it is taking . . . the Ways and Means Committee, in considering the bill, 6 months now. The civil rights bill only went up about 6 weeks ago, 5 weeks ago, and that will take I should think, a substantial amount of time." The president closed his discussion of the subject by stating, "What I am interested in seeing is before the end of this year both bills enacted. That is what we will be judged on."[63]

Seven of the fifteen Democrats on the Ways and Means Committee were southerners, including its chairman, Wilbur Mills of Arkansas. After discussing the southern legislative problems existent with the pending civil rights bills, Mills warned the president, "These fellows will do anything. They'll make any kind of a trade just to try to stop it."[64] The legislative warnings from the southern side of the Democratic party were not to be taken lightly, but at this juncture they could not get the president to alter his position on the issue.

Most Democrats and Republicans were committed to civil rights legislation. On June 13 Senator Mike Mansfield, the Democratic majority leader, worked out an agreement with Senator Everett Dirksen, the Republican minority leader, to jointly introduce a bill covering all of the legislation proposed by the administration with the exception of a public-accommodations provision. Thomas Kuchel, the Republican whip, agreed to join Hubert Humphrey in sponsoring public-accommodations legislation. Mansfield wrote that without Dirksen's agreement to the proposed legislation "the whole legislative effort in this field would be reduced to an absurdity."[65] On June 17 Senator Dirksen publicly announced his commitment to the civil rights package, except for the proposed public-accommodations section.[66] Dirksen was a key actor to have on the administration side. Only a bipartisan effort would secure a bill. To this end, the administration and the Democratic leadership worked diligently to round up key Republican support.[67]

On June 18 Harris Wofford wrote to Martin Luther King, Jr.: "The great thing now is that the logic of events has taken hold in civil rights. That will, I trust, produce the response you—we—have been seeking."[68] The country was moving to deal with the issue. "Never before had there been so much support—grass roots, editorial, political—for a new civil rights bill," concluded one ADA report. "The prime mover in developing support for the bill was the Negro himself—his increased determination, organization and effort—and his potentially dangerous impatience."[69]

Black impatience was overflowing into the streets. In the ten weeks following the president's June 11 speech, there were an estimated 758 protests and demonstrations in 186 different communities, and more than 15,000 blacks were arrested.[70] "Every day that summer," Schlesinger wrote, "new and ominous tendencies seemed to appear in the colored masses."[71] Moderate leaders like King were booed when they appeared before northern audiences, while radicals like Malcolm X and the Black Muslims appeared to be getting an ever-larger following.

John Kennedy was concerned about the impact of black demonstrations and outbursts on the public mood and on the mood of the Congress. His June 19, 1963, civil rights message to the Congress included a plea for restraint by black protestors. He argued that the black "demonstrations have increasingly endangered lives and property, inflamed emotions and unnecessarily divided communities. They are not the way in which this country should rid itself of racial discrimination." The president continued: "This problem is now before the Congress. Unruly tactics or pressures will not help and may hinder the effective consideration of these measures. If they are enacted, there will be legal remedies available; and, therefore, while the Congress is at work I urge all community leaders, Negro and white, to do their utmost to lessen tensions and to exercise self-restraint."[72]

The administration's proposals received mixed reviews in the civil rights community. The president endorsed pending fair employment legislation, but his bill omitted a fair employment practices section [FEPC]. The president proposed allowing the attorney general to sue on behalf of individuals who were discriminated against with respect to access to schools, but only in cases where citizens filed written complaints and demonstrated that they could not afford to bring suit on their own. This was a very limited application of the Title III approach proposed by the Eisenhower administration in 1956. The Eisenhower Title III proposal would have allowed the attorney general to go into court on behalf of any individual who was the victim of racial discrimination. The Kennedy proposals banned discrimination in public accommodations in enterprises having a "substantial effect" on interstate commerce. The president's proposals also allowed for a discretionary cutoff of federal aid to discriminatory school districts. There were no substantial voting rights proposals in the president's package. The administration bill called for a Johnson-inspired local conciliation service, which would allow racial disputes to be mediated before they got out of hand. The president's bill was a victory for those who called for compromise on the issue; for those who argued that this approach would win bipartisan Congressional support.[73]

Civil rights advocates were pushing for a fair employment

practices section; a Title III section covering all racially discriminatory practices; a comprehensive public-accommodations
section; a Powell-type amendment (named after New York congressman Adam Clayton Powell, who repeatedly introduced it
in the House), prohibiting federal aid to schools practicing racial discrimination; and a federal voting-registration procedure. These proposals were a limited advance for the
administration. Some black rights supporters believed it was
too little, while others saw it as a critical shift in the Kennedy
position. As a Southern Regional Council report put it: "A national administration with no prior intention of seriously sponsoring civil rights legislation in 1963, mobilized its thinking and
its supporters and put before Congress a far-reaching civil
rights bill."[74]

After the legislation was sent up, John Kennedy asked his
brother, "Do you think we did the right thing by sending the
legislation up? Look at the trouble it's got us into." Robert Kennedy responded that the issue "really had to be faced up to."[75]
Some adverse reaction had already occurred, and there was
fear of further negative reaction across the nation both to parts
of the bill and to black unruliness. "White backlash" was a new
term coined to describe hostile white reaction to black demands.[76] Republican support for the bill wavered. "Republicans
are flirting with the possibility of being cool or even hostile to
the civil rights program in the belief that they have already lost
the black vote and have a chance of taking the Southern vote," a
Humphrey aide reported. "There is also a suggestion of hostility among suburbanites who fear an encroachment on their
housing."[77]

"When President Kennedy sent up that bill every single person who spoke about it in the White House—every one of
them—was against President Kennedy sending up that bill;
against his speech in June; against making it a moral issue."
That is how Burke Marshall remembers the White House discussion of civil rights during that season of high passions. "The
conclusive voice within the government . . . Robert Kennedy
was the one. He urged it, he felt it, he understood it. And he
prevailed."[78] Robert Kennedy argues that his brother went with
this position even though he believed that the legislation was

"maybe going to be his political swan song."[79] Whether the president went with the legislation or went for a stand-pat position, the political costs had to be faced and the political choices had to be made.

The administration mobilized its resources behind the proposed legislation. From late May through mid July, the president met with nearly sixteen hundred leaders from a variety of business, professional, and political organizations to sell them on the importance of the proposed legislation.[80] One meeting attended by the chair of the National Business Council, Frederick Kappel, reflects the president's tone at these sessions. Kappel reports the president said, "he believed . . . that unless the emotion that is now behind the demonstrations is relieved fairly soon any real long-range solution is going to be increasingly difficult and less satisfactory." The attorney general argued that the "proposed [legislation] was the minimum that would be required to overcome the obstacles to getting people off the streets and the situation under control." The president also believed the business leaders should be "going out and finding qualified Negroes in order to get programs started and established." The president urged the leaders to round up support for his program and help him get the situation under control.[81]

JFK was very concerned about proposals for a black march on Washington. Rumors abounded that the march leaders planned to stage sit-ins and to generally disrupt life in the capital. The origins of the march lay with A. Philip Randolph, the head of the Brotherhood of Sleeping Car Porters, and Bayard Rustin, a longtime rights activist and committed socialist. Randolph had organized a march on Washington in 1941 to demand equal employment opportunities for blacks engaged in federal contract work. The 1941 march was canceled when President Roosevelt agreed to sign an executive order establishing the Fair Employment Practices Commission. Now it was Rustin who in December 1962 proposed the idea of a new march to Randolph.[82]

The date and the specific program of the march were changed several times.[83] The objectives of the march, upon King's urging and support from the NAACP and the Urban League, changed from a focus on jobs to a focus on broad civil rights issues.[84] March plans changed from a massive exercise in civil disobedience and militant tactics into a massive but orderly and peaceful demonstration for legislation. Whitney Young, director of the National Urban League, wrote to Randolph: "Under what ever name we might call it, the impact and significance of the March would be to pressure for immediate legislative action and Congressional activity."[85] All of the five big movement organizations—the NAACP, the Urban League, CORE, SCLC, and SNCC—agreed to participate in the March on Washington for Jobs and Freedom.

This is precisely what the president did not want to happen. Rumors flew about Washington that massive sit-ins in the Congress or traffic blockages in the streets would be used to disrupt the nation's capital. Fear was in the air. "How can this country endure," asked Senator Richard Russell of Georgia, "when we legislate on the basis of threat and intimidations from mobs?"[86] Such mainstream civil rights supporters as AFL-CIO president George Meany and NAACP president Arthur Spingarn opposed the march. Liberal black congressman Charles Diggs, Jr., of Michigan wrote to King:

> I view with increasing concern certain preliminary statements which have been made with respect to the proposed "March on Washington." . . .
>
> First of all, as you undoubtedly know there are certain limitations upon any demonstrations in the Nation's Capitol. These limitations have been imposed . . . to preserve the dignity of the Federal Government and to protect its branches from threats and intimidation. There can be, for instance, no demonstrations, picketing, or placard carrying in the Capitol Hill Area. . . .
>
> Secondly, if the proposed "March on Washington" involved anywhere near the number suggested, which from the announcements range from 100,000 to 300,000 people, a tremendous logistics problem would arise. Where would they assemble for instructions? Where would they be housed? How would they be fed? Where would they take care of their personal hygiene? . . .
>
> Thirdly, how would this operation be financed? . . . In view of the need for money to finance freedom money operations on a local level, would it be prudent to expend such a large sum in view of such unpredictable dividends? . . .

Fourthly, can we be assured that disciplinary problems will be minimized with such diverse groups converging on Washington? . . .

I hope you will give very serious consideration to the points I have raised and which, in addition to others, are making a lot of people nervous about the prospects of the "March."[87]

The core of Martin Luther King's reply to Congressman Diggs reflects the inalterable position to which he and other march leaders had come:

I sincerely feel that this can be one of the greatest demonstrations for freedom that has ever been held in America. Since Negroes all over this country are so aroused now, it is constantly necessary to develop creative channels through which this legitimate discontent can be expressed. A failure to do this will cause the Negro to express this discontent in ominous outbreaks of violence. I feel that the March on Washington will serve as that creative channel through which thousands of Negroes can nonviolently articulate their longing for freedom and human dignity. It will also give masses of people an opportunity to participate in the shaping of their own destiny and to make a personal witness as they could not otherwise make.[88]

On June 20 the civil rights leaders publicly announced their intention to pursue a huge march on Washington to support their demands for legislation and jobs. On June 22 the president brought the activists to the White House. He had three major concerns. First, the president wanted to discuss the role the civil rights leaders could play in getting the proposed legislation through the Congress. Second, the president was fearful of congressional and public reaction to a march, and he wanted to dissuade the leaders from pursuing their plans. Finally, the president was concerned about increasing FBI information that communists were active in key positions in the civil rights movement—especially in King's organization.[89]

The president succinctly summarized the legislative situation. He emphasized the need for western and Republican help with the legislation and noted the reluctance of the smaller states to support any move for cloture. Whitney Young brought

up the administration's repeated warnings about demonstrations and the president's hints that he was opposed to the
march on Washington. JFK responded, "We want success in
Congress, not just a big show at the Capitol. Some of these
people are looking for an excuse to be against us. I don't want
to give any of them a chance to say, 'Yes, I'm for the bill, but I'm
damned if I'll vote for it at the point of a gun.'" The president
made his opinion about the march explicit: "It seemed to me a
great mistake to announce a march on Washington before the
bill was even in committee. The only effect is to create an atmosphere of intimidation—and this may give some members
of Congress an out."[90]

Randolph responded to the president, "The Negroes are already in the streets. It is very likely impossible to get them off.
If they are bound to be in the streets in any case, is it not better
that they be led by organizations dedicated to civil rights and
disciplined by struggle rather than to leave them to other
leaders who care neither about civil rights nor about nonviolence?" While the president agreed that the demonstrations
had brought results up to this point, he countered: "Now we
are in a new phase, the legislative phase . . . To get the votes we
need we have, first, to oppose demonstrations which will lead to
violence and, second, give Congress a fair chance to work its
will." The vice-president added, "We have about 50 votes for us
in the Senate and about 22 against us. What counts is the 26 or
so votes which remain. To get those votes we have to be careful
not to do anything which would give those who are privately
opposed a public excuse to appear as martyrs. We have to sell
the program."

Robert Kennedy was afraid that the black rights forces
would try to strengthen the administration's proposals and end
up bringing out a bill that could not be passed. "For a moment I
was stricken with a sense of *deja vu*," recalls Roy Wilkins. "At
last we had some real legislation to work on, but the strategic
considerations of the administration made it sound as if we
were back in 1957."[91] James Farmer, while acknowledging the
administration's problems, pointed out to the president, "The
civil rights forces have their problems too. We would be in a
difficult if not untenable position if we called the street demon-

strations off and then were defeated in a legislative battle."
King's response to the Kennedy position was straightforward.
"Frankly, I have never engaged in any direct action movement
which did not seem ill-timed. Some people thought Bir-
mingham ill-timed." The president interjected, "including the
Attorney General."

"This is a very serious fight," the president observed. "The
Vice President and I know what it will mean if we fail. I have
just seen a new poll—national approval of the Administration
has just fallen from 60 to 47 per cent [this poll has never been
found]. We're in this up to the neck. The worst trouble of all
would be to lose the fight in the Congress. We'll have enough
troubles if we win; but, if we win we can deal with those. A good
many programs I care about may go down the drain as a result
of this—we may go down the drain as a result of this—so we
are putting a lot on the line." Civil rights had become a moral
issue that the president believed he had to support. The president concluded, "What is important is that we preserve confidence in the good faith of each other. I have my problems with
the Congress; you have yours with your own groups. We will
undoubtedly disagree from time to time on tactics. But the important thing is to keep in touch." With those words JFK left
the meeting.

With the president out of the meeting, Joseph Rauh addressed the vice-president: "We are for FEPC and the addition
of Title III. Would the administration have any objection to
our trying to strengthen the bill?" Johnson responded in the
presence of the attorney general, who remained silent, "We
have no objection to your trying to get a stronger bill." The
liberals believed they had won a crucial agreement, the administration's go-ahead for pursuing stronger legislation. But they
were to find that other bargains were going to be made that
precluded administration support for a stronger bill.[92]

As he departed from the meeting, JFK asked Martin Luther
King, Jr., to talk with him outside in the White House Rose
Garden. Kennedy told the black leader, "You're under very
close surveillance." The FBI believed that two of King's close
associates, Stanley Levison and Jack O'Dell, were communist
agents.[93] Levison was the editor of King's books and a longtime

confidant of King. He was also known as "Solo" to the FBI and was believed to be a top-level communist agent. O'Dell, upon the recommendation of Levison, was made a top SCLC executive. King knew that O'Dell had been a member of the Communist party in the 1940s and 1950s. The president's conveyance of this information to him in the Rose Garden convinced King that "Hoover must be buggin' him [JFK] too."[94]

"You've read about Profumo in the papers," the president said to King as he reminded him of the fall of a British minister who had recently made the headlines. "That was an example of friendship and loyalty carried too far. Macmillan is likely to lose his government because he has been loyal to a friend. You must take care not to lose your cause for the same reason. They're communists [Levison and O'Dell]. You've got to get rid of them. . . . If they [the opponents of civil rights] shoot *you* down, they'll shoot *us* down too—so we're asking you to be careful."[95] King refused to commit himself until he saw some hard evidence substantiating the charge against Levison. None was ever produced for King, but the pressure was on him to act.

Robert Kennedy believed that communists were attempting to infiltrate the black movement.[96] J. Edgar Hoover had long suspected communist attempts to infiltrate the civil rights movement, and now he believed he had hard evidence of a linkage between King and the communists.[97] Rumors of communist activity in the black movement were rife, especially in the South. But a top-level FBI report in August 1963 concluded: "There has been an obvious failure of the Communist Party of the United States to appreciably infiltrate, influence, or control large numbers of American Negroes in this country."[98]

Fundamentally, as John Kennedy told King, this was a political question. Was King willing to risk his movement and, in turn, an administration sympathetic to the movement for the sake of protecting an alleged communist or two? King agreed to break relations with Levison, although he resumed telephone contact within weeks when Burke Marshall told him the administration would not produce the evidence that Levison was a communist. O'Dell, with his prior history of membership in the party, had to go. At first O'Dell temporarily resigned his SCLC position. Then, on July 3, King wrote to him:

We conducted what we felt to be a thorough inquiry into these charges and were unable to discover any present connections with the Communist Party on your part. . . .

The situation in our country is such, however, that an allusion to the left brings forth an emotional response which would seem to indicate that SCLC and the Southern Freedom Movement are Communist inspired. In these critical times we cannot afford to risk such impressions. We, therefore, have decided in our Administrative Committee, that we should request you to make your temporary resignation permanent.[99]

O'Dell quickly complied with the request.

The president was aware of these events. A political quid pro quo now occurred as Kennedy bolstered the black movement in return for King's removal of O'Dell. At a July 17 news conference, a reporter brought the communist issue before the president. "Mr. President," he stated, "in the last week the Governor of Alabama, the Governor of Mississippi, and the Attorney General of Arkansas have all testified before the Senate Commerce Committee insisting that the integration movement was Communist-inspired. . . . Will you comment on it?" JFK replied, "We looked into this matter with a good deal of care. We have no evidence that any of the leaders of the civil rights movement are communists. We have no evidence that the demonstrations are communist-inspired." He went further. "I think it is a convenient scapegoat to suggest that all the difficulties are Communist and if the Communist movement would only disappear that would end all this. . . . The way to make the problem go away, in my opinion, is to provide for a redress of grievance."[100] But in October 1963, after Hoover informed Robert Kennedy that King had resumed contact with Levison, the attorney general agreed to authorize a wiretap on King's telephone.[101]

The president referred to "we" in his June 22 talk with the civil rights leaders. But JFK's "we" had its limitations. When off-duty uniformed air force servicemen asked for and received permission to demonstrate against discrimination in South Dakota, the president was furious. He berated presidential assistant Lee White, who had authorized the servicemen's participation. "It was the worst beating I ever took," recalls

White. "It was my worst moment on staff and I'll never forget how awful it felt." The White House made sure that nothing like this would happen again. Governor George Wallace's testimony before the Senate Commerce Committee had prompted the sharp presidential reaction. "Perhaps," Wallace told the committee, "we will now see Purple Hearts for street brawling."[102]

In another incident, a Louisiana state highway official complained to Senator Russell Long and Congressman Hale Boggs, both of Louisiana, when federal funds were withdrawn from construction contracts because of racial discrimination in the employment of workers. This was done under a presidential executive order barring the use of such funds on projects that practiced racial discrimination in employment. Long talked with the president, and the requirement was waived. "Of course," Lee White wrote JFK, "the less that is said about this in the newspapers, the better off everyone will be."[103] The president's "we" had its political limitations.

Civil rights leaders also understood that the president's "we" was not synonymous with "us." After the June White House meeting, Roy Wilkins released a statement that the Kennedy proposals were "more comprehensive than any previous Presidential recommendations for civil rights . . . [but] they do not fully meet the needs of the times." He also noted that the president's "call for suspension of civil rights demonstrations" was inappropriate because "such demonstrations are a part of 'the American tradition of freedom and protest.'"[104] On June 25, at a rally in Harlem, the black leaders announced August 28 was to be the day for the "March on Washington for Jobs and Freedom."[105]

However, a significant change occurred in the tone of the planned demonstration and in the role played by the administration. The black leaders were convinced by the president and his brother that, rather than have sit-ins or lay siege to the Capitol, they should engage in a planned, orderly march and rally.[106] "Instead of a menacing sit-in in the legislative galleries," writes Sorenson, "it was to be a peaceful assembly on the Washington Monument grounds, marching from there to the Lincoln Memorial."[107]

While planning for the march went forward, the civil rights

leadership was also working to strengthen the president's proposed legislation. In a joint press release, Wilkins, Young, Farmer, King, and James Forman of SNCC acknowledged that "no President has recommended a bill of this scope before," but they also pointed out that the proposed "civil rights legislation [is] not enough."[108] In a July 2 meeting with members from more than seventy civil rights organizations, the Leadership Conference on Civil Rights decided to open a full-time office in Washington, D.C., to coordinate the lobbying efforts on behalf of civil rights. By the end of July the Washington office was in operation, with funding substantially provided by Walter Reuther's United Automobile Workers Union.[109] This was the beginning of "the greatest period of activity that the Conference ever sustained."[110] The chairman of the Executive Committee of the ADA told the national board members, "This is the most important legislative fight in ADA history."[111]

Robert Kennedy was the administration strategist and lead man on the bill, and his initial testimony before House Judiciary Subcommittee no. 5 was an indication of the administration's uncertainty over how to handle the matter.[112] On June 26, after introducing of the administration bill to the subcommittee, the attorney general committed gaffe after gaffe. When asked if he was familiar with a public-accommodations bill introduced on June 3 by Congressman John Lindsay (R-N.Y.), the attorney general replied, "I am not. As the Chairman [Emanuel Celler] said, there are 165 bills or 365. I have not read them all." Lindsay broke in, "I am quite deeply disturbed, Mr. Attorney General, that you have never bothered to read this very important legislation." Kennedy replied, "Congressman, I am sorry that I have not read all of the bills, and I am sorry that I have not read your bill."

But Lindsay, an ardent liberal, was not satisfied. "In view of the fact that you apparently did not consider these bills at all, I can't help but ask the question as to whether or not you really want public accommodations legislation. . . . Let us be frank about it. The rumor is all over the cloakrooms and corridors of Capitol Hill that the administration has made a deal with the leadership to scuttle the accommodations." Kennedy angrily responded, "I am surprised by this, but maybe I shouldn't be, that you would come out here in this open hearing and say that you heard these rumors in the cloakroom. I think it has been made clear. . . . I want this legislation to pass. I don't think, Congressman, that I have to defend myself to you about this matter."

If Republican votes were the necessary element for passage of civil rights legislation, Robert Kennedy's testimony did not help to secure these voters. The attorney general was not adequately prepared for the hearings. The Republicans wanted recognition for their legislative role in civil rights, and the attorney general cavalierly dismissed their efforts in public. In addition, RFK, even before the heated exchange with Lindsay, referred to a member of the committee as "Congressman." This was an affront to the dignity of the House, whose members are carefully acknowledged as "Distinguished" or "Mr. Congressman."

The next day, Secretary of Labor Willard Wirtz went before the subcommittee and stated, "I hope this testimony will be identified with a thorough reading of . . . [all the proposed] legislation and that the approach to this matter will continue as it was throughout the past decade to be absolutely nonpartisan." Chairman Celler responded, "I think the statement is well taken. I have come to rely greatly on the support I have received on civil rights legislation from not only the Democrats but from the Republicans. Frankly, it would be impossible to get a civil rights bill without the support of those on the other side of the aisle." The peace offering was made and acknowledged, but mistrust of the administration—by the Republicans and by strong civil rights supporters— was never far below the surface.

With the agreement of the president, Celler stalled the civil rights bill in his committee. The president wanted to give the House Ways and Means Committee time to get the tax bill out before civil rights proposals dominated the legislative agenda.[113] After the Labor Day recess and after the march was over, the House Judiciary Committee got to work seriously on the proposed legislation. This occurred soon after the tax bill was reported out of committee. In the interim, the prorights leaders had lined up the support of George Meany and the AFL-CIO for the inclusion of the FEPC in the omnibus civil rights bill.[114] The serious legislative maneuvering was yet to get under way.

The march could not be "headed off," but, the White House was determined to at least make it an orderly demonstration.[115] "It was awfully disorganized at the beginning of the summer," recalls Burke Marshall. Once the administration decided to go along with it, "the Attorney General wanted to make sure it was a success and that it was organized right."[116] John Douglas, an assistant attorney general, was assigned full time to provide logistical support for the march. He worked closely with Jack Conway of the United Auto Workers; and labor, religious, and white political leaders joined with the black leadership in an evocation of national unity.[117] In the wake of the Evers shooting, Stephen Currier, with Whitney Young's help, established the United Civil Rights Leadership Council to coordinate black movement efforts. Currier raised eight hundred thousand dollars to be used by the council to support the march.[118]

"People were talking about sitting in on Capitol Hill and the floor of Congress," writes one activist sympathizer. "They were ready to bring the country to a halt, but Jack Kennedy called in the top 'civil rights leaders' and before the people knew what was happening, the march was Kennedy-sponsored and proclaimed as being 'in the American tradition.'"[119] There was increasing talk of white "cooptation" of the black movement.[120] While some of the black leadership in CORE and SNCC opposed extensive white participation, others in the SCLC, the NAACP, and the National Urban League saw the shift as a splendid opportunity. An internal Urban League memorandum, "The March as a means to a New Coalition," argued that this broadened participation

> can completely change the overall civil rights climate almost overnight. . . . We have a major chance to help our whole society . . . [by] testing at once the chance for a broad coalition that can surround and penetrate the power elite with moral and intellectual and political and aesthetic pressure. . . . Power elite members who see in the parade familiars carrying solid signs instead of strangers . . . are wide open to accepting the challenge they've never "heard" before. . . . *All can join at some point or other right now in the basic good work of this freedom movement,* which is being mounted for the good of *all* at a time when *all* of us are affected by discrimination whether we know it or not.[121]

At a July 18 news conference, the president publicly endorsed the march. He called it a "peaceful assembly calling for a redress of grievances." "I think," he remarked, "that's in the great [American] tradition." JFK continued, "We want citizens to come to Washington if they feel they are not having their rights expressed. But, of course, arrangements have been made to make this responsible and peaceful." The president closed his remarks by saying, "I would suggest that we exercise great care in protesting so that it doesn't become riots."[122]

Cardinal Francis Spellman of New York endorsed the march, and the National Catholic Conference for Interracial Justice helped sponsor it, as did the American Jewish Congress and the National Council of Churches of Christ in America. "We need allies," A. Philip Randolph told James Reston of the *New York Times*. "People who are victims must take the leadership. But the Negro cannot win the fight alone, no more than the Jew or the labor leader could win his fight alone."[123]

The August 28 march on Washington, originally viewed by the White House as a massive, threatening mob action, became a celebration of a shared dream.[124] *New York Times* writer Russell Baker described the day: "For the most part they came silently during the night and early morning. . . . Instead of the emotional horde of angry militants that many had feared, what Washington saw was a vast army of quiet, middle-class Americans who had come in the spirit of the church outing. And instead of the tensions that had been expected, they gave this city a day of sad music, strange silences and good feeling in the streets."[125] The march of one quarter of a million Americans, at least for the moment, transformed the black movement. The white middle class embraced the movement, and their children joined it.[126]

Up to the last moment the administration was fearful that the march might not go off as planned. The president turned down an invitation to address the marchers.[127] After the march was over and the television networks had beamed the huge assemblage across the country, the president issued a statement: "This nation can properly be proud of the demonstration that has occurred here today."[128] He also greeted the march leadership at the White House with a refrain from King's magnificent "I have a dream" speech.[129] Sandwiches were ordered from the White House mess. Wilkins noticed that John Kennedy "was very relieved."[130] The march helped the president and the movement; it was now politically sound to espouse the goals of the black movement.[131]

The president discussed legislative strategy with the march leaders as they basked in the afterglow. Randolph told JFK, "It is going to take a crusade to win approval of the civil rights measures. It is going to be a crusade that, I think, nobody but you can lead."[132] But neither John Kennedy nor Robert Kennedy wanted to lead a crusade. "What I want is a bill," said Robert Kennedy, "not an issue."[133]

King, Randolph, Whitney Young, Wilkins, and Walter Reuther, among others, tried to persuade the president to strengthen the equal employment section of his bill with a strong Fair Employment Practices Commission section (FEPC) and to add a section giving the Justice Department the ability to intervene in cases of alleged discrimination (Title III). The president responded, "We've got 158 to 160 Democrats," and 60 more "hard to get" Republican votes needed to be found. "Congressman McClintock [McCulloch] indicated to the Justice Department that he thought he could vote for our bill with some changes. He's the chief fellow. He won't vote for it unless he's got the green light from Halleck. If we can get him, we will get the 60 Republicans."[134]

The president was referring to Congressman William M. McCulloch, the ranking minority member of the House Judiciary Committee, and Charles Halleck, the minority leader in the House. The administration planned to create a strong bipartisan bill. "If I wanted to beat your bill," JFK continued, "I would put FEPC in. And I would vote for it and we would never pass it in the House." The important thing was to bring the Republicans along, and Kennedy believed the Republicans would never support a bill containing a strong FEPC and Title III.

Two days after the march, Arnold Aronson, the executive secretary of the LCCR, wrote to the leaders of the major civil rights organizations: "The March in Washington as a great and moving experience is secure in history. . . . What is still in doubt is what effect the March will have on the fate and shape of the civil rights bill." Aronson's concern focused on JFK. "The President has previously acknowledged the need for two of the key amendments the March leaders asked to have added to the bill. He supports pending FEPC legislation [and] something like 'across the board Part III.' . . . Unquestionably," Aronson believed, "Mr. Kennedy will accept both provisions if they are included in the bill. But he is hesitant to urge their addition and prefers to leave that decision with Congress."[135]

But before much could be done in committee, outside events again played a major role. Governor Wallace repeatedly refused to desegregate Alabama's public schools in the fall of 1963. Finally, under court order and after the White House federalized the Alabama National Guard, which the governor had used to block the entry of the black children into the school, the schools were desegregated. Wallace's blatant appeals to hysteria created the atmosphere that led to the Sunday morning bombing of the Sixteenth Street Baptist Church in Birmingham. Four black children were killed on that September 15, and twenty others were injured.

The country was again outraged at the violence in the South. King called for the "United States Government to restore a sense of confidence in the protection of life, limb and property." He pointed to the need for Title III "legislation empowering the Attorney General to file suit on behalf of citizens whose civil rights have been violated."[136] A new, moral grassroots pressure on legislators was being brought to bear by the liberal groups. "The major new factor is the church participation," wrote David Cohen, the legislative representative of the LCCR. "Some of the denominations, the Episcopal most recently and the Presbyterian earlier, have brought in lay and religious leadership to speak directly to Congressmen and Senators." Congressman Robert Kastenmeier (D-Wis.) noted a "change in attitude among at least a critical number of members of the [Judiciary] Subcommittee toward a fuller commitment. . . . Gradually the bill shaped into something even stronger—in fact much stronger than the Administration bill."[137]

The White House strategy was to concentrate on a bill that would appeal to the swing-vote Republicans. During July and

August, McCulloch met secretly with top Justice Department officials to work out a joint legislative package. But the Birmingham bombing and the moral fervor that black rights was now generating swung a majority of the subcommittee over to a stronger civil rights position than the McCulloch-Kennedy package.

Despite an earlier pledge to McCulloch and the Republicans that he would back a circumscribed public-accommodations section, Celler now backed the extension of this section to include every form of business—even private schools, law firms, and medical associations. Celler also backed the addition of a strong Title III to the proposed legislation. By the end of September, the subcommittee had added a series of major strengthening amendments.[138]

The liberals were delighted. As the finishing touches were being put on this subcommittee bill, Arnold Aronson wrote to the LCCR constituent organizations: "The civil rights bill coming out of subcommittee is so comprehensive that in spite of the pitfalls ahead, it is hard not to feel a jubilant sense of victory."[139] Roy Wilkins wrote to the NAACP affiliates, "A good civil rights bill, containing important additions to the Package proposed by President Kennedy last June, has been reported favorably."[140]

McCulloch was livid. He recalled that the moderate Republicans had been sold out once before—in 1957, when they had put themselves on the line and voted to support a strong civil rights bill, only to watch as Johnson scuttled it with the connivance of the southerners and some conservative Republicans. Now the moderate Republicans thought they had a deal with the chairman and the administration that insured bipartisan cooperation on every major aspect of the proposed legislation. It appeared that this deal was not going to be upheld and that they were again being put into a no-win position. They now had to vote to cut back the strong liberal amendments and thus look as if they opposed civil rights. Or they could vote to sustain the liberal amendments and watch the bill go down to defeat in the full committee, the House, or the Senate.[141]

The southerners, on the other hand, appeared to be delighted with the movement of events. They believed that a strong bill would be defeated in a Senate vote, or a strong bill would never get to a final vote on the Senate floor. The southerners now lined up with the more ardent liberals to support the stronger legislation.[142]

The administration leadership was dumbfounded. "We had everything under control, and then he [Celler] collapsed in the face of the Liberals," Katzenbach recalled.[143] "Can Clarence Mitchell and the Leadership [LCCR] group deliver 3 Republicans on the Rules Committee and 60 Republicans on the House floor?" President Kennedy asked an LCCR leader. "McCulloch can deliver 60 Republicans. Without him it can't be done. McCulloch is mad now because he thinks an agreement he had with us on the language of compromise has been thrown away by the subcommittee. . . . Once McCulloch is mad then it ceases to be bipartisan. I'll go as far as I can go, but I think McCulloch has to come with us or otherwise it is an exercise in futility."[144] More moderate leadership had to be brought to bear or, the Kennedys believed, the entire civil rights legislative program was doomed to defeat.

Celler accepted the White House position after a meeting with the attorney general. McCulloch was appeased after Katzenbach and Marshall agreed that the subcommittee Democrats would support the necessary changes in the bill and the administration would back no watering-down proposals in the Senate without McCulloch's approval. In addition, the attorney general again went before the subcommittee and recommended the specific changes that were now proposed. One Republican member of the subcommittee, James Bromwell of Iowa, "was impressed with his [Robert Kennedy's] forthrightness. There was no equivocation. He took full responsibility for the cut backs."[145] The administration presented the strong liberals with a stark choice: take their civil rights proposals or take no bill at all.

The committed liberals felt betrayed by the Kennedys. They had believed the White House would accept a strong FEPC and Title III if it could be sold to the committee. They had obtained a stronger bill, and the administration was gutting it. Roy Wilkins argued that the administration's "maneuver now seems to be to pull the teeth out of the bill before you even get a chance to chew. . . . The Kennedys want to remove all obstacles before there is even a test."[146] Joseph Rauh recalls, "A terrible brawl [ensued] between the Administration and us."[147] "There is no reason for this kind of sell out," Clarence Mitchell argued. "The Administration should be in there fighting for the subcommittee bill."[148] Mitchell wrote to Celler, "Some of the Attorney General's suggestions have done incalculable harm to civil rights because they were . . . described as efforts to get a bill 'more reasonable' than that reported by the House Judiciary Subcommittee No. 5." The revised subcommittee bill was reasonable, argued the black leader.[149]

The administration was intent on getting through a bill it considered reasonable, with the allies it considered necessary to achieve success. By October 23 the president had brought Halleck around to go along with the proposed legislation. The Republican House leader promised to call the White House later in the day when he was sure that his followers were on board. The president waited for Halleck's call. When it did not come by the promised hour, JFK finally called the minority leader. "Mr. President," Halleck said, "I've got enough votes for you."[150]

On October 29 the White House and the Judiciary Committee chairman were ready for the full committee to vote on the revised compromise package that had been put together with the Republicans. It was a substantially different piece of legislation than the bill passed by the subcommittee. FEPC and Title III were eliminated from the measure. The revised bill was similar to the original administration measure, with some additional refinements, especially the public-accommodations section modeled after Congressman Lindsay's proposals, added by the Republicans.[151]

Chairman Celler led the full committee through the required votes to have the substitute bill put in place of the original. The motion to retain the original, stronger subcommittee bill was defeated by a vote of nineteen to fifteen, with the diehard liberals and the southerners voting for retention. McCulloch, with Halleck's strong assist, brought along nine Republicans to join Celler's Democrats to provide the majority needed to bring the compromise motion forward.[152] On November 20 the Judiciary Committee sent the new bill to the clerk of the House. The clerk, in turn, sent it on to the House

Rules Committee chaired by the irascible Howard Smith of Virginia.

The administration turned its attention to the Senate. Everyone understood that the more difficult battle was now under way. Senator Eastland's Judiciary Committee commenced hearings on the president's civil rights proposals in July. The committee recessed in mid September subject to the call of the chair. The southern Senate members were not rushing forward to deal with this legislation. They believed the emergent white backlash would ultimately come to the aid of their cause.[153]

On November 2 the administration received some positive news. Nicholas Katzenbach had extracted from Republican Senate minority leader Everett Dirksen the promise that the civil rights legislation would have his support to come to a vote on the Senate floor.[154] The Republican Senate leaders were still committed to support some form of civil rights legislation, but they were going to have to be brought along on the specifics of what they would support.

Virginia's Democratic senator Harry Byrd, chair of the Senate Finance Committee, was applying his own pressure on the White House. He was intent on conducting a leisurely paced hearing on the president's tax package and thus holding it hostage to the civil rights program.[155] At a November 14 press conference, JFK was asked about the linkage of the tax bill to civil rights. "I think it is unfortunate," Kennedy responded. "The fact of the matter is that both these bills should be passed. . . . The tax bill hearings have been quite voluminous. It would seem to me that it might be possible to end those hearings and bring the matter to the floor of the Senate before the end of the year." He continued, "There may be a very long debate [on civil rights]. The tax bill may be caught up in that. And I think the economy will suffer. . . . I would like to get the tax bill out of the way quickly."[156]

The administration was having problems with the South, as expected, and many Republicans and liberals were uncomfortable with the House bill. Conservative Republicans were unhappy with the cooperation Halleck extended to the administration. They believed the Republican leadership had helped the administration out of a politically difficult situation.[157] Many liberal Democrats were unhappy with the watered-down bill the administration was supporting.[158] Bayard Rustin wrote to Martin Luther King, Jr.: "Partly from a moderate liberal orientation, but largely as the President himself has said, because of the mass revolt of the Negro people, civil rights bills have been introduced into Congress. But there are few, if any, who claim that the Administration is putting its full weight behind even these measures."[159] True or not, Rustin's words mirrored the continuing mistrust between the administration and a large portion of the civil rights leadership.

It was November of 1963, and the 1964 presidential election was looming on the horizon. John Kennedy told one black leader, "This issue could cost me the election, but we're not turning back."[160] In the fall of 1963 JFK's approval rating remained high in the North, and his support among blacks was at phenomenal levels of 80 to 90 percent. In the South, however, his approval level was generally in the 40 to 50 percent range. The battle over civil rights was the key to this shift.[161]

Barry Goldwater, a staunch states' rights advocate, was increasingly being mentioned as the GOP nominee, and polls showed him to be considerably stronger than Kennedy in the South. The early summer polls had indicated that any Republican but Rockefeller could beat JFK in the South.[162] Nationwide, Goldwater was no match for JFK according to the Gallup Poll trial heats.[163] The more Barry Goldwater moved to the fore as his likely adversary, the more incredulous John Kennedy became. "I can't believe we will be that lucky," Kennedy told Ben Bradlee.[164] Arthur Schlesinger, Jr., wrote: "Plainly the President could not wait for 1964." And Tip O'Neill recalls, Kennedy "simply relished the prospect of running against Goldwater."[165]

Planning for the 1964 campaign was under way. Larry O'Brien recalled, "We were absolutely convinced John Kennedy would be President for eight years. We had no fear of reelection. The President and a group of us who had been active in the previous campaign, Ken O'Donnell, Steve Smith and others, sat in the Cabinet Room and we had our first conversation about '64. We said we would soon have to focus on '64, but we were *very* confident."[166] A week after this first precampaign meeting, JFK went to Texas to deal with intra-party rivalries and to get a firsthand sense of the southern electorate's feelings about his administration.[167] It was all not to be. John Kennedy's reelection campaign and his maneuvering over civil rights came to an end as an assassin's bullets ripped into him. Lyndon Johnson took over the stewardship of the nation and the Democratic party.

PART TWO

Lyndon B. Johnson: Coincident Hero of the Second Black Reconstruction

When you're dealing with all those senators . . . you've got to know two things right away. You've got to understand the beliefs and values common to them all as politicians the desire for fame and the thirst for honor, and then you've got to understand the emotion most controlling that particular senator when he thinks about this particular issue.

Lyndon B. Johnson, 1964

5

From Texan to National Politician

LYNDON JOHNSON was known as a friend of the poor, black or white, when he served as a Texas congressman. But in 1948, when he ran for the United States Senate, Johnson's voice resonated with the southern chorus of racism. He denounced President Harry Truman's civil rights proposals and repeatedly declared, "I voted against the so-called and mis-named civil rights bills; and I expect to continue fighting them in my six years as a Senator."[1] The South was in revolt against the president's civil rights proposals, and Johnson was running as a southerner.

His segregationist rhetoric continued when he entered the Senate. Johnson courted the southern leadership and planned to use his first floor speech to ingratiate himself with this group by attacking Truman's civil rights proposals. LBJ asked a long-time ally and Roosevelt appointee, James Rowe, to help him draft this speech. But Rowe, who favored Truman's program, refused and admonished Johnson, "It is not enough for you to be a Senator, a leading politician, and an able man of great influence . . . . Your old friends, who remember the high stepping, idealistic, intelligent young man who came here as a bright new Congressman in 1938, expect more of you than that. . . . Someone like you had better grab hold of it [the civil rights issue] and if you can get even 20% of it solved in the next 20 years you will be one of the great men of American history."[2]

Johnson's foray into racism was a rare exception in his political career, but it reflects the pathway he took in his vocation. He used race when he had to use it to further his ambitions, and he ignored race when it was of no consequence for those ambitions. Johnson's hopes ultimately lay not with a racist South but with the progressive South of his origins.

Gillespie County, Johnson's birthplace, voted 398 to 16 against secession from the Union.[3] The Texas hill country in which Johnson grew up did not have "plantations and darkies," and as LBJ further recalls, "[I] never sat on my parents' or grandparents' knees listening to nostalgic tales of the ante-bellum South."[4] His grandfather, Sam Johnson, Sr., was an organizer for the biracial People's party and a staunch campaigner for its 1892 presidential nominee, General James B. Weaver. His father, Sam Early Johnson, played a leadership role in the 1920s that resulted in the Texas legislature passing an anti–Ku Klux Klan statute making it a crime "to parade and otherwise to operate in masks."[5] In 1923 Sam Early Johnson walked off the floor of the Texas House rather than support a bill that excluded blacks from participation in the Democratic party primary election.[6] Overt racism was not a part of LBJ's family background or early social environment.

Sympathy for those who were down-and-out was part of the Johnson family inheritance. His grandfather's association with the populist movement and his mother's "belief that the strong must care for the weak" held sway over Johnson throughout his life.[7] He identified with the poor; he perceived himself as having the origins of a poor person. In 1960 he told a black reporter, "My family was poor and I was poor. . . . When time came for us kids to go to college, the money wasn't there. We couldn't go to the university. We had to scuffle through a state teachers college. Because of all that I had to suffer."[8] Johnson believed he was brought up in a family that lived on the economic margin of society. He told his aides how his "father came every morning at 5:30 and would say, 'Lyndon, all the kids are up and ahead of you— you've got to get moving—you've got to make money. We need everyone working to make a go of it.'" And going to San Marcos State Teachers College while the better-off kids went to the University of Texas was a humiliation that he always carried with him.[9] When LBJ worked as a school-teacher with poor Mexican-Americans in Cotulla, Texas, he used his own money to help them with their schoolwork. As he told his biographer, Doris Kearns, "you never forget what poverty and hatred can do when you see its scars on the hopeful face of a young child."[10] Poverty and racism were twin evils for Johnson, and he was always to claim that he opposed them both. But Johnson had political ambitions, and he was quick to learn that the fulfillment of political ambitions sometimes required the subordination of personal beliefs to the necessity of election and political bargaining.

Johnson began his years in Washington in 1931. Without his prior knowledge, one of Sam Early Johnson's political allies, Welly K. Hopkins, moved to have young Johnson placed on the staff of newly elected congressman Richard Kleberg.[11] Immediately prior to the appointment, Johnson was the speech teacher and debating team coach at Sam Houston High School. His speaking abilities and the help he provided Hopkins in his 1930 state senate campaign gave him the opportunity to move to Washington. He ran with it, and with his storehouse of energy, talent, and ambition, he became a Washington personage in his own right, even though he was nominally just a congressional aide.

LBJ used his position on Kleberg's staff to get to know the powerful men of Texas and the House of Representatives, and they soon helped the young Texan. In July 1935 Congressman Sam Rayburn and other Texas New Dealers intervened to arrange for the appointment of Lyndon Johnson as the National Youth Administration (NYA) director for Texas. During his eighteen-month tenure in this position, he struggled for "his" people and he felt for them. His brother, Sam Houston Johnson, recalls, "Lyndon would make you think that his people in Texas were suffering more than any other." And he meant both poor whites and poor Negroes. Frank Horne, an NYA administrator and uncle of black singer Lena Horne, recalls "this guy in Texas, who was really something . . . . Johnson didn't think the NYA was for middle-class people the way a lot of Congressmen did; he thought it was for people, including Mexican-Americans and Negroes."[12] LBJ crossed the color line when it came to basic economic aid, but he went no farther. Johnson, like other southerners, never appointed a black to a supervisory role in the NYA. Mary McLeod Bethune, the NYA national deputy director and member of Franklin D. Roosevelt's black kitchen cabinet, cajoled and implored Johnson to cross the color line with a black appointment, but she could not get him to violate the region's norms.[13]

Johnson was a southerner in Washington, and he needed no special prodding to explicate his beliefs about the "Negroes'" place. His "Special Report of Negro Activities of the National Youth Administration in Texas" aptly summarized his position. "The question during the past one hundred years in Texas . . . has resolved itself to a definite system of customs which cannot be upset over time. There is peace and harmony between the races in Texas, but it is exceedingly difficult to step over a line so long established, and upset a custom so deeply rooted by any act which would be shockingly against precedence."[14] This was Johnson's answer to the question of whether or not there should be black supervisors in the Texas NYA. This was not a virulent, race-obsessed position; it was an ordinary statement by a southerner about the order of things and why they could not be changed.

Change, however, especially in race relations, was coming as nothern blacks joined the New Deal Coalition. The race issue was not a matter dealt with directly on the New Deal agenda, and President Franklin Roosevelt never gave public support to either poll-tax ban proposals or antilynching legislation; but FDR recognized the right of blacks to equal treatment under his programs. He established a civil rights section in the Justice Department; and after much black pressure, he established by executive order the first Fair Employment Practices Commission. To push for southern black civil rights would have meant a Roosevelt challenge to the southern political barons of the House and Senate. This confrontation was never undertaken; FDR always believed he could not risk the loss of his southern support as he led the nation out of depression or took on the role of "Dr. Win-the-War."[15] Roosevelt's commitment to aid the poor was never in doubt once the New Deal took hold. Black Americans, whose members were disproportionately among the poorest of the poor, moved into the Democratic column when Roosevelt made his bids for reelection.

Johnson did not need to be prodded to aid his black constituents. His basic fairness in dealing with race-related issues gave him a following among blacks in his home area and throughout Texas. In addition, Johnson initially and repeatedly ran for Congress as an unabashed Roosevelt man and New Dealer. Roosevelt became a father figure, a near idol for Johnson.[16] LBJ remained a Roosevelt supporter throughout his political career. In 1944 the anti-Roosevelt Texans who were opposed to the New Deal's liberalism planned to place an "uninstructed" set of electors on the Texas general election ballot. These Texas regulars were opposed by FDR loyalists, who stormed out of the Texas state convention. At the national convention the loyalists, with Congressman Lyndon Johnson in their ranks, challenged the seating of the regulars. The Credentials Committee recommended seating both delegations and splitting the Texas state vote between them, and this was accepted by the convention. Johnson's comments about the regulars left no doubts about his loyalties. "A man publicly acknowledges his allegiance to his country and to his church and to his party. . . . Republicans who posed as Democrats in the Texas Democratic convention have the comfort of knowing their consciences are clear. They did not take, and refused to take, the pledge [oath] of allegiance [to the Democratic party]."[17] The loyalist position of Johnson was well received by the White House and Texas's black citizens.[18] From the time of his first election to the House in 1937 through his election to the Senate in 1948, LBJ would always receive substantial support from black voters.

Johnson's election to Congress was received as the arrival of an ally by the black leadership. Black rights were not an issue in the contest that sent him to Congress. The key election issue was that he was a Roosevelt Democrat against a field of anti-Roosevelt Democrats. Johnson stayed a Roosevelt man, and FDR always remained a Johnson hero. Mary McLeod Bethune, despite her earlier rebuff from Johnson, wrote that she was pleased to see elected to the House a white southerner "who had proven himself so conscious of and sympathetic to the needs of all the people."[19]

Throughout his years in the House, Johnson almost always met these expectations of racial evenhandedness in the economic realm. As a freshman member of Congress, he went directly to FDR to complain when the head of the Agricultural Adjustment Administration did not adequately pass on benefits to black Texas farmers.[20] In his first term he also used his Washington connections and "go-gettedness," as Leon Keyserling, then deputy administrator of the United States Housing Authority, called it, to have one of the first three low-rent, federally subsidized housing projects built in Austin.[21] Sixty of the units went to black families and forty to Mexican-American families. Throughout his years in the House, Johnson backed almost every piece of New Deal economic legislation that came to the floor. He maintained his commitment to the poor of all races.[22]

Still, Congressman Lyndon Johnson scrupulously observed southern legislative norms when it came to race relations. He voted against every piece of civil rights legislation that came to the floor of the House. This included votes against antilynching proposals (1938 and 1940); poll tax abolition bills (1942, 1943, 1945); a fair employment bill (1946); and an antidiscrimination amendment to the federal school lunch program (1946). Johnson later wrote: "One heroic stand and I'd be back home, defeated, unable to do any good for anyone, much less the blacks or the underprivileged. As a Representative and a Senator, before I became a majority leader, I did not have the power [to do otherwise]. That is a plain and simple fact."[23] He believed he had to stand fast with the South. It was not only that his election and reelection depended on it, but so did his career within the Congress. His southern friends were his passport to a successful congressional career, and he could not offend them. For example, Congressman Carl Vinson of Georgia helped freshman Johnson get an appointment to the important House Naval Affairs Committee.[24] Speaker Sam Rayburn of Texas and Senator Richard Russell of Georgia became powerful mentors who intervened time and again to abet Lyndon Johnson's political career.

Congressman Johnson stuck with the white South on the race issue, but he did it quietly, without race-baiting in either his reelection campaigns or his speeches on the floor of the House. His posture appeared to be: I will do what I can when I can for blacks, but the timing is not right for any public support. He gave blacks support for their economic needs, and they gave him their support at the ballot box.[25]

When Johnson ran for the Senate in 1948, he changed his public position on the race issue and ran as a vocal segregationist. He was in a hard-fought campaign with a well-known conservative, antiblack opponent, Coke Stevenson, and he was not going to cede the segregationist position to his foe. With Texas, not the hill country, as his constituency, Johnson campaigned with a southern voice. He had run for the Senate once before, in 1941, and had been defeated when he downplayed race. This time he kicked off his second Senate campaign with a statewide radio hookup of a speech in Austin in which he denounced President Truman's civil rights proposals as "a farce and a sham—an effort to set up a police state in the guise of liberty." Johnson proudly reminded his audience he had voted against every piece of civil rights legislation that came to the House floor, and he promised to continue to do so as a senator. He repeated this boast in speeches across the state.[26] In this campaign Lyndon Johnson became a staunch advocate of states' rights and a vocal opponent of federal intervention into the southern racial domain.

The battle against civil rights was not the focus of Johnson's 1948 Senate election campaign. But given the racist oratory of his major opponent, Coke Stevenson, LBJ believed he did what he had to do in order to win the election. Stevenson led Johnson in the first primary election by a vote of 477,077 to 405,617; but Johnson came back to win the runoff election by a reported margin of 87 votes.[27] The black leadership believed that Johnson's racist rhetoric, so out of character with his prior record, was solely a creature of the campaign. National black leaders such as Mary McLeod Bethune and Robert Weaver urged blacks to vote for Johnson. Texas black leaders also rounded up votes for LBJ. One Texas newspaper editorial aptly summed up the black perspective on Johnson: "Though he is no angel, he is about as good as we have seen in the race."[28] LBJ carried the black precincts of Texas's cities by a margin of thousands of votes. Given his narrow overall victory margin, black leaders and black voters believed they had an IOU due them from the new Texas senator. They were to be sorely disappointed.

Johnson's maiden speech in the United States Senate, with the prior agreement of the southern Senate leader, Richard Russell, was ostensibly an attack on a proposal to liberalize Senate Rule 22, the filibuster rule. The liberals wanted to permit debate to be halted—that is, to have cloture invoked—for procedural matters as well as for the consideration of actual legislative proposals.[29] The strict maintenance of Rule 22 was the southern weapon to keep civil rights legislation from ever becoming a reality. The southern filibuster, or the threat of a filibuster, had always been successfully invoked in the past. Now it was Truman's civil rights proposals that were moving toward the center of the legislative arena, and the South wanted to make sure that they would never be enacted into law.

When James Rowe refused to help Johnson write his first Senate floor speech, Johnson wrote to Rowe in reply: "I think that all men are created equal. I want all men to have equal opportunity." But he found liberals like Hubert Humphrey, the mover of the strong minority civil rights plank at the 1948 Democratic convention, and southerners like Strom Thurmond, the 1948 Dixiecrat presidential candidate, both too extreme. The Truman civil rights proposals came directly out of the extremist liberal position. Johnson argued for a "frontal assault on the 'ill-housed, ill-clad, ill-fed' problem facing our nation. Until this problem is met all your other [civil rights] legislation is built upon sand."[30] The government needed to play a role to ensure those at the bottom a better shot at economic well-being, not to make sure that racial equality was achieved. But Rowe did not buy Johnson's economic arguments without the coupling to racial equality, and Johnson proceeded to formulate his Senate speech without Rowe's help.

Lyndon Johnson made his debut on the floor of the Senate on March 9, 1949. His speech was a strong defense of the right to filibuster and the traditional southern view of civil rights: "When we of the South rise here to speak against this resolution or to speak against the civil rights proposals, we are not speaking against the Negro race. . . . This is not the way to accomplish what so many want to do for the Negro race." Johnson continued, "Racial prejudice is dangerous because it is a disease of the majority endangering minority groups." But the liberals were intent on "depriving one minority of its rights in order to extend rights to other minorities." He then reasserted his opposition to lynching, poll taxes, and racial discrimination in employment. However, he noted that under the Constitution these were state matters, not federal matters. These recommendations, especially the proposed Fair Employment Practices Commission, "would necessitate a system of Federal police officers such as we have never before seen."[31]

Richard Russell denounced the commission as "a new department of the government to . . . [form] an army of lawyers to direct the F.B.I. in the prosecution of anyone who might seek to enforce segregation. The marshall of the humblest village in the South . . . would be the object of attack by this federal gestapo."[32] While Russell's attack was more bitter than Johnson's and more typical of the Deep South reaction, Johnson, at least for the moment, moved into the ranks of those who used the rhetoric of race in pursuit of their political careers.

Johnson's speech solidified his relations with white Texans. But blacks reacted adversely to the new message, and this bothered him. He wrote to one black NAACP Texas activist, it is "a profound regret to me that many Negro citizens of Texas have viewed my speech in the Senate as an affront to them."[33] Yet he did not apologize for his speech or indicate any words of regret about its content. Throughout the early 1950s Johnson voted against civil rights legislation that came to the Senate floor, and he opposed all attempts to weaken the filibuster power. In 1950 the San Antonio branch of the NAACP reproached Johnson for his anti–civil rights record and demanded that he support such legislation in the future because blacks were "being denied the rights of first-class citizenship." The senator's response was consistent with his career aspirations. "I cannot agree that the civil rights legislation, as it is currently written, would extend to any citizen 'the rights of first-class citizenship.' First-class citizenship," he continued, "begins at the meal table, in the school, at the doctor's office, and many other places other than in court. . . . In the future, as in the past, I shall work to equalize opportunity and reward for all Americans through better housing, better schooling, better health, all those things which are the true rights of first-class citizenship."[34] He later told a group of black Texas businessmen that he "was not going to stick his neck out to do anything for Negroes and get defeated."[35]

More and more, as Joseph Rauh, saw it, Lyndon Johnson sounded and acted like "a conservative Senator from a conservative state."[36] Johnson was a southerner in both time and place at this point in his career. He believed his Senate political career depended most specifically on the good offices of Richard Russell, much as his House career was provided support by Speaker Sam Rayburn. Richard Russell, as the leader of the South in the Senate, was considered to be one of the most powerful men in Washington. Johnson wanted access to Russell, and Congressman Carl Vinson of Georgia intervened to have Johnson placed on the Senate Armed Services Committee, where Russell sat as the second ranking member. "I knew there was only one way to see Russell every day," recalled Johnson, "and that was to get a seat on his committee. Without that we'd most likely be acquaintances and nothing more."[37] Now Johnson had access to Russell.

LBJ wanted more than access to the southern commander; he wanted to be his apprentice. LBJ arranged for Russell to become a regular visitor to the Johnson household. Russell was a bachelor without family in Washington, and Johnson wanted Russell to become part of his family. The Georgia senator, upon the Texan's request, became a regular Sunday visitor to the Johnson household. As Lady Bird Johnson recalls, "Early in our Senate years he became part of the pattern of our lives." Russell took to the Johnson girls, and they took to him. With the prodding of their father, they called him "uncle." As Mrs. Johnson further recalls, Lyndon "was a great friend of Dick Russell's. I'm sure there was nobody he admired more."[38] Russell became Johnson's political godfather.

Lyndon was the up-and-comer who could possibly serve as the bridge between the northern and southern wings of the Democratic party. Russell believed that the South and the North had not yet become truly reconciled since the Civil War and that the only way for that to happen was for a southerner to be elected president. Johnson was Russell's choice for the role of southern reconciliation president. LBJ was never to have another benefactor who could do as much for him as Richard

Russell. According to the famed Senate reporter William S. White, "The association between the two became, in fact, one of the most important of all Senate realities."[39] It was to become important not only for Lyndon Johnson and Richard Russell but also for the nation.

Time after time Russell eased Johnson's way up the national political ladder. When the Senate Democratic whip, Francis Myers of Pennsylvania, was defeated in his 1950 Senate re-election bid, Russell intervened at Johnson's behest and helped him obtain the whip position.[40] After Russell had raised the southern standard in his failed 1952 bid for the presidency, at LBJ's request he spoke with the victor, Adlai Stevenson, and put Johnson's name forward for the second place on the Democratic ticket. Although he rejected the Texan, Stevenson did give the vice-presidential nod to Senator John Sparkman of Alabama, Russell's convention floor manager. Russell had considerable power, and Stevenson deferred to it in 1952, although not quite in the way Johnson would have found most preferable. The national Democratic party's relationship with the South was in political disarray after the 1948 presidential election, and the Democrats and Republicans each positioned themselves to deal with the situation.

Stevenson's selection of Sparkman, combined with a party pullback from the strong 1948 civil rights platform, generally assured the Democratic ticket of southern support. However, the combination of Dwight D. Eisenhower's personal popularity with the emergence of middle-class Republicanism in the developing urban centers of the rim South helped carry the Republican ticket to victory. In addition, Stevenson came out against the southern states' claims to oil rights in the tidelands of the Gulf of Mexico. As a consequence, some Texas Democratic leaders, including Governor Alan Shivers, came out against the Democratic ticket. Other Texans, like Lyndon Johnson, were not about to come out against the Democratic ticket; but they also would not campaign actively for an anti–Texas oil candidate.[41] On the whole, despite the loss of Texas, Florida, Virginia, and Tennessee to Eisenhower, Johnson and the South stayed with the Democrats in 1952.

Of the 1952 election results, the reelection defeat of Senate majority leader Ernest McFarland of Arizona had the greatest consequences for Lyndon Johnson. Right after the election results became known, LBJ approached Booth Mooney, a speech writer for Coke Stevenson during the 1948 Texas Senate campaign, and asked him to join his Senate staff. "Landslide Lyndon," as he became known after his victory of 1948, had to improve his image in Texas before his Senate term came to an end; and he had an idea about how to do it. Mooney recalls, "Johnson [told me] he was not really the all-out-New Deal-Harry-Truman-liberal that many Texans believed him to be. He wanted to— he must—project a more conservative image." How? "If he was elected Democratic floor leader, he would have an opportunity to lead his colleagues in support for the Republican president when matters affecting the general welfare—and especially the welfare of Texas—were at stake."[42]

The position of party leader generally was not regarded as particularly powerful in the 1940s. Richard Russell, in fact, was regarded as the most powerful Democratic senator, no matter who was leader. Many Senate Democrats were committed to Russell's taking the formal leadership position, but he had declined it amidst a spate of publicity in 1950. "I could not accept any position," he wrote a political colleague, "that would jeopardize my independence of thought and action and I have consistently declined to be considered for this position." His leadership of the South and his advocacy for the South would be restricted. In addition, many ardent liberals would be outraged at Russell's appointment. At Johnson's request Russell backed him for the formal party leadership position. As Ralph Huitt, a leading Senate scholar, recalls, "He [LBJ] and Russell were on the telephone all night long, and he had the job."[43] Afterwards, Johnson gratefully wrote his mentor: "My few years in the Senate have been rich and rewarding in experience and I have many fond memories. But of them all, the greatest is our friendship and how much your kindness meant to me."[44] A large portrait of Russell standing beside the door of his Georgia law office held a place of prominence in the new Democratic leader's office. Richard Nixon, the Senate's presiding officer from 1953 through 1960, recalls that Johnson almost always "had Russell as his own—very closest advisor. I don't think

Johnson made a move on any very major issue without talking to Dick Russell."[45] Russell's desk on the Senate floor was situated directly behind the new leader's desk.

Johnson was the minority party leader in 1953; but in 1955 when control of the Senate came into Democratic hands, Johnson moved into the majority leadership position. His maneuvering and use of the majority leader position was a feat of political mastery acknowledged by friend and foe alike. Yet it was a mastery within the context of a particular era and network of political leaders and mores. Russell and Rayburn remained Johnson's ever-present advisors, but LBJ came to the leadership position already regarded as a first-rate inside political operator in his own right.[46]

Johnson transformed the majority leader's position into a powerful operation. When he became party leader the Democrats were in disarray. On labor issues, civil rights, and McCarthyism, the Democrats were embattled among themselves. Eisenhower had won the presidency with a large majority, and he was a consistently popular president. Johnson developed a strategy to bring the Senate Democrats together. First, he would not oppose the popular president unless there was a consensus for doing so within the party. It made no sense to him to "fight the good fight" for the sake of a fight and get stuck with the tag of opposing a popular president for the sake of "mere" opposition. Second, he compromised and compromised again whenever he believed there was a chance of victory on a piece of legislation important to the Democrats. Lyndon Johnson knew how to count votes. If he sensed the Democrats had a victory in their hands, he made sure they won. Third, the "Johnson treatment," grabbing someone and extravagantly asking, imploring, or demanding his vote—given the situation—became a hallmark of his leadership. Finally, the Rayburn axiom "You have to go along to get along" became a Johnson touchstone.

With the prior agreement of Richard Russell, one of Johnson's first acts as leader was to persuade the Democratic Steering Committee to allow freshman senators to have an appointment to one major committee before a senior member would be given an appointment to a third major committee.

As a result of the Johnson-promoted rule changes, newly elected liberals such as Hubert Humphrey of Minnesota, Mike Mansfield of Montana, Herbert Lehman of New York, John F. Kennedy of Massachusetts, and Stuart Symington of Missouri all received choice committee assignments. And all were now somewhat indebted to the Democratic party leader. Across party divisions new alliances were being formed.[47]

The manner in which Johnson seduced and entranced liberals to go along with the party position nearly drove some of the more avid ideologists to distraction. "I don't believe Johnson was ever a particularly ideological guy," recalls Joe Rauh. "He was a guy who always wanted to have his bill or his amendment passed. And he had a genius for finding that point where you'd get the most people and then rounding them up. That was our complaint." It was a complaint about the LBJ recruitment of almost unholy alliance partners. Rauh: "He would get some right-winger and Hubert Humphrey to agree. A lot of what he did in finding that middle ground was painful to [those of] us who were fighting for issues." One instance of particular pain is recalled by the veteran liberal: "He persuaded Hubert Humphrey to persuade the liberals not to make the fight [on Rule 22 in 1955]." In another instance, Bob Oliver, the CIO lobbyist, "accepted the Johnson theory of the half-way position. . . . Bob was more Lyndon Johnson's lobbyist back to the labor movement than he was the labor movement's lobbyist to Lyndon Johnson." Rauh concludes, "The people who are supposed to tell you to go further, go back and tell [you] . . . they really don't want to go that far and that he's [LBJ] getting them the best deal possible."[48] The liberals were oftentimes brought over to Johnson's view of the art of the possible in politics. The Democratic leader was a southerner with strong ties to northern leaders of all political hues.[49]

On the other side of the regional-ideological divide, Johnson often mustered southern support for issues that most observers believed they would not support. Perhaps his most outstanding achievement on this score was when he brought a united Senate Democratic party to vote for the condemnation of Joe McCarthy. For liberal northerners, a vote against McCarthy was a vote against rabid anticommunism, and they needed little else to

I   A drinking fountain in the segregated South. Bettmann Archive.

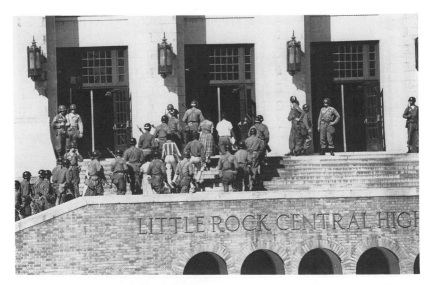

2   The federal government brings the races together in Little Rock Central High
     School. September 25, 1957. UPI/Bettmann.

3   In a Greensboro, North Carolina, F. W. Woolworth store, black students sit in
     to stand up for their rights. February 2, 1960. UPI/Bettmann Newsphotos.

4   The Kennedy campaign receives a frenetic greeting in Los Angeles. November 1, 1960. National Archives.

5   The Johnson Special, at a stop in Greenville, North Carolina, toured the South throughout the campaign. October 11, 1960. UPI/Bettmann.

6   Until the morning hours of the day after the election, no one knew who won in 1960. CBS television election eve broadcasting. National Archives.

7   The presidential inauguration of John F. Kennedy generated high expectations as the nation reacted to his youth and the vigor of his words and ideas. January 20, 1961. National Archives.

8   The Freedom Rides generated a civil rights crisis early in the Kennedy
     administration. Outside of Anniston, Alabama, a white mob burned this
     Freedom Ride bus. May 14, 1961. UPI/Bettmann Newsphotos.

9   Martin Luther King, Jr., peers between the bars of his jail cell after he was arrested on a trespass charge in St. Augustine, Florida. June 11, 1962. UPI/ Bettmann Newsphotos.

10   In Birmingham, Alabama, firehoses sprayed peaceful marchers and the
     pictures went out over the national airwaves. May 3, 1963. UPI/Bettmann.

11   The Justice Department leadership plans civil rights strategy. *Left to right*:
     Robert F. Kennedy, attorney general; Nicholas deB Katzenbach, deputy
     attorney general; Harold K. Reiss, Office of Legal Council; Harold Green, Civil
     Rights Division; and Burke Marshall (with his back to the photographer),
     assistant attorney general. National Archives.

12   **Attorney General Robert Kennedy remained with black leaders to discuss strategy for the newly introduced civil rights bill after President Kennedy had to leave the meeting. June 22, 1963. *Left to right*: Robert Kennedy, Martin Luther King, Jr., Roy Wilkins, and A. Phillip Randolph. National Archives.**

13   The March on Washington, black and white together in a call for change.
      August 28, 1963. National Archives.

14   After the March on Washington was over—and deemed a success by the
      president—the leaders were invited to the White House. JFK greeted them
      with the words, "I have a dream," August 28, 1963. National Archives.

15 Richard Russell and Lyndon Johnson went head-to-head in the White House when the president told his old mentor, "Dick, you've got to get out of my way." Russell responded, "It's going to cost you the South." December 7, 1963. Lyndon Baines Johnson Library.

16 President Lyndon Johnson repeatedly invited black leaders to the White House to discuss legislation. At this meeting with the president are (*left to right*) Roy Wilkins, executive secretary of the NAACP; James Farmer, national director of CORE; Martin Luther King, Jr., head of the SCLC; and Whitney Young, executive director of the National Urban League. January 18, 1964. UPI/ Bettmann.

17   Joseph L. Rauh, Jr., stands up before the Credentials Committee at the 1964 Democratic National Convention in Atlantic City, New Jersey, to plead for the seating of the Mississippi Freedom Democratic party. August 22, 1964. UPI/Bettmann.

18   Lyndon Johnson's theme at the 1964 Democratic National Convention, "Let Us Continue," stressed his place in the line of Democratic party legitimacy. Lyndon Bains Johnson Library.

19 Barry Goldwater's campaign theme, emphasized on a billboard placed in Atlantic City, New Jersey, at the time of the Democratic convention, stressed he would do what was "right"—and be right. UPI/Bettmann.

20 Lyndon Johnson's exuberance during the 1964 presidential campaign could hardly be contained. He saw himself, his political party, and his political program—the Great Society—all coming together with a resounding election victory. Lyndon Baines Johnson Library.

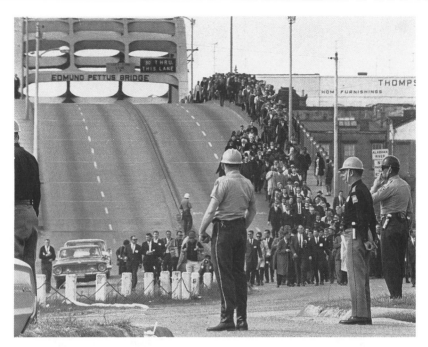

21   Martin Luther King, Jr., led a march over the Pettus Bridge in Selma, Alabama, stopped, held a brief prayer vigil, then turned around rather than violate a federal court order and risk a confrontation with Alabama law officers and the federal courts. March 9, 1965. UPI/Bettmann.

22   Governor George Wallace of Alabama visited the White House during the Selma crisis and left as the leader of a defeated cause. President Johnson told the governor he "would not hesitate to send in federal troops" to maintain order in Selma. He also informed the nation, "This Monday I will send to Congress a request for legislation." March 13, 1965. National Archives.

23 In the Capitol rotunda, President Johnson takes Martin Luther King, Jr.'s hand after the signing of the Voting Rights Act of 1965. August 6, 1965. Lyndon Baines Johnson Library.

garner their support. For southerners, many of whom had staunch anticommunist and strong nationalist constituencies, the vote against McCarthy had to take on another dimension, and Johnson made it happen. He made the McCarthy vote for southerners a vote for the defense of the honor and integrity of the United States Senate. Every Democrat on the Senate floor voted for condemnation.[50]

One of Johnson's top aides, Harry McPherson, notes that LBJ often had to first convince the southerners that they had to give in a little on an issue or they would eventually get overwhelmed by northern votes. But as William S. White notes, LBJ had an advantage in dealing with the South: he was one of the South's sons. The southerners "had not only affection for Johnson, they also had a paternal interest in him and a curiously mixed and modified regional pride in him."[51] However, Roy Wilkins, of the NAACP, points out that LBJ was "different from most Southerners. It was always possible to talk to him . . . . and he was not a classic race-baiter."[52] Johnson's correspondence and discussions with blacks were very limited at this point in time, but he never publicly stirred the racial pot after his initial Senate speech was over. In fact, in the face of the 1954 Supreme Court decision to desegregate the public schools of the nation, *Brown v. Board of Education of Topeka, Kansas*, Johnson became a truly well tempered spokesman on the race issue.

The *Brown* decision pushed the nation to deal with the civil rights problem, and it pushed the majority leader to grapple with one of the most divisive issues ever to come to the Hill. On the day after the Supreme Court announced its decision in *Brown*, Richard Russell went on the floor of the Senate to denounce this "flagrant abuse of judicial power" and "clear invasion of the legislative branch." He was the first to denounce *Brown* on the Senate floor, but almost every southerner then rose in turn to declare his opposition to the decision. Privately and publicly, Russell and almost all of the other southern leaders denounced "the decision of the Supreme Court as the most dangerous perversion of power in the Court's history."[53] Mississippi's James Eastland stated on the Senate floor "that the Southern people, by and large, will neither recognize, abide by, nor comply with this decision. . . . I know that there will be no compromise."[54] Southern political leadership became southern demagoguery.

Johnson, however, was not simply a part of the South in the Senate; he was a national party leader. LBJ had to respond to the mood of his party in the Senate, or he was liable to lose his effectiveness as leader. On the same day that Russell took to the Senate floor to denounce *Brown* and the court, Johnson took to the floor to acknowledge, "First, the decision is an accomplished fact. However we may question . . . this ruling, it has been made: It cannot be overruled now, and it is possible that it can never be overruled. Second," the Senate leader continued, "the Supreme Court in its ruling has recognized the complexity of the problem. It has delayed the actual decree that will turn a general ruling into a specific order." Johnson then gave his mild disapproval to the ruling. "I think it could have been sounder judgement to allow that progress [that has been made] to continue through the processes of natural evolution. However, there is no point in crying over spilt milk. . . . Our people [will] work this matter out within the boundaries of the Supreme Court decision and in a manner that will be satisfying to both races."[55] Lyndon Johnson as Senate leader could not and would not speak the words that Lyndon Johnson as southerner would have, perhaps, spoken. His position on *Brown* and his position on future civil rights issues would have to reflect the need to balance the Democratic party coalition.

The *Brown* decision went to the very heart of the southern system of race relations. It mandated that the young of both races had to be with each other in schools and therefore deal with each other on a daily basis and, possibly, interact socially. The Supreme Court's implementation decision for *Brown v. Board of Education*, which was announced on May 31, 1955, allowed for integration "with all deliberate speed." The interpretation of this dictum was to be worked out in the local school districts of the South. There were some areas in Texas, Tennessee, and Arkansas that, following the leadership on integration in Washington, D.C., provided by the White House, proceeded to peacefully desegregate in the fall of 1955. But southern politicians were getting ready for the 1956 elections in their home states and in the nation, and in the tradition of southern politics going back for nearly a century, they would not allow race mixing to occur without first stirring up the populace with some race-baiting.

In the Senate, Richard Russell, after consultation with Senators Sam Ervin of North Carolina and John C. Stennis of Mississippi, wrote the final draft of the Declaration of Constitutional Principles, which was to become popularly known as the Southern Manifesto. They attacked the *Brown* decision as "a clear abuse of judicial power" and took up the cry "to use all lawful means to bring about a reversal of this decision which was contrary to the Constitution." On March 12, 1956, Senator Walter George of Georgia introduced the Southern Manifesto on the Senate floor.[56] Only three southern senators, Estes Kefauver and Albert Gore of Tennessee and Lyndon Johnson of Texas, did not sign the document.

Johnson publicly declared he could not sign the manifesto because as majority leader of the Senate, he could not place himself in opposition to the law of the land. As John Stennis, one of the most avid segregationists, recalled, "Just Senator to Senator, of course, we wanted him to sign it, but at the same time we recognized that he wasn't just a Senator from Texas. He was a leader and had a different responsibility to that degree." Johnson did what he had to do by senatorial standards; and as Stennis concluded, "It wasn't held against him . . . by the Southerners."[57] His friends from the South understood and excused his actions. In the very month in which Johnson declined to sign the manifesto, Richard Russell wrote to a fellow southerner to promote Johnson as a man who would make "an infinitely better President than any of the present active or 'inactive' candidates, and his views are much closer to mine than any of the other candidates."[58] Russell was quite correct in his assessment. In July of 1956, after an Eisenhower administration civil rights package passed the House, Russell and Senate leader Johnson agreed to consign the proposals to the Senate Judiciary Committee chaired by Mississippi's Senator Eastland. They believed that a Senate brawl over the civil rights bill would hurt the Democrats in the fall elections.[59] Under Eastland's careful supervision the bill would no longer be a concern during this election year because it would remain buried within the committee's private domain.

Throughout all of this maneuvering in the Senate, Johnson

still had a Texas constituency that was often not aware of the political nuances of the Senate but was aware of his reluctance to stand forthrightly with the South against outside interference on the race issue. His reaction to these constituents was to remind them that he had never voted for any "so-called civil rights bill" and that he was a man "who had lived in the South all his life, and both of whose grandparents fought on the Confederate side in the War Between the States."[60] On the whole, however, the Texas press and the Texas political leadership were not bound up in a seething cauldron of opposition to *Brown* at all costs. In fact, sixteen of the twenty-two Texan House members in Washington, including Speaker Sam Rayburn, had refused to sign the manifesto. They were the only southern delegation in which a majority of representatives did not sign the document; seventy-seven southern House members signed it. Back home, Johnson's mildly heretical civil rights stance was cloaked in the company of many of his fellow Texans' actions.

In the nation, Johnson's Senate leadership style was generally receiving favorable press, and he believed he was now becoming a possible contender for his party's presidential nomination if a deadlock developed among the leading contenders. He appeared on the cover of *Time* magazine; and the publisher of the *Washington Post*, Philip L. Graham, believed Johnson was the possible future president "who could heal the" racial and regional "divisions within the country."[61] However, Governor Adlai Stevenson of Illinois was again the solid favorite for the Democratic presidential nomination, and Estes Kefauver, the antisegregationist Tennessean, won the convention's nod for the vice-presidential slot. Johnson ran as Texas' favorite son per an agreement with Sam Rayburn to keep the Texas delegation united.[62] He won 80 votes on the first presidential ballot—56 of them from Texas and 22 from Mississippi. Johnson had shown his flag in Democratic presidential politics, but the Senate was the national stage for his ambitions.

The Eisenhower-Stevenson presidential campaign of 1956 turned out not to be very much of a contest at all. The popular incumbent added votes to his earlier winning margin and added Louisiana to the roster of southern states that he carried in 1952. Even more ominous from the point of view of the northern Democrats was that Eisenhower lowered the Democratic black vote margin to its lowest point since 1936. The liberal demand for civil rights legislation was, once again, in line with the strategic political needs of the big-city bosses. The big-city political machines and the needs of Democratic presidential aspirants were too dependent on black votes to cede them to the Republicans.

Lyndon Johnson was acutely aware of the black vote shift, and as Harry McPherson notes, this was one of the critical factors that led LBJ to support civil rights legislation in 1957. In addition, George Reedy, another Johnson Senate staffer, urged his boss that "some effort should be made [on] civil rights . . . simply because the issue has reached a point where some action is necessary." Johnson, Reedy argued, had to provide the "moderate leadership" for a broadly acceptable bill. If LBJ could get the "edge taken off the civil rights issue, the Democratic Party could then fall back on economic issues where, with Negro voters, it has a decided advantage." Johnson knew he had to be recognized as a national leader, not just a Senate leader, if his presidential dreams were ever to become reality. Civil rights were the most critical issue separating North from South, and positive leadership on civil rights legislation would immeasurably help Johnson's pursuit of a nationwide constituency.[63]

Soon after Eisenhower was inaugurated into his second term of office, Johnson wrote to a friend that he had "come to the conclusion that we are going to have the civil rights controversy with us for many years. However it may have started, it has now gone beyond the point where it can be called off." Johnson told his biographer, Doris Kearns, "One thing had become absolutely certain: the Senate simply had to act, and I simply had to act; the issue would wait no longer."[64] The Eisenhower civil rights proposals were again before the Congress, and this time they would not be consigned to the Judiciary Committee deep-six. Johnson's job was to mold the legislation in such a fashion as to keep the Democratic party intact and yet to have the measure popularly received as a step forward in resolving the bitter issue.

The Eisenhower administration proposal included four parts or titles: (1) the creation of a fact-finding Civil Rights Commission; (2) the creation of a civil rights division with an assistant attorney general in the Department of Justice; (3) the granting of injunctive powers to federal court judges in cases involving civil rights violations; and (4) the granting of injunctive powers to federal court judges in cases involving voting-rights violations. Title III of the proposal particularly outraged the southerners because it provided a blanket commitment to civil rights protection by the federal government in language that was markedly similar to Reconstruction legislation. Richard Russell spoke of this legislation as "cunningly designed to vest in the Attorney General unprecedented power to bring to bear the whole might of the Federal government, including the armed forces, if necessary to force a commingling of white and Negro children."[65]

Johnson devised a legislative strategy to reconcile the South and the North over these proposals. The party had to be held together. That was critical if he wanted to run for the presidency. He told Hubert Humphrey, "The right to vote with no ifs, ands, or buts, that's the key. When the Negro gets that, they'll have every politician, north and south, east and west, kissing their ass, begging for their support." Thus, he would mold this legislation into a voting bill. Who could oppose voting? The North and the South would have to go along with it. "It would be possible to pass a civil rights bill if you limited it to voting rights," George Reedy advised LBJ. Southerners "were defensive about the vote thing. That they couldn't justify. One of the characteristics of Southerners is that they really do believe in the Constitution as written. And . . . it was clearly unconstitutional to deprive these blacks of their votes. And the Southerners know that." Reedy later added, "The Southerners were constitutionalists not only out of principle, but also because they understood the Constitution protected minorities and they were a minority themselves. They could not openly favor the deprivation of a basic right like voting from a minority group."[66] This was Johnson's route to achieving a compromise civil rights bill.

Johnson set out to convince his southern colleagues that a

voting bill was the route to legislative success—in Southern terms. He believed, as did many others, that no one could be openly opposed to the right to vote. Johnson prevailed upon the Dixie Senate contingent to hold off on the use of the filibuster. He argued that this time the filibuster might be counterproductive. He reminded the Senators from this fiercely nationalist region that a filibuster on civil rights would hurt the American image abroad and aid communist propaganda depicting blacks in the United States as only half-free. He followed this up with the contention that GOP senators who had previously gone along with the South on its states' rights, anti–civil rights argument would now be obliged to support a bill sent to the Hill by their own president. Finally, LBJ argued, southerners had to accept a "mild" civil rights bill, or they would find that a much stiffer piece of legislation was going to be "crammed down their throats."[67]

In the end Johnson got Russell and all of the other southern senators, with the exception of South Carolina's Strom Thurmond, to agree that they would not pursue a filibuster if Title III of the bill was eliminated and a jury-trial amendment in criminal cases added to Title IV.[68] After all, what southern jury would convict a white person of a criminal charge related to denying black rights? Johnson now turned his attention to rounding up a majority of the nonsouthern senators on behalf of his version of civil rights legislation.

First, Johnson, with Russell's help, brought a crucial group of Republicans into line with his concept of a bill. During the Senate debate on the issue, Russell, with Johnson's prior agreement, focused the southern attack on Title III as an unprecedented extension of federal power into the domain of the states. At LBJ's suggestion, Eisenhower invited Russell to the White House to discuss this issue. Russell, as Eisenhower's attorney general, Herbert Brownell, recalls, "was persuasive. He had a point to a certain extent. Title III did give the Attorney General a new power to broadly enforce civil rights. It did mean the Attorney General could enforce civil rights without going to the Congress for legislation." The president assured the Georgian that "the overriding provision of the bill that he wanted to set down in law [was] the citizen's right to vote."

Upon leaving the mansion, Russell told the press, "The President's mind was not closed to possible amendments to clarify the bill." Brownell adds another item to this episode: "Johnson had convinced the president that he had the votes to extract Section III from the bill, and perhaps the votes to kill the package in its entirety. At this point Eisenhower believed he had to accept the elimination of Section III to save the bill." Eisenhower told a press conference about his view of Title III: "I was reading part of that bill this morning and there were certain phrases I didn't completely understand. So, before I make any remarks on that, I would want to talk to the Attorney General and see exactly what they mean."[69] The president called the attorney general, informed him of his concerns, and backed away from his support of Title III of his administration's proposal. Moderate and conservative Republicans who wanted a bill and who wanted to support their party leader could now be easily brought around to vote against Title III. Republican Senator Everett Dirksen of Illinois had almost "endless meetings" with LBJ during this period. He agreed with LBJ to alter the bill so that what eventually emerged "was not an extreme bill," in Dirksen's eyes, "but it did make a start in that whole civil rights picture."[70] The Republicans were in the Johnson fold.

Now the western Democrats had to be brought along. LBJ straightforwardly recalled his strategy with this group. "I began with the assumption that most of the Senators from the mountain states had never seen a Negro and simply couldn't care all that much about the whole civil rights issue. But if they couldn't care about the Negro, I knew what they did care about and that was the Hell's Canyon issue."[71] Johnson talked with the westerners, and he talked again with Russell. Then, in the middle of the civil rights debate, with the Georgian's permission and the voting support of the southern Senators, enabling legislation for the Hell's Canyon project was brought to the Senate floor and passed. Democrats from the Mountain States now came through with support for Johnson's civil rights plan. Clinton Anderson, a liberal Democrat from New Mexico, and George Aiken, a moderate Republican from Vermont, jointly sponsored an amendment to eliminate Title III from the Eisenhower legislative package. The amendment carried by a fifty-two to thirty-eight margin, with the mountain Democrats, moderate Republicans, and southerners all together on the winning side.

The jury-trial proposal was the next item to which Johnson turned his attention. Everyone understood that the South wanted a jury-trial amendment because southern juries were generally picked from the almost all-white voting rolls. It would be all but impossible to get such a jury to convict a white person for violating the voting rights of a black person. Johnson, with the aid of a group of famed liberal lawyers—Dean Acheson, well known for his State Department work during the Truman years, and Ben Cohen and Abe Fortas, both New Deal stalwarts—proposed that a judge should be able to impose a fine or jail sentence for civil contempt citations, but penalties for criminal contempt should be imposed by a jury. It was "un-American," Johnson argued, to have a citizen be labeled a criminal without a right to a trial by jury. "This was all a smoke and mirrors debate," George Reedy argues. "The southerners needed to get a jury trial into the bill, but judges were almost always going to be handling these matters as civil contempt cases. Almost everyone missed the point of what was happening: The southerners were getting a jury trial provision to take back home and the liberals were getting a useable civil contempt process for civil rights cases."[72] To the consternation of civil rights supporters, John L. Lewis, the head of the United Mine Workers of America, and George Meaney, the president of the AFL-CIO, supported this proposal. They always opposed the power of federal judges unilaterally to issue contempt citations against union leaders who defied federal strike-injunction orders. With union leaders providing support for liberal defections to the southern side on this issue, LBJ was now ready to have the Senate do its work.

Liberal senators Frank Church of Idaho and Estes Kefauver of Tennessee were joined by the less-predictable Joseph O'Mahoney of Wyoming to bring the jury-trial amendment to the Senate floor. Church added an amendment to the original proposal that juries could not be drawn from all-white jury lists. On August 1 the jury-trial amendment to the original part 4 of the bill passed the Senate by a fifty- one to forty-two vote. Harry F. Byrd of Virginia wrote to LBJ the next day about this southern triumph: "No one living but yourself could have accomplished what was done last night. It was due to your wonderful leadership and strategy." Russell wrote of the precarious southern position: "Men who had taken great political risks in sticking their necks out to help us were restive and were insisting that we let the bill out to come to a vote. . . . [We] had to find nine votes for the jury trial amendment who had voted against us on Part III." He confided to another supporter, Johnson "did give us tremendous help on the jury trial amendment. We would have lost everything if he had not turned two or three liberals around in the Senate on it."[73] The Johnson magic worked again, and the bill was now ready for passage in its new incarnation.

The final margin of passage for the entire civil rights package was 72 to 18. Except for Estes Kefauver (Tenn.), George Smathers (Fla.), and Ralph Yarborough and Lyndon Johnson (Tex.), the Southerners opposed passage. Only two maverick liberals—Pat McNamara of Michigan and Wayne Morse of Oregon—joined them in opposition. After further conference committee modification of the jury-trial provision, the final bill passed the House on August 27 by a 279 to 97 vote margin and the Senate on August 29 by a 60 to 15 vote. Eisenhower publicly complained that he was "bitterly disappointed" by the Senate metamorphosis of the original civil rights package. "Rarely," he inveighed, "have so many extraneous issues been introduced into the debate to confuse both the legislators and the public." The Johnson machinations disturbed the president, but there was little he could do about them. He could either sign a much-weakened bill or face criticism for the veto of the first civil rights legislation passed by Congress since the end of Reconstruction. After much public and private argument, Eisenhower quietly signed the 1957 Civil Rights Act into law. He believed it was at least a beginning place for black voting rights to be achieved.[74]

Frank Church provides a brief, close-up description of how the Johnson system worked to create this bill.

When I first came into the Senate in 1957, I had no sooner taken the oath and stepped down and started to walk up the central aisle to my seat in the rear of the chamber when I encountered the long arm of Lyndon Johnson grabbing me as I passed and pulling me into his desk there, front and center and saying to me, "Now Frank, you are the youngest member of this Senate, and you have a great future. There's a lot going for you. But the first thing you ought to learn is that in Congress you go along to get along. . . ."

He said, "Now we've got a motion here that Clinton Anderson offered and it relates to a matter that is not important to your state. People of your state don't care how you vote on this . . . but the leadership cares. It means a lot to me. So I just point this up to you. Your first vote is coming up, and I hope you'll keep it in mind, because I like you, and I see big things in your future, and I want for you to get off on the right foot in the Senate."[75]

Johnson believed he now had Church's vote, but Church maintains he never made that commitment and voted otherwise. "For the next six months he simply ignored me. When I was present with other Senators, he talked to the other Senators. It was clear to me that I was persona non grata with Lyndon Johnson." Then Church came up with the idea for his jury-trial proviso, which gave LBJ the additional votes he needed to pass the amendment.

After my role in the passage of the civil rights legislation Lyndon Johnson was warmly and massively grateful, so much so that I was almost stifled in his embrace. All at once I was in the Garden of Eden and Lyndon Johnson could not be lavish enough.

Johnson got the bill through Congress, but precisely what this meant for him and the nation became a matter of what was in the eye of the beholder. From Johnson's perspective the consequences of his maneuvering were mixed. He repeatedly stated: "I got all I could on civil rights in 1957. Next year I'll get a little more and the year after that I'll get a little more. The difference between me and my northern friends is that I believe you can't force these things on the South overnight." From this perspective, Johnson took the position that the bill represented the best that could be done for civil rights at the time, and he hoped to get more in the future. Of course, Johnson and other leading politicians believed that passage of the first civil rights bill in the twentieth century could help his presidential ambitions. As his friend Richard Russell told other southern leaders, "The victory would help Johnson in his 1960 bid to be the first Southerner since the Civil War to win the Democratic Presidential nomination."[76] Perhaps with a different Senate leader a stronger civil rights measure would have become law, or perhaps no legislation at all would have gotten past a determined southern filibuster. But under Johnson's leadership, a civil rights bill did emerge, and his stature in the Senate and in the nation was enhanced.

Lyndon Johnson's and Ralph Yarborough's ayes in favor of final passage of the Civil Rights Act were the first pro–civil rights votes cast by Texas senators since the end of Reconstruction. As a consequence, for Johnson the act meant he had to mend fences and redefine what had been done for his Texas constituents. He had no wish to end up a politician sacrificed on the altar of civil rights. He wrote to a complaining constituent: "We cut out the notorious 'troops in the South' provision. We defeated a maneuver that would have given the President the authority to obtain an injunction that would place people in jeopardy of fines or jail sentences." And he concluded: "What we have . . . now is a right-to-vote measure." Time and again he repeated this message to his constituents. Chiding them for the thought that they could be against "right-to-vote" legislation, he agreed with them in that he was opposed to any "so-called civil rights" bill.[77]

On the whole, the Texas press remained relatively calm about the civil rights legislative struggle and generally praised Johnson's Senate efforts in the matter.[78] Thus, for Texas, he did not produce a civil rights bill; he helped destroy such a noxious proposal. He did support a voting-rights bill, and his actions were understood by most of those concerned.

The 1957 Civil Rights Act was met with scant enthusiasm by many civil rights liberals, but they respected Johnson's handiwork. The chair of the House Judiciary Subcommittee, Emanuel Celler, accepted the Johnson bill as the best civil rights act that could be obtained. "You have to compromise and Johnson had to do just that in order to get the bill through in the Senate. This was a revolutionary bill—this first breakthrough against the barrier of civil rights."[79] The *New York Times* praised Johnson's "courage and skill to break with the past" and called the act "incomparably the most significant domestic action of any Congress in this century."[80] C. Vann Woodward, a leading liberal scholar, wrote to Johnson about his "magnificent work" in getting the bill out and compared his leadership role to that of Henry Clay.[81] Six times since the end of Reconstruction, civil rights legislation had been filibustered to death on the floor of the United States Senate. Johnson had prevented a seventh death-by-filibuster, and eighty years after the end of Reconstruction the Senate finally passed civil rights legislation again. The 1957 act created a new Justice Department division of civil rights, headed by an assistant attorney general who could pursue suits in court, and it established a temporary Commission on Civil Rights. The public influence of the commission proved to be a surprise to everyone. In sum, therefore, from the perspective of some liberals, both civil rights and Johnson's standing were enhanced by passage of the Civil Rights Act of 1957.

While the southerners were aghast at the very idea of a civil rights act, let alone one passed under the aegis of a Texan Senate majority leader, they also believed that a balance was achieved with this legislation. Senator Russell wrote:

The so-called compromise bill is wicked, but it is not as bad as it could be. We have eliminated the provision which would have put the full power of the Federal government behind mixing our children in the schools and mixing the races in hotels, swimming pools and all places of entertainment. This bill is so shot through with politics that we never at any time had the thirty-two senators that are necessary to prevent us from being gagged. . . . The great danger which faced us is an amendment that would bring back the power of the Federal government to move into our schools and mix the races there [Title III]. The elimination of that provision was my primary aim throughout the fight. We can handle our voting situation over a period of years . . . but once the schools are mixed under Federal domination our society is destroyed.[82]

From this perspective the greatest of the civil rights horrors was avoided by the Johnson legislation, and what was now upon the South could be dealt with in good time.

As the legislative struggle over the Civil Rights Act came to a close, the confrontation over integration in Little Rock's Central High School began. Arkansas Governor Orval Faubus refused to obey a federal court order to permit the integration of the Little Rock school and called out the Arkansas National Guard to enforce his position. This provoked the most bitter federal-South confrontation since the Union troop withdrawal of 1877. President Eisenhower's consequent decisions to support the court order, federalize the Arkansas National Guard, and bring in federal troops to Little Rock set off a wave of southern hysteria.

Richard Russell protested to the president and the secretary of defense against "the high-handed and illegal methods being deployed by the Armed Forces of the United States under your command who are carrying out your orders to mix the races in the public schools of Little Rock Arkansas." Russell resorted to histrionic absurdity as he continued: "The troops are . . . applying tactics which must have been copied from the manual issued the officers of Hitler's Storm Troopers."[83] Absurdity turned into demagoguery as Russell issued a public statement decrying this "sort of totalitarian rule" and sent message after message to his Georgia constituents protesting the "President's actions in copying the Storm Trooper tactics which brought Hitler to power."[84]

Johnson's approach to the Little Rock crisis was markedly different from that of his longtime mentor. On the same day that Russell and most of his southern colleagues took to the floor to play to the rednecks, Johnson took to the floor to play to the nation. His statement was brief: "With millions of other Americans I am concerned and disturbed by the situation in Little Rock. It is filled with dangerous emotional tension and marked by extremely complex questions. In the absence of full knowledge of the actual facts, one can only call upon men of good will to act with restraint and with traditional American respect for law and order."

He closed his remarks with the note that "there should be no troops from either side patrolling our schools."[85] While expressing concern for the situation, Johnson used the traditional southern respect for law and order to argue in effect, that, the South should respect the law of the land. He was also lecturing Governor Faubus, because the Little Rock confrontation began with the calling out of the Arkansas National Guard to stop the entry of the black children into the school. Had there been "no troops from either side present," the showdown would have most likely never involved the use of federal troops. In his private correspondence with constituents, LBJ took a harsher line concerning the "unrevocable [*sic*] steps" of the Eisenhower "intervention," but he always maintained, "I am against mob violence."[86] His was among the mildest of southern responses to Little Rock; he was a southerner wary of the conflagration brought forth by simmering hatreds.

Johnson had become a different politician from most of his southern colleagues, but there were other Texans, such as Speaker Rayburn, and other senators, such as Gore and Kefauver of Tennessee, who also staked out a moderate nontraditional position on civil rights. They were among the few exceptions in the region. Harry Ashmore, the Pulitzer Prize–winning Arkansas newspaper editor, wrote a letter in December of 1958 to John A. Blatnik, a Minnesota representative, which expressed the prevailing mood of the South:

> The Southern leaders have [almost all] cut themselves off from the possibility of meaningful compromise; they have whipped their followers into a mood where any man who yields to any degree on the segregation issue invites immediate retaliation. In the case of Faubus, it is essential to understand that he does not lead the people, but follows them . . . . I believe the same thing applies, with only insignificant variation in degree, to most of the other Southern office-holders.[87]

Johnson was different. He was master of the Senate and a possible future president. His Senate colleagues, as well as other southern and national leaders, and news media people recognized this fact. His ambitions and the expectations that others held of him and his ambitions moved Lyndon Johnson further away from a southern position on civil rights. As the Eighty-sixth Congress got under way, the liberals once again wanted to change Rule 22. The southerners, again led by Russell, threatened to filibuster if such a motion was introduced on the Senate floor.[88] Johnson, with the concurrence of Republican leader Everett Dirksen, proposed that Rule 22 be altered by "striking out 'two-thirds of the Senators duly chosen and sworn' and inserting in its place, 'two-thirds of the Senate present and voting.'"[89] Senator Paul Douglas of Illinois, a staunch civil rights liberal, proposed allowing floor debate to be brought to a halt after fifteen days by a vote of a simple majority of the Senate membership. The motion was defeated twenty-eight to sixty-seven, with only twenty-one Democrats supporting the proposal. Then, by a vote of thirty-six to fifty-eight, with twenty-five Democratic ayes, an alternative liberal proposal to permit the closure of debate by vote of three-fifths of those present and voting was defeated. The Johnson proposal, by a margin of seventy-two to twenty-two, with fourteen southerners and five liberal Democrats among the dissenters, passed the Senate.[90]

The "meaningless sham" change, as Wayne Morse of Oregon called it, was accomplished.[91] On the other hand, the *New York Times* understood that this change was Johnson's attempt "to satisfy pressure on Congress for a change in the filibuster rule without splitting his party in the process."[92] This was another Johnson foot-in-the-door measure that satisfied Democrats of the South, the North and the West, with one group, the strong civil rights supporters, taking notable exception.[93] Roy Wilkins, called the Johnson modification of Rule 22 "a fraud in so far as it pretends to make possible the passage of civil rights legislation." Furthermore, Wilkins asserted, if the Democrats wanted "Negro support" in the 1960 elections they would have to demonstrate that "effective civil rights legislation" could come out of the Senate.[94]

Not only were black leaders demanding civil rights legislation, but they were being joined by an increasing number of Democrats and Republicans. Dean Acheson, President Truman's highly regarded secretary of state, for example, wrote

the Senate leader to "use his rare gifts of leadership and courage" to pass another measure. This, he argued, was critical for
Democratic success in the 1960 presidential elections.[95] Within
days of his victory in the rules fight, Johnson brought out *his*
civil rights measure. It was a mild measure, but it was also the
first civil rights bill since Reconstruction to be introduced in the
Congress by a southerner.[96] The Johnson proposal contained
four sections: (1) the establishment of a community relations
service to act as a conciliator in racially tense communities;
(2) the extension of the life of the Civil Rights Commission;
(3) the outlawing of the interstate transportation of explosives for
purposes of violence or intimidation; and (4) the extension of the
attorney general's subpoena power in voting-rights cases.

The liberals saw the Johnson proposal as a palliative measure
designed to forestall any real civil rights legislation.[97] Johnson
anticipated this objection. When he introduced his proposal he
told the Senate, "I can sympathize with those who feel that everything should be done at once. . . . Rome was not built in a
day. And compared to the promotion of human understanding, the building of Rome was a minor and relatively simple
job."[98] On the other side of the civil rights divide, some of Johnson's Texas constituents were writing to him of the outrage
they felt at the very idea that he, a southerner, would introduce
civil rights legislation. His reply to these complaints was that he
offered "a reasonable proposal around which men of all
sections of the country could rally." He wanted to take the issue
away from "extremists" who believed in "forced integration
and harsh, punitive legislation" and have it reflect more of what
"men of reason" found acceptable."[99] This was LBJ operating as
party leader, as negotiator, and as presidential aspirant. He was
attempting to bring as much of his party together as he could
for the upcoming presidential year, and he was doing it as a
leader who was responsive to the national mood.

Two weeks after the Johnson proposal was introduced, the
Eisenhower administration brought forward its new civil rights
recommendations. The Eisenhower measure (1) made it a federal crime to interfere with a federal court order involving
school desegregation; (2) made it a federal crime to cross state
lines to avoid prosecution for bombing a church or school;

(3) required the preservation of federal voting records by state registrars and allowed the attorney general to inspect these records; (4) established a Commission on Equal Job Opportunity under Government Contracts; and (5) extended the life of the Civil Rights Commission.[100] The Republican package was also viewed as a relatively moderate civil rights program.

The Eisenhower proposals, after passing through Emanuel Celler's House Judiciary Committee, never emerged from the Rules Committee, chaired by Democrat Howard Smith of Virginia. In the Senate, no civil rights proposals emerged out of Senator James Eastland's Judiciary Committee. That was the end of civil rights for the first session of the Eighty-sixth Congress. But by prearrangement with the Senate majority leader, Senator Jacob Javits of New York inquired about bringing civil rights legislation before the body in the next session. Johnson replied, "I serve notice to all members that on or about 12 o'clock on February 15 [1960] I anticipate that some Senator will rise in his place and make a motion with regard to the general civil rights question."[101]

On February 15, 1960, an innocuous bill to allow the town of Stella, Missouri, to use old army barracks as a temporary public school facility became the focus of Johnson's second round of civil rights maneuvering. "This bill," the majority leader announced, "has been selected as the one . . . to begin discussion of civil rights proposals." Johnson avoided sending the Civil Rights bill to Eastland's Judiciary Committee by permitting it to be added as an amendment to the Missouri school bill on the floor of the Senate. He declared, "The bill is open to amendment," and Senate minority leader Dirksen introduced the administration's 1959 proposals, with the addition of technical assistance to schools undergoing desegregation and a plan to have federal voting referees appointed by federal judges if a finding of racially based voter-registration discrimination was made by a federal court. Johnson and Dirksen remained allies in the ensuing legislative struggle.[102]

This time the Texas leader found that most of his southern colleagues were distinctly unhappy with his actions. Russell denounced Johnson's actions as a "lynching of orderly procedure" and proceeded to lead a filibuster with almost all of the southern senators lined up with him.[103] When LBJ told Russell about the plan to bring up civil rights legislation, "he was rather cool, aloof and said, 'Yes, I understand that you let them jockey you into that position. I understand.' And a little later I reminded him again, and he said, 'Yes, I know that. Go ahead, do whatever your judgement tells you. That's your business, your responsibility. I'm not the leader.'" Johnson recalled how, after he made the motion to introduce the matter, Russell not only called it a "legislative lynching," but more importantly he said, "You have just heard a motion that I thought would never be made in the Senate by the leader of my party."[104] Harry McPherson, a Senate aide and admirer of Johnson and Russell, points out that to Russell "that move by Johnson—offering a civil rights bill to an unrelated amendment was anti-institutional." It obviated the usual processes of the Senate as an institution. The Johnson maneuver "struck a blow at everything Russell worked for in the Senate—reliability, predictability. Johnson's move responded to the outside." McPherson continues, "Russell believed and worked for the institution to be hermetically sealed from the outside. He wanted no outside presence, no pressures that would impede on the Senate working its will in its way."[105] Johnson was part of the inner circle of the Senate and had always been mindful of its ways and manners. Now he had violated these conventions. The obligation of leadership and the pursuit of ambition had moved Johnson, at least for the moment, into opposition to his longtime mentor.

Johnson was not the only southern leader moving forward on black rights. Sam Rayburn also used his leadership position to move civil rights legislation through the House. The Eisenhower legislative package, with the Federal Contracts Commission section deleted, passed the House on March 24.[106] By now the Senate civil rights debate, with eighteen southerners united in filibuster, had been in progress for over five weeks. Johnson proceeded to get the business of the Senate to move beyond civil rights. Johnson persuaded Russell and twelve other southerners to agree that the House bill would be sent to the Senate Judiciary Committee with a proviso that it be reported back to the full Senate no later than midnight, March 29.[107] With the aid of the Republican leadership and the southerners, all amendments to strengthen the House civil rights bill, including the addition of a part 3 similar to that removed from the 1957 bill, were defeated.[108] When the demolition of the liberals was complete, Dirksen announced to the press that the president and the attorney general were "quite happy with the bill." On April 8, with eighteen southerners opposed, the Civil Rights Act of 1960 passed the Senate by a seventy-one to eighteen vote that closely resembled the coalition put together for passage of the 1957 act.[109]

The 1960 Civil Rights Act received mixed reviews. The committed liberal contingent vented its unhappiness with the result. Democratic Senator Joseph Clark of Pennsylvania termed the 1960 act "a pale ghost of our hopes." Democratic Senator Paul Douglas remarked that the Senate "passed what can only by courtesy be called a civil rights bill." Johnson's view was, in the now familiar litany: "I got the best bill I could with the votes I had, and if they [the liberals] could have gotten a better bill, we would have gotten it." Johnson was pushing for a "minimal" civil rights bill.[110] When he reported back to Texas on the matter, he told his constituents that it was a "victory for fair play."[111] It was a bill the South could accept. That is what the nation got in 1960.

The liberal appraisal of the 1957 and 1960 acts was fundamentally correct. Both had more show than substance. The enforcement of the 1957 and 1960 Civil Rights Acts did not lead to a single black voter added to the southern registration rolls under the auspices of the Eisenhower administration. Progress under the acts was painfully slow during the Kennedy administration—only 37,146 blacks were directly registered as a consequence of actions taken under the acts, while 2.2 million age-eligible southern blacks remained off the voting rolls. Thurgood Marshall, the chief attorney for the NAACP Legal Defense Fund, examined the 1960 act and stated, "It would take two to three years for a good lawyer to get someone registered [to vote] under this bill."[112] It would take another five years of national crises before southern blacks had equal access with southern whites to the voting rolls.

No politician was hurt too much by the enactment of the Civil Rights Act of 1960, and no politician was helped too much.[113] Johnson minimized the political fallout that could have ensued from congressional involvement with civil rights. On the other hand, Theodore White notes, "The fact that the subject is open to reasonable discussion and minimally open to legislative management, however cautious, is Johnson's achievement."[114] It was an achievement wrought of necessity. LBJ had a badly divided Democratic party to lead in the Senate, and civil rights were at the core of the division. He had to hold the South in the party and to appease the northern majority's need for civil rights legislation. He held the coalition together as the issue moved onto the national legislative agenda—an accomplishment that provided him with national recognition as a party leader. His leadership ability and his ambitions coincided with his party's needs and the movement of the national political agenda.

Sam Rayburn and Richard Russell agreed that Johnson was "the strongest candidate the Democrats could nominate [in 1960] and the one most likely to defeat either Nixon or Rockefeller."[115] They also believed Johnson was the individual who could heal the increasingly bitter division between the North and the South and find a solution to the civil rights imbroglio.[116] But 1960 was not to be the year of Johnson's accession to the presidency. His strategy for capturing the executive office was not equal to John F. Kennedy's tact. From the end of the 1956 presidential contest until hours prior to his first-ballot nomination, Kennedy continuously campaigned for delegates across the states. The political machine that the Kennedys put together was a work of wonder to Theodore White, the chronicler of the campaign.

Johnson, on the other hand, used an insider strategy to pursue the presidential nomination; unbeknownst to him, this approach was bypassed by developments beyond his control. Although Johnson labored almost continuously to demonstrate his leadership abilities in the Senate, he never established a nationwide political network that could secure convention delegates. While Johnson worked his magic in the Senate, Kennedy worked his magic in the primaries and in the media. Johnson's strategy was to go to the Democratic National Convention with a solid base of southern delegates. This would serve as his springboard to capture the nomination once a deadlocked convention moved into the serious work of selecting a candidate brokered by the party leadership. He believed that a Catholic could not be the Democratic nominee. The disastrous 1928 Al Smith candidacy was part of the party lore on this matter.[117] But it took only one ballot for John F. Kennedy to win a majority—806 of the 1521 convention votes—secure the nomination, and undo party lore on this matter. Johnson mustered 409 votes, but the regional nature of his candidacy was obvious; 351.5 votes of LBJ's total came from southern and border state delegates. Despite his best efforts to broaden his base of support, Johnson remained fundamentally a southern candidate.

A southern candidate was what John Kennedy wanted and needed as his running mate. But first he had to reassure the liberals and the blacks that he was faithful to their cause. The black leadership, especially, did not trust Kennedy on the civil rights issue.[118] He had cast two key votes against their positions in the fifties—one to send the civil rights bill to Senator Eastland's Judiciary Committee and one in favor of the jury-trial amendment— and he avidly courted the South in his pursuit of the presidential nomination. To remedy this problem, the Kennedy camp pushed through the strongest civil rights plank ever endorsed by a Democratic National Convention.[119] This infuriated many southerners. To smooth things over with the southern wing of the party and to round up electoral votes in a region where the Republicans were making inroads, John Kennedy, with Rayburn's help, named Johnson as his running mate.[120]

Why Johnson, a man of tremendous ego and ambition, would allow himself to move from being *the* leader of the Senate to vice-president is not completely clear. When he discussed the Kennedy offer with Homer Thornberry, a close family friend and Democratic congressman from Texas, Johnson said, "Well here's my problem. If I refuse it and go back as majority leader and Kennedy chooses somebody else, and he loses, they'll blame me for it, and then my position as majority leader might be in jeopardy. If he wins, they'll say, 'He won without your help,' and then I'll have some problems. Finally, I may owe a responsibility to try to carry this country for the Demo-

cratic party." It was a powerless position that LBJ would oc-
cupy. He believed, however, as he told another colleague, that
it need not remain powerless. "Power is, where power goes," he
argued.[121] He had, after all, created a power base in the Senate
leadership position where none had previously existed. As vice-
president perhaps he could again create power where none had
been. It may also be that Johnson came to the conclusion that,
no matter what he did, in national electoral politics he was always going to be a southerner; and a southerner could not get a
presidential nomination on his own. This was his chance, possibly his only chance, to make it to the presidency. From vice-
president to president, or at least presidential nominee, had
been the route of both Truman and Nixon in recent years. It
could be the route for a southerner.

The liberal and the black reaction to the LBJ vice-presidential nomination was generally one of disbelief, outrage, and betrayal. JFK had personally promised Joe Rauh and other
liberals that LBJ would not be on his ticket. Clarence Mitchell,
the head of the NAACP's Washington lobbying effort, believed
that Kennedy needed a vice-president who "could act as a
bridge between us and the White House." But with Johnson on
the ticket, "the chance of Senator Russell and others [of the
South] getting to tell their story would be increased." James
Farmer, the head of the Congress of Racial Equality (CORE),
called the Johnson nomination "a disaster." Leonard Woodcock, a leading liberal unionist, believed, "Kennedy had betrayed us all. . . . Our whole theme had been to unite behind
Kennedy to stop Johnson." Joe Rauh sums up the bitter liberal
disappointment: "Here was the man who watered down every
liberal proposal of the 1950s and now he was being put on the
national ticket. I could not believe it."[122] It was done, and now
all eyes turned toward the fall campaign.

The South's anger over the Democratic platform was not
completely assuaged by Johnson's placement on the ticket. But
the Republicans aided the Democratic cause in the South when
their convention also produced a strong civil rights plank. Furthermore, their presidential nominee, Richard Nixon, had a
liberal civil rights record as vice-president and as a member of
Congress, and his running mate, Henry Cabot Lodge of Massa-

chusetts, was a staunch civil rights advocate born of a family with a long history of such advocacy. The Lodge force bill, an 1890 proposal for federal enforcement of black voting rights in the South, was named after Lodge's grandfather, its author.

Immediately after the passage of the Democratic plank, Russell wrote to a Georgia ally: "I am just as shocked and embittered as you are about the complete surrender of our political party to the NAACP." The day after the Republicans adopted their civil rights plank, Russell wrote to another Georgian: "I devoutly pray that we will be able to find some way to spare our Southland from the evil threats of the platforms of the two major parties." Russell noted: "I am not enamored of Kennedy, but I am frank to say that I cannot see any reason to prefer Nixon to Kennedy. On matters of vital concern to us, their thinking is almost identical."[123] But the Democrats had Johnson on the ticket; in the end, that made a vital difference.

During the campaign, Lyndon and Lady Bird Johnson made a whistle-stop train tour of the South. The Johnson Special visited cities and hamlets by the score. And almost everywhere it appeared that Mrs. Johnson had kinfolk. The Kennedys also made forays into the region, especially to deal with the Catholic issue; but the South was basically Johnson's to win—or to lose— for the ticket. LBJ called on the South's leaders to campaign for the ticket; when turned down, he would call again and again. "When my friend Lyndon Johnson called me the third time," Richard Russell wrote, "and said that he was really in trouble and I could help, I stopped weighing issues and went."[124] For the first time since 1936, Russell actively supported the national ticket—and so did many other southerners who would never have campaigned but for the siren call of Lyndon Johnson. And it paid off.

The Kennedy-Johnson slate carried the 1960 election by less than one percent of the popular vote. The Johnson contribution cannot be given an exact measurement, but in the rim South only the states of Florida, Tennessee, and Virginia went Republican. Texas and Louisiana were back in the Democratic fold after their 1956 defections. The Deep South, with the exception of Mississippi, which cast its ballots for segregationist Harry F. Byrd of Virginia, went solidly Democratic. By any standard, Johnson had done the job he was supposed to do for the ticket. But as vice-president, he realized with gloom, he was to play second fiddle.

"The night he was elected vice-president," Margaret Mayer, the Washington correspondent for the *Dallas Times Herald*, recalls, "I don't think I ever saw a more unhappy man. . . . It was clear to me and a lot of other people that even then he didn't want to be vice president." The vice-presidential years for LBJ were often simply "a nightmare."[125] This was the period of the "Johnson eclipse," and he suffered terribly. His relations with the president were generally good, but time and again he withheld his views when the chief executive asked for discussion among his advisors. Bobby Kennedy had opposed Johnson's placement on the ticket, and he and almost all of the so-called Irish Mafia who were closest to JFK resented LBJ's presence in the administration. Lady Bird Johnson's secretary and family confidante, Elizabeth Carpenter, sums up the situation: "Lyndon figured correctly, I think, if he volunteered any advice [to JFK] it would guarantee Bobby's opposition to what ever he proposed."[126] LBJ never had the opportunity to establish the vice-presidential position as anything resembling a powerful office.

Johnson did make an effort to create something out of his post. He used his position as chairman of the President's Committee on Equal Employment Opportunity to make his first real positive contacts with national black leaders. "I began to see the first real change in Johnson when he was Vice-President," recalls Roy Wilkins. "He had always been capable of a constructive personal response to race issues, but suddenly it became possible for his feelings and his future to coincide. . . . As Vice-President he began to think about himself and the entire country—he no longer held back on civil rights." Whitney Young, the executive director of the Urban League, recalls that soon after LBJ took over the chairmanship of the Equal Employment Committee, he hired a black, Hobart Taylor, Jr., the son of a wealthy Houston family and a longtime close Johnson supporter, to become its executive director. Johnson also came to the reception given in honor of Young's appointment as director of the Urban League, and he came to the league's annual dinner. Young fondly recalls that at the dinner "he made a speech that made mine sound like a moderate."[127] James Farmer's view of the vice-president also changed for the better when he discussed the Equal Employment Committee's work with him. And Louis Martin, the politically savvy black editor of the *Chicago Defender*, thought Johnson's leadership of the committee "showed exceptional realism in dealing with the [racial discrimination] problem."[128]

Johnson launched the Plans for Progress program to obtain voluntary compliance by government contractors to meet increased black employment goals. Although many black leaders were pleased with Johnson's actions, he had one consistent and very powerful critic—Robert Kennedy. RFK wanted Johnson out of the administration, and he was not going to let the vice-president thrive in his committee notch. The committee, RFK believed, needed "some direction. . . . It accomplished a good deal more than it had accomplished under Nixon. But a lot of it was public relations."[129] The committee record, given its leadership, was not good enough for Robert Kennedy. In May of 1963 RFK came to a committee meeting and bombastically attacked its work. "It was," said Jack Conway, a labor union member of the committee with ties to the Kennedys, "a pretty brutal performance, very sharp. It brought tensions between Johnson and Kennedy right on the table and very hard."[130] Soon after this encounter, Johnson told Ted Sorenson, "Bobby came in the other day to our Equal Employment Committee and I was humiliated." The attorney general attacked the leadership of the committee and told all those present that they had to do more. They had to make firms with federal defense contracts hire blacks. But Johnson complained, "Obviously the President and the Attorney General can get twenty-six or twenty-six hundred [jobs] if they tell them, 'Put them on.' We can't make them do anything."[131] Robert Kennedy recounts that, after telling the president of Johnson's work on the Equal Employment Committee, JFK responded, "That man can't run this Committee. Can you think of anything more deplorable than him trying to run the United States? That's why he can't ever be President."[132] Robert Kennedy kept pressing his brother to dump Johnson from the ticket.

Despite Robert Kennedy's attacks on Johnson as weak on the civil rights work of his committee, the vice-president was increasingly reaching out to blacks. He became a vocal and articulate administration spokesman for civil rights. On January 1, 1963, at Wayne State University in Detroit, he declared, "While we Americans have freed the slave of his chains, we have not freed his heirs of their color. Until justice is blind to color, until education is unaware of race, until opportunity ceases to squint its eyes at pigmentation of human complexions, emancipation will be a proclamation, but it will not be a fact."[133] While Birmingham was under a virtual state of siege in the spring of 1963, Johnson delivered a Memorial Day speech at Gettysburg, Pennsylvania, that made front-page headlines across the nation. "One hundred years" after the battle of Gettysburg "the Negro remains in bondage to the color of his skin. The Negro today asks Justice. We do not answer him—we do not answer those who lie beneath this soil—when we reply to the Negro by asking, 'Patience.'"[134] Johnson had gone national and liberal in his civil rights proclamations.

Privately, Johnson's civil rights tone had also changed since his Senate days. Soon after the Gettysburg speech, Theodore Sorenson asked LBJ what advice he would give the president on how to handle civil rights. The administration was preparing a new, stronger civil rights bill for congressional consideration, and the president was concerned about how to proceed. Until this point, Johnson had remained outside the picture of White House civil rights strategy discussions. Now that he was asked directly by one of the president's most trusted advisors, Lyndon Johnson was not going to hang back on the issue. The vice-president began by saying the president ought to go into the South; then he laid out his view of what ought to be said and when it ought to be said:

When he talks, say, "Now I don't come here without talking about our constitutional rights. We're all Americans. . . . When I order men into battle I order the men without regard to color. They carry our flag into foxholes. The Negro can do it, the Mexican can do it, others can do it. We've got to do the same thing when we drive down the highway at places they eat. I'm going to have to ask you all to do this thing. I'm going to have to ask the Congress to say that we'll all be treated without regard to our race. . . . "

I believe that he'd run some of these demagogues right in the hole. This aura, this thing, this halo around the president. Everybody wants to believe in the president and the commander in chief. I think he'd make the Barnetts and the Wallaces look silly. The good people, the church people, I think have to come around to him. . . . It would really unify the North. He'd be looking them straight in the face, not lecturing them as a father but what his responsibilities were as president. I'd do it in San Antonio. I'd let a Mexican congressman [introduce him]. I'd just show them that there's not anything terrible about this business. That here, right in the heart of the southland, you've got a fellow whose father and mother were born out of this country and he's in the Congress. I'd let him introduce him with that white suit on and every television in America [would be tuned in] for maybe a fifteen-minute stop at a space medical center.[135]

Johnson understood the political implications of his recommendations, but he told Sorenson the hazards had to be confronted if the country was to get through the civil rights crisis intact.

I know these risks are great and it might cost us the South [in 1964], but those sorts of states may be lost anyway. The difference is, if your president just enforces court decrees the South will feel it's yielded by force. But if he goes down there and looks them in the eye and states the moral issue and the Christian issue, and he does it face to face, these southerners [will] at least respect his courage. They feel that they're on the losing side of an issue of conscience. Now. . . . the whites think we're just playing politics to carry New York. The Negroes feel and they're suspicious that we're just doing what we got to do. Until that's laid to rest I don't think you're going to have much of a solution. I don't think the Negroes' goals are going to be achieved [solely] through legislation. . . . I think the Negro leaders are aware of that. What Negroes are really seeking is moral force and [to] be sure that we're on their side and make them all act like Americans, and until they receive that assurance, unless it's stated dramatically and convincingly, they're not going to pay much attention to executive orders and legislative recommendations.

Sorenson intervened at this point: "I agree with that and I think that's very sound." But Johnson was not about to let go of his chance to tell the president what had to be done.

And I think he's got to have his bill. . . . We haven't passed anything! I think he ought to make them pass some of this stuff. . . . This is just what the Republican Party, if I was their manager, this is what I'd recommend they do. And this is what they're doing. They're sitting back giggling. . . .We got civil war going on in the South; they move Kennedy in and they cut off the South from him and blow up the bridge. That's what they want to do. If I were Kennedy I wouldn't let them call my signals. I'd pass my program, make them stand up and vote for it. While I was doing that I'd go into the South a time or two myself. While I was doing that I'd put the Republicans on the spot by making them buy my program. . . . I would try to call in my southern leaders. . . . I can't sit idly by and say, "What do you recommend Senator?". . . I would be sure that I got a good solid program, that I got the Republicans with me if I can get them, that I got my [Senate] leader with me. Then when I move, I wouldn't be stopped.

Johnson and Sorenson briefly discussed the legislative fiasco that attended a civil rights bill the administration had sent to Congress earlier in the year. "They messed around there four of five days, had a little perfuncto [*sic*] vote. . . . It was hypocritical and disgraceful." Sorenson agreed, "We could have done better." "I don't think we're at that stage now," Johnson went on, "I told the attorney general that and I tell you that." Sorenson replied, "I think we're in agreement on substance [with this new proposal]. . . . I think it's the minimum we can ask for and a maximum we can stand behind. But the question is one of timing, and I think that this—" LBJ interrupted, "I don't agree." Sorenson continued on, "—thing is hot enough and now it's pretty tough to—" Again LBJ interrupted, "I don't agree with that. I don't know that, I haven't seen it [the proposed legislation]." Johnson now went on with his lecture. He had touched

upon a sore point—his exclusion from civil rights discussions—
and he was going to come back to it in the context of the administration's overall handling of civil rights.

Now I want to make it clear, I'm as strong for this program as
you are, my friend. But you want my judgment now, and I don't
want to debate these things around fifteen men and have them
all go out and talk about the vice-president and how he is, because I haven't talked to one southerner about this. I haven't
been able to talk with [one member of the] executive about it
except the attorney general and you and Ken[neth O'Donnell]
very briefly this morning. I haven't sat in on any of those conferences they've had up here with the senators. I think it would
have been good if I had.

I don't think it's impossible to pass a good constructive
bill along the lines that you've got. I think it's possible to pass
probably a stronger one. But I don't think it's been thought
through. . . .

Now, summarizing everything, I'd say the legislation ought to
be screened much more carefully, ought to be added to and
taken from. . . .

Second, I think he ought to talk to the Negro leaders and give
them the moral commitment right in the horse's mouth that he's
going to get off their back. . . .

Three, I think he ought to talk to Republican leaders from
Eisenhower on down, particularly legislative leaders. . . .

Four, I think he ought to get his own team on line about
chairmen of [congressional] committees. He got Humphrey.
What the hell is Humphrey? . . . He's done voted. We've got to
get some other folks in this thing to get that cloture. You've got
to get a good many of your westerners. You got to sit down with
them, help them have a reason [to support you]. . . .

Fourth [Fifth], I think he ought to look men in the eye and
say this in the South . . . [in] a place of his choosing and a time of
his choosing with the image of his choosing and leading. That
will pulverize a good many of them [southern demagogues like
Wallace]. . . . So I make a point, that you haven't done your
homework on public sentiment, on legislative leaders, on the
opposition party, or on the legislation itself. . . . I don't know
who drafted it; I've never seen it. Hell, if the vice-president
don't know what's in it, how do you expect the others to

know what's in it? I got it from the *New York Times*. . . . I've never seen anything else.

It was this last item that particularly galled LBJ and was probably the source of his testy telephone conversation with Sorenson. But the conversation paid off for Johnson. He became an active member of the White House civil rights team now that a serious civil rights bill was under consideration. He was going to let the administration hear about civil rights strategy as only a southerner could understand it. He participated in White House discussions with blacks, union leaders, business leaders, and others from all walks of life as part of a concerted effort the administration now put forth to have its civil rights proposals become law. Contrary to Robert Kennedy's hopes, at a White House campaign-planning meeting held in mid November of 1963, the president indicated that he had every intention of keeping Johnson on the ticket for the next election go-around.[136] On November 22, within hours of John Kennedy's assassination, Johnson was sworn in as president aboard Air Force One.

6

Creating a Liberal Presidency

UNLIKE JOHN KENNEDY and in marked contrast to his own Senate record, in 1963 Lyndon Johnson did not hesitate on civil rights. The morning after he became president, LBJ told two of his closest aides, Bill Moyers and Jack Valenti, that his "first priority is passage of the Civil Rights Act."[1] Johnson wanted his aides and the American public to know that he was resolutely committed to passage of this legislation. On November 27, five days after the assassination, he delivered a televised address before a joint session of Congress calling for the enactment of civil rights legislation. "No memorial or eulogy," he orated, "could more eloquently honor President Kennedy's memory than the earliest possible passage of the civil rights bill for which he fought so long." The memory of the martyred president was now indelibly tied to the civil rights proposals. The new president continued, "We have talked long enough in this country about equal rights. We have talked for one hundred years or more. It is now time to write the next chapter—and to write it in the books of law."[2]

On the evening of Thanksgiving Day, LBJ again went on national television to appeal for support of the pending civil rights legislation.[3] This was the president's public commitment to civil rights, and he remained constant to both the public and the private commitment.

President Johnson's strategic problem with civil rights was fundamentally different from that of his predecessor and what he had faced as the Senate leader of the 1950s. JFK's base of support was with most of the liberal establishment, despite the occasional conservative actions that weakened their attachment to him. Throughout his rise to national prominence, LBJ's base of support was with the' southern establishment. Now Lyndon Johnson had to reach out to the liberals to establish his legitimacy with them. "Johnson was our enemy all of the years that he was Senate majority leader. He cut the heart out of the [1957 civil rights] bill," lamented Arnold Aronson, the secretary of the largest national coalition of pro–civil rights organizations in the country, the LCCR.[4] Civil rights was *the* liberal issue, and LBJ had to grab onto it and undo his image as the politician who had devastated the civil rights legislative agenda of the 1950s. As such he was almost always at odds with the more liberal Democrats. "I knew," Johnson recalled, "that if I didn't get out in front on this issue they [the liberals] would get me. They'd throw up my background against me. They'd use it to prove I was incapable of bringing unity to the land. . . . I had to produce a civil rights bill even stronger than the one they'd have gotten if Kennedy had lived. Without this, I'd be dead before I could even begin."[5]

The presidential election season was but a few months away when Johnson took office; before he could be elected in his own right, he had to ensure his legitimacy. Lawrence O'Brien, head of congressional relations and a key political advisor to both John Kennedy and Lyndon Johnson, believed that Johnson's fear of the liberals played a major role in explaining the immediacy with which he moved on civil rights as president. "The eastern liberals didn't trust Johnson," O'Brien commented, and "he believed he had to prove to them he was a liberal." O'Brien was convinced "Johnson believed the Kennedy people were going to try to deny him the nomination in '64. At Atlantic City he [LBJ] and his people believed a coup might be pulled to stop him from being nominated."[6]

LBJ also had concerns beyond his immediate political self-interest. He was a southerner concerned about his native region. "This concern for civil rights," O'Brien argued, "also went back to his roots. He had it in his gut. The fit between his personal feeling and his political needs was there."[7] Many northerners viewed the South, with its rural poverty and overt racism, as somewhat of a national embarrassment. In the wake of the repeated scandals of black lynchings and the brutal repression of black demonstrations in Birmingham and across the South, the region was increasingly an international embarrassment, at best, and a criminal blot upon the nation, at worst. LBJ acutely felt the "disdain for the South" and for southerners that was "woven into the fabric of northern experience." He felt for its burdens and its crises.[8] Time and again he remarked that the stigma of racism had to be removed from the South and that passage of this civil rights legislation would help eliminate many of the social and economic burdens wrought by the southern race system. "I want the ordeals to end," the southern president told the nation, "and the South to stand as the full and honored part of a proud and united land."[9] Johnson knew that his newly found civil rights crusade "was destined to set me apart forever from the South. . . . [and] likely to alienate me from some of the Southerners in Congress who had been my loyal friends for years."[10] But as Harry McPherson, a longtime Johnson Senate aide pointed out, "Lyndon Johnson knew he could not be a national leader as long as there was any doubt about his commitment to civil rights."[11] He could not be a southerner on civil rights and be president of the United States.

Soon after he decided that there would be no compromise on civil rights, Johnson asked his Senate mentor, Richard Russell, to visit the White House. Johnson explained in his memoirs: An "important consideration was my old friend, the Southern legislative leader, Richard Russell. . . . He had to realize that I meant to obtain a meaningful civil rights bill."[12] There would be no "compromise in any way." The president told his old ally as they stood face to face in the mansion, "Dick, you've got to get out of my way. I'm going to run over you. I don't intend to cavil or compromise. I don't want to hurt you, but don't stand in my way." "You may do that," the Southern leader replied, "but, by God, it's going to cost you the South and cost you the election."[13] On the day Johnson delivered his first presidential speech to Congress, Russell wrote to a Georgia friend: "I am afraid we are in for a hard time as President Johnson seems to be committed to pushing every aspect of the Kennedy program."[14]

The die was also cast by Johnson because, like John Kennedy, he was fearful of the violent and almost uncontrollable rage that was overtaking the civil rights movement. "The biggest danger to American stability," he told Doris Kearns, "is the politics of principle which brings out the masses in irrational fights for unlimited goals, for once the masses begin to move, then the whole thing begins to explode." Furthermore, LBJ believed that the civil rights issue undermined both the Democratic party and the United States Senate as accepted, legitimate institutions.[15] The speed and authority with which he moved on the issue and the total commitment of his political prestige to passage of the Civil Rights Act of 1964 was new for Johnson. He was a politician who was known for caution and consultation before action was taken. When the Senate took action on the 1957 Civil Rights Act, LBJ wrote to an ally: "The civil rights controversy . . . has now gone beyond the point where it can be called off." Yet, in 1957 and again in 1960, he used his political skills to eliminate much of the substantive legislation that would effectively deal with the issue.[16] He believed that this was necessary to get any semblance of civil rights legislation through the Senate. More would come, he argued, as it became possible for more to be accomplished. "I did not think there was much I could do as a lone Congressman from Texas," LBJ explained in his memoirs. "One heroic stand and I'd be back home, defeated, unable to do any good for any one."[17] He had expounded on this theme time and again as a senator. His approach to the civil rights legislative agenda as president was different from his approach as a senator in both substance and process. The transformation of Lyndon Johnson was under way. He had to act differently.

Johnson moved to establish his administration as the natural successor to the Kennedy administration and the guardian of Democratic liberalism. Arthur Schlesinger, Jr., the biographer and resident liberal intellectual of the Kennedy White House, was seated next to Lady Bird Johnson during LBJ's televised address to the Congress. Also in Mrs. Johnson's company were liberal New York City mayor Robert Wagner and Georgia governor Carl Sanders, a vocal opponent of racism.[18] LBJ not only used the imagery of the Kennedy legacy in his early presidential speeches, but he also maintained the Kennedy staff and the

Kennedy cabinet in his White House. He kept the Kennedy men on despite the visceral dislike between himself and Robert Kennedy and some of the other members of the Irish Mafia.[19] Robert Kennedy, Dean Rusk, Robert McNamara, and the other major Kennedy appointees were all known to the public and respected as policymakers. Political insiders such as Lawrence O'Brien and Kevin P. O'Donnell, JFK confidants, were savvy political operators. All were important for the transition to function smoothly and for Johnson to be viewed as the rightful inheritor of the presidency and the leadership of the Democratic party. While Robert Kennedy, O'Donnell, and others broke with Johnson after the initial transition period, other Kennedy appointees stayed on after the 1964 election. Some individuals such as Lawrence O'Brien, who became a key Johnson political operative, Sargent Shriver, the Kennedy-in-law who headed up LBJ's War on Poverty program, and Richard Goodwin, a JFK presidential aide who served as a Johnson speech writer were very influential after the 1964 election.

The touchstone, however, on which Johnson depended above all else for liberal legitimation would be his actions with respect to the proposed civil rights legislation. The Johnson whirlwind propelled his association with the civil rights recommendations, and he moved on several fronts. First, he courted the black leadership. One by one the leaders of the major mainstream black organizations were invited to the White House. On November 29 Roy Wilkins, the executive secretary of the NAACP, was ushered into the president's office and given the famous "Johnson treatment." LBJ pulled up his chair, as Wilkins recalls, to within inches of the NAACP leader and "he talked quickly, earnestly. It was the first time I had really felt those mesmerizing eyes of Texas on me." Johnson was "leaning forward, almost touching me, he poked his finger at me and said quietly, 'I want that bill *passed*.'" LBJ told Wilkins he wanted a strong bill and was prepared to suffer defeat rather than take a watered-down act. He also warned the black leader that his organization and its allies were going to have to lobby Congress, particularly the Republican side of the aisle, because the president, constitutionally, could not be the chief lobbyist. Wilkins "left the White House that day convinced that Johnson was willing to go much further than he had ever gone before."[20]

The president's meetings with black leaders continued. On December 2 he met with Whitney Young, the executive director of the NUL. The next day, having already spoken with him on the telephone soon after President Kennedy's funeral, Johnson met with Martin Luther King, Jr., the head of the SCLC and de facto leader of the black civil rights movement.[21]

December 4 was the presidential meeting day set aside for James Farmer, head of CORE and leader of the famed freedom rides of 1961. "Mr. Farmer," the president said as he turned fully toward him, "I've got to get this civil rights bill through Congress, and I'm going to do it. If I never do anything else in my whole life, I'm going to get this job done." Again the president spoke of his need for the civil rights leaders to help him. "You all should tell the Republicans that if they vote for this bill, you'll tell your people to vote for them. And I think you should too." As Farmer was leaving the Oval Office, LBJ turned to him and said, "By the way, Jim—you don't mind if I call you Jim, do you?" "Not at all, Mr. President," Farmer replied. "You may call me Lyndon." "Thank you, Mr. President," came the courteous reply. Johnson asked Farmer what part of Texas he was from and, when told it was Marshall, LBJ responded, "Marshall! Doggone, Jim, do you realize that's Lady Bird's hometown? Her father had a filling station there." As he left LBJ, Farmer recalls, they "shook hands warmly—two Texans reaching out across the invisible railroad tracks of the Lone Star State." Farmer was flattered by the "Johnson treatment." He knew he had been "buttered up. . . . The fact that I knew what was happening did not lessen its effectiveness."[22] On December 5 the president met with A. Philip Randolph, the near-legendary president of the Brotherhood of Sleeping Car Porters, and again the president stressed his need for help with the civil rights bill.[23]

Throughout his meetings with black leaders, Johnson emphasized the need to secure Republican support and his absolute commitment to a strong civil rights bill. He also emphasized the need for restraint, if not a total suspension of activities, on the part of black demonstrators. The president wanted Congress and its "usual" processes to operate without undue outside agitation. Anything that threatened to undermine this process was unacceptable. As a consequence, no leader of the Student Nonviolent Coordinating Committee (SNCC) was invited to the White House, even though SNCC was considered to be the fifth major black organization. The SNCC leadership was young and constantly pushing mainstream black leaders for more demonstrations and direct action. Finally, as its leaders had confirmed at the March on Washington when John Lewis's proposed denunciation of the Kennedy administration's lack of commitment to civil rights was stopped at the last moment, SNCC was unpredictable. Only those individuals and groups who abjured demonstrations and who could be relied upon to work within the established processes, at least until the 1964 presidential election was over, were acceptable at Johnson's White House.[24]

Next came the white leadership. An internal ADA memorandum of early December made it clear that these liberals were wary of LBJ. They believed it would "probably be in the liberal movement's interest to help elect Johnson." But they set up two criteria LBJ had to meet to get their support: First, "will Johnson support a civil rights bill no weaker than the present House bill?" Second, "will Johnson's candidate for Vice-President be acceptable to the liberals? . . . ADA itself can have only one choice—Hubert Humphrey." Johnson was to meet, even exceed, these expectations.[25]

Johnson had close personal ties with Hubert Humphrey, a central figure in the labor–civil rights–liberal coalition, and he now assiduously courted another leading white liberal with ties to the mainstream civil rights movement, Joe Rauh. "Imagine my surprise," Rauh wrote, "when, in a matter of days after Johnson became President, he invited me to go with him to Senator Herbert Lehman's funeral in New York and on the plane asked me to come to the White House in a day or two [December 8] to plan strategy on the pending civil rights legislation. . . . Imagine my surprise, too," Rauh continued, "when [on December 19] he opened our Oval Office talk with what appeared to me at least, to be an apology for his past civil rights performance and with what was certainly a direct request to let bygones be bygones so that we could work together to get the bill passed."[26]

Rauh brought with him a copy of the latest Civil Rights Commission report on school segregation. He pointed out to the president that Texas, his home state, was still one of the most segregated states in the nation. "I suggested that this might be used as a Republican line of attack in 1964 and he better push his old friend, [Texas] Governor Connally, into some action." Rauh went on, "For the first time I saw a glint of admiration in Johnson's eyes—civil rights like everything else was part and parcel of politics to him and he was surprised to find one of his erstwhile do-gooder opponents with even a trace of political sense. He asked me to prepare a memorandum to send to the governor over his own name, hardly a task I would have expected some years earlier." Soon after this meeting, Rauh, a man who regarded Senate leader Johnson as the major "nemesis" of civil rights legislation in the 1950s, wrote to President Johnson of his "admiration and respect for the outstanding way in which you have taken hold of the problems of the nation."[27] The Johnson treatment had worked again.

LBJ enveloped the Democratic and Republican congressional leadership in his push to assure the liberals that he was earnestly committed to civil rights legislation. He pushed the leaders of both parties to grapple more assertively with the pending bill. Yet there was more work to do on the Hill. At the beginning of December the president's legislative liaison staff informed him that "between 90 and 100 Democrats will be off the reservation [in House support for the civil rights proposals]. This means we need sixty to seventy Republicans to get a bare majority."[28] In addition, the White House had to do work on the Senate side if civil rights legislation were to become a reality.[29] On December 3 LBJ held his first Tuesday White House breakfast meeting with the Democratic congressional leadership. He told the assembled leaders that after Kennedy's tax-cut proposals were enacted into law, civil rights was to be the top legislative priority. He was thorough, pointed in his remarks that he wanted the Congress to move on civil rights. He insisted that the Democrats had to work closely with the Republicans to get the support needed to enact this measure into law.[30]

The next day, December 4, the president met with Senate minority leader Everett Dirksen. LBJ was concerned that the

Senate minority leader understand his commitment to move forward with the civil rights package as soon as it came to the Senate from the lower house. After his visit to the White House, Dirksen publicly acknowledged that the Senate "certainly would act on the bill early next year."[31] On December 5 Johnson led an early morning presidential motorcade to the residence of House Republican leader Charlie Halleck. The minority leader then accompanied LBJ to the White House for breakfast. Kennedy had secured Halleck's agreement to support the legislation, and Johnson now discussed the need to schedule a floor vote as quickly as possible.[32]

In between his meetings with the Senate and House Republican leaders, Johnson managed to get in a meeting with the Executive Council of the AFL-CIO; and he told them, "You must help me make civil rights in America a reality. . . . I ask you to hurry."[33] He also received ninety members of the Business Advisory Council and told them: "I appeal to you for your support of legislation that will help to destroy discrimination."[34] This was Johnson rounding up support for a civil rights bill, in much the same way he had rounded up support to water down such legislation when he was Senate leader. He assured one and all of his commitment to civil rights—much as he had previously reassured them of the need to move slowly and carefully in this area.

At the beginning of the second session of the Eighty-eighth Congress, the president reemphasized the need for civil rights legislation. In his State of the Union Address, he told the assembled legislators: "Let this session of Congress be known as the session that did more for civil rights than the last hundred sessions combined. . . . It is a moral issue—and it must be met by passage this session of the bill now pending in the House."[35] The *Afro-American* responded editorially to Johnson's speech: "Not even the most bitter-end obstructionists like Mississippi's James Eastland or Virginia's Howard Smith now doubt that Congress will pass a civil rights bill." But the black editors, like many in the civil rights community, were concerned that the president still had "to convince thousands of voters . . . he can be trusted to be the President of all the people" and that he would not settle for a watered-down bill.[36] Distrust of Johnson and worry about the possibility of a sellout by him remained a concern for many black rights advocates throughout the early months of 1964.

Of course, it was not only Johnson who had to win the trust of the civil rights proponents, but also the Congress itself that had to prove its commitment to a strong civil rights bill. In the early fall the more fervent civil rights supporters had added several strengthening amendments to the original Kennedy proposal, but under White House pressure almost all of these had been removed from the pending bill.[37] Black leaders were now adamant with Johnson and the Congress; they did not want to lose any more of substance out of this proposed legislation.

In mid January rumors flew all about Washington that the president and members of the congressional leadership on both sides of the aisle were going to compromise away a strong civil rights bill in order to avoid a full-blown filibuster in the Senate. William McCulluch, the Ohio Republican congressman who shepherded the bill through the House Judiciary Committee in exchange for administration pledges that no changes would be made without his consent, reassured the civil rights defenders that no compromise would be permitted in the Senate.[38] LBJ also moved to control the rumors. He held a White House meeting with Roy Wilkins, James Farmer, Martin Luther King, Jr., and Whitney Young, as a group, to reiterate his position on civil rights. Afterwards, the black leaders reported to the press, "This [civil rights] bill should not be watered down any further. We are not prepared to compromise in any form."[39]

In a further effort to reassure blacks that there would be no more compromises, on January 21 Johnson discussed legislative strategy with Joseph Rauh and Clarence Mitchell. The president "said he wanted the [civil rights] bill passed by the House without a word or a comma changed." LBJ told the two rights advocates the House vote was scheduled to be taken immediately prior to the Lincoln Day recess. Rauh noted, "Clarence assured the President that we would have our troops in Washington the week before the Lincoln Day recess helping get the bill passed." However, the president disappointed Rauh and Mitchell when he told them that he would not support strengthening amendments to the bill. If he altered the bill, McCulloch would lead the House Republicans in a revolt that would mean the end of civil rights legislation in the Eighty-eighth Congress. But LBJ delighted his two guests when he also told them "that he wouldn't care if the Senate didn't do another thing for two or three months until the civil rights bill was enacted." Johnson was unequivocal, "You can tell Mansfield, you can tell anybody, the President of the United States doesn't care if this bill is there forever. We are not going to have anything else hit the Senate floor until this bill is passed." Rauh was now persuaded that "the President wanted the bill just as badly as we all do."[40]

This was "the key meeting that convinced me that we were going to get the bill and the president was absolutely committed to it," recalls Rauh. The president "wanted them to know it was hopeless. . . . That's the most important thing he did—telling us how to break the filibuster by making sure everyone understood that there was not going to be a compromise and nothing was going to move in the Senate until we had a vote on the civil rights package. Clarence and I backed the no cloture vote. One thing we didn't want to do was lose on a cloture vote."[41] Johnson and the civil rights leadership had one critical part of their Senate strategy established: there was going to be no quarter given in this legislative battle.

Johnson continued his private and public campaign to convince others of his devotion to civil rights. As H.R. 7152 moved to a vote in the House, LBJ wrote to John A. Hannah, the chairman of the United States Civil Rights Commission: "I believe the most important consideration is enactment of the civil rights bill and that all of our efforts should be undertaken with that in mind."[42] On January 25 the president publicly stated, "I was hopeful we would get civil rights out and get voted on in the House, getting at least half of the job done so that we could take it up as soon as we finish the tax bill in the Senate." LBJ closed with a reiteration of his private commitment to Rauh and Mitchell. "When we take it up, we expect to stay on it until they [the Senate] act upon it." On February 1 Johnson again publicly stated his support for the bill as reported out of committee. When asked by a reporter, "Do you think in order to pass it in the Senate the bill will have to be substantially trimmed?" he replied, "No. . . . And yes, I do expect a filibuster."[43]

The president's activity soon paid dividends for him and the bill. For him came liberal recognition of his positive role. Arnold Aronson wrote to the seventy-five groups associated with the LCCR: "Much of the credit for this welcome spurt of [supportive] civil rights activity must go to President Lyndon B. Johnson. He made it unmistakably clear that he wants the House to act."[44] For the bill, movement in the House was assured. After the Rules Committee Republicans threatened to join the liberal Democrats to ensure that the bill would be voted out of committee, chairman Howard Smith of Virginia scheduled a committee vote to bring H.R. 7152 to the House floor by January 30. The president received assurances that a House floor vote would be quickly scheduled, and he publicly expressed his support for a prompt floor vote.[45] On January 30 the Rules Committee voted eleven to four, with only southern Democrats dissenting, to bring the bill to the House floor.

By a vote of 290 to 130, with 152 Democrats and 138 Republicans voting aye, the bill passed the House on February 10. Of the ninety-six Democrats who voted no on final passage of H.R. 7152, only ten were from outside the eleven states of the old Confederacy. Thirty-four Republicans, including ten non-southerners, voted against passage of the bill. Democratic congressman Jamie L. Whitten of Mississippi voiced the chagrin of his southern colleagues at the bipartisan support for the bill. "It is unfortunate," he intoned, "that we see agreement between the Republican leadership over here and the Democratic leadership over there to pass through this House every last bad provision that is in this bill."[46] As one House staff member recalls, "Congressman Halleck explained to us, 'We don't know what the politically okay position would be, so we had to all stick together.' This was the real strategy for both sides [Democrats and Republicans]: to develop a position for their respective parties so that there would be minimal risk of getting blamed for what happened."[47]

McCulloch's insistence that nothing was going to be "traded

away" in the Senate held the Republicans for the bill. The Democratic Study Group, an association of liberal House Democrats headed by Frank Thompson of New Jersey and Richard Bolling of Missouri, created a whip organization that mustered the votes to keep the bill intact as amendment after amendment was offered on the House floor.[48] Unlike 1957, when the House Republicans believed they had gone all out to support legislation and then saw their work demolished in the Senate, this time there was going to be bipartisan responsibility to keep a strong, unaltered civil rights bill. The administration, acting through Robert Kennedy and Nicholas Katzenbach, repeatedly reassured the GOP House members of its commitment to this position.

Clarence Mitchell, the head NAACP lobbyist, believed "there were many times when we could have lost on the House floor if we had not had the kind of attention that the President was giving to the bill."[49] His conversion to the Johnson choir was completed when the president called him and Joe Rauh on a corridor pay phone as the House finished voting on the bill. LBJ had tried to reach Mitchell and Rauh at the LCCR office near the Hill, and a messenger rushed over to the House and had Rauh and Mitchell ready for the White House call in the hallway.[50] Mitchell later recalled, "He was calling to say, 'All right, you fellows, get on over there to the Senate because we've got it through the House and now we've got the big job of getting it through the Senate.'"[51]

Johnson was ready to go after civil rights in the Senate, but he was not sure how to proceed. The votes for passage of the civil rights bill were there, but the votes for cloture to end the forthcoming southern filibuster were not apparent. Of the eleven previous votes to impose cloture when a civil rights bill was pending, not one was successful. The day after H.R. 7152 passed the House, Johnson convened a White House meeting with the top administration people involved in civil rights: Robert Kennedy, Nicholas Katzenbach, Burke Marshall, Lawrence O'Brien, and Press secretary Pierre Salinger.[52] Back in early December he had told the leaders, "We all know the real problem is in the Senate."[53] Johnson was still not sure they would ever get the votes necessary for cloture. The meeting ended without agreement, but later that evening Johnson and Katzenbach resumed the argument at a White House diplomatic reception. They sat in the middle of the hall debating whether the votes for cloture were ever going to be there as the guests milled around them. Katzenbach told his chief they needed seven of the eleven votes that were uncommitted on cloture. The president adamantly repeated that he did not think they could get the votes. "Mr. President," Katzenbach retorted, "I think we can." LBJ agreed to give it a try. "And he went to work on those eleven votes," Katzenbach recalls. Soon after, Katzenbach continues, LBJ was asked at a press conference, "'What are you going to do with the civil rights bill?' He replied, 'We're going to get cloture.' And when Lyndon Johnson, with all his experience in the Senate said, 'We're going to get cloture,' that made it believable."[54] Whether or not the president believed it is beside the point. He was committed to the bill, and he was going to do all he could to get it out.

Early on during the strategy discussions, Johnson pointed out that Senate minority leader Everett Dirksen held the key to getting the necessary votes for cloture if they ever were to be gotten. At least partly as a result of Johnson's urging, President Kennedy had consulted with the Republican leader before sending his civil rights proposals to the Hill.[55] "How great a price should the administration pay for Senator Dirksen's cooperation?" was the question posed to JFK by his counsel, Theodore Sorenson.[56] This was now the question before Johnson, but he was determined to do everything in his power to coopt the senator from Illinois into the civil rights camp without having to pay him much of anything.

The gravelly voiced minority leader was ardently courted by the White House and its agents. The Republicans had to be brought along, and Dirksen was the keeper of the Republican course. Katzenbach wrote to O'Brien: "We should make every effort to point out that Republican support will be needed for passage of the bill and that we can only fail if that support is not forthcoming."[57] Dirksen was regularly brought to the White House through the Diplomatic Reception Room entrance so that no one would know he was there; and then, according to Jack Valenti, the two old friends would sit down and parley.

"The President was trying to get Dirksen to do certain things and Dirksen would [eventually do them] . . . exacting his price for it."[58] Johnson avoided involvement in the internal Senate parliamentary struggle, and he turned over to Robert Kennedy responsibility for heading the Justice Department team that was directly involved in the strategy and negotiations.[59] The top Justice Department leaders met with Dirksen, and they negotiated with him as he made his concerns about the bill known. The administration and the Senate Democratic leadership were all in accord on this strategy.

Hubert Humphrey, the designated floor leader for the civil rights bill, became Dirksen's chief courter and Senate strategist for the bill. Mike Mansfield, the majority leader, wanted to be able to mediate between the forces involved in this battle, and Humphrey wanted the floor leadership position as the capstone to his career of support for civil rights. Mansfield gave it to him for the asking.[60] "Now you know that bill can't pass unless you get Ev Dirksen," the president told Humphrey. "You and I are going to get Ev. It's going to take time. We're going to get him." The president continued, "You've got to spend time with Ev. You've got to play to Dirksen. You've got to let him have a piece of the action. He's got to look good all the time."[61] This was to be one key part of the Johnson-Humphrey strategy.

The floor leader never let up in his pursuit of Dirksen. Clarence Mitchell recalls, "Humphrey said to me in a meeting: What we want to do is get some blue lights and pink lights and dress up this little spot on the stage. And when everything is set we want to have Everett Dirksen walk out there, stand in the spotlight, and be the man who rescues the whole operation."[62] In a March appearance on "Meet the Press," Humphrey was asked about whether Dirksen would vote for the bill when he publicly opposed Title II, the public-accommodations section, and Title VII, the equal employment opportunity section. The Minnesotan responded, "I think Senator Dirksen is a reasonable man. Those are his current opinions and they are strongly held, but as the debate goes on he'll see that there is a reason for what we're trying to do." And then came the kicker, "Not only that, Senator Dirksen is not only a great senator, he is a great American, and he is going to see the necessity of this legislation. I predict that before this bill is through Senator Dirksen will be its great champion." Humphrey remembered, "Johnson called me after that and said, 'Boy, that was right. You're doing just right now. You just keep at that. . . . You drink with Dirksen! You talk to Dirksen! You listen to Dirksen!'" Day after day Humphrey reminded the GOP leader, "Everett, we can't pass this bill without you. We need your leadership in this fight, Everett." "Oh, I was shameless," Humphrey acknowledged, but "he liked hearing it all, and I didn't mind saying it."[63]

Within the Senate, Humphrey created an ad hoc organization that was remarkable for its effectiveness. The southerners were a tightknit band of nineteen led by the unwavering Richard Russell. Humphrey, with his core of fifty-five supporters, had a much greater organizational task before him. He had to make sure that the pro-rights forces always had a majority of senators available to meet quorum calls. He had to make sure that everyone understood and abided by the developing parliamentary strategy. He had to hold a bipartisan majority together. He appointed captains to lead the debate on each section of the bill. The leaders of the pro–civil rights forces of both parties met together each morning to discuss strategy. A daily newsletter reviewing major concerns with the pending legislation and continually singing the praises of Dirksen's civil rights efforts was issued jointly by Humphrey and Thomas Kuchel, the liberal Californian who was appointed the GOP floor leader for the bill. Humphrey publicly proclaimed, "Everything is going to be talked over with the Republicans— strategy, tactics, timing. . . . We have obligations not only to the Republicans in the Senate, but also to those of both parties in the House who were so faithful and effective."[64]

"The way Humphrey set up the whole operation in 1964 had the Lyndon Johnson kind of care to it," recalled the NAACP chief lobbyist, "a care that hadn't been present in the Senate liberal effort up to that point."[65] Humphrey's organizational efforts earned him the respect of the New York Times, which noted: "As militarily precise as the Southerner's three platoon system, the Humphrey forces are organized down to the last man."[66] Humphrey learned his lessons on Senate strategy from Lyndon Johnson, and he was now master of the Senate and its civil rights forces.

Outside the Senate, Humphrey and Johnson often paralleled their efforts to bring pressure on the uncommitted senators. Humphrey used his ties to the LCCR, labor unions, liberal church organizations, and other liberal groups to develop a powerful, grassroots lobbying effort. LCCR leaders Clarence Mitchell and Joseph Rauh attended the morning Senate leadership briefings twice a week. They were indefatigable workers during the Senate battle. In addition, the NAACP leadership worked tirelessly to have members write letters of support for the bill, lobby on the Hill, and keep the pro–civil rights forces working in the system.[67] Humphrey knew he also "needed more active participation from . . . church groups." In early March he met with Jewish, Catholic, and Protestant leaders. He prodded them to lobby their senators, and he promoted their use of public pressure to move the Senate on civil rights. "We selected the date of April 28 at that time for the inter-faith civil rights convocation to be held at Georgetown University."[68] On April 19 trios of Catholic, Protestant, and Jewish seminarians began a round-the-clock civil rights prayer vigil at the Lincoln Memorial. The National Council of Churches spent approximately four hundred thousand dollars in its efforts on behalf of the civil rights bill.[69]

These groups were, according to journalist Murray Kempton, "Mr. Humphrey's Conquering Hosts."[70] The church leaders pressured U.S. senators from midwestern and western states to support black rights. Individual visits to senators by ministers from their home state were organized.[71] This was a new phenomenon for many of these senators, they had few or no black constituents and had never had constituency pressure on this issue.[72] As Joseph Rauh pointed out, "It was one thing for these guys [in Congress] to brush past Clarence [Mitchell] and me and vote against us, but it was another thing to brush past the high church and vote against them."[73] The church lobbying was intense. For example, the Catholic Convocation for Civil Rights held in Omaha, Nebraska, in early May laid out the following strategy for its members: "(1) have bishops issue pastoral letters; (2) form interfaith work groups; (3) take ads in newspapers; (4) have constituents contact their senators; distribute literature supporting the bill at churches; (5) have sermons delivered 'on the moral basis of the bill.'"[74] Russell, speaking for the South, acknowledged the effectiveness of the religious leadership's mobilization. "We have seen cardinals, bishops, elders, stated clerks, common preachers, priests and rabbis come to Washington to press for passage of the bill. They have sought to make its passage a great moral issue."[75] Humphrey's exertions were paying off.

Johnson also appealed to religious groups for help in this effort. For example, on March 25 he addressed the members of the Southern Baptist Leadership Seminar in the White House Rose Garden. He pressed them to lobby for civil rights. "I am proud to say that in this cause [civil rights] some of our strongest allies are religious leaders who are encouraging elected officials to do what is right. But more must be done," he intoned, "and no group of Christians has a greater responsibility in civil rights than Southern Baptists." He reminded them that they led southern congregations, and "their attitudes are confirmed or changed by the sermons you preach and by the lessons you write and by the examples you set." LBJ also reminded the preachers, "In the long struggle for religious liberty Baptists have been prophets. . . . Help us to pass this civil rights bill and establish a foundation upon which we can build a house of freedom where all men can dwell."[76] The national bully pulpit was in strong hands.

Johnson and Humphrey repeatedly worked together to position the Senate for the upcoming Senate battle. When Humphrey left the White House after a meeting with Johnson on March 3, he told reporters that the bipartisan leaders and the president were committed to the bill as passed by the House.[77] At a March 7 press conference, LBJ was asked to "assess the chances" of the civil rights bill that would be in the Senate the following Monday. He responded, "I think we passed a good civil rights bill in the House. I hope the same bill will be passed in the Senate." Another reporter asked the president, "How long do you think the battle in the Senate may take?" Johnson replied, "I don't think anyone really knows how long the matter will be discussed but [all senators] . . . will be given adequate opportunity to express themselves. Then I believe the majority of the Senate will have an opportunity to work its will."[78] On the same day, Humphrey told reporters, "If it takes until September to pass the House bill, it's perfectly all right with us. We'll be there."[79] At the United Automobile Workers Convention in late March, the president echoed Humphrey's remarks: "We are going to pass a civil rights bill if it takes all summer."[80] Procedural maneuvering over the bill began on the Senate floor on March 9, and on March 15 the president told a national television audience, "I know of nothing more important for this Congress to do than to pass the Civil Rights Act as the House passed it."[81]

Humphrey had always been a civil rights champion, but Johnson's conversion to the cause changed the course of the struggle. Russell understood the basis for Johnson's conversion and what it meant for the South. On March 1 the Georgian remarked, "President Johnson feels that if he loses any substantial part of it, that will cast all of his statements in support of it in doubt as to their sincerity." Russell's conclusion: "This really makes it a much more difficult position as to any compromise than there would have been had President Kennedy not met his tragic fate."[82]

On March 26 by a vote of sixty-seven to seventeen, H.R. 7152 moved to the Senate floor. Only the southerners voted in opposition. Throughout the ensuing Senate debate, Johnson publicly reiterated his no-compromise-keep-the-Senate-at-work position.[83] He also kept pushing leaders from business, unions, churches, and minority groups to round up their constituents to support the bill.[84] The president had a legislative agenda he wanted to move on, including the War on Poverty, which he introduced in his State of the Union message.[85] Yet, aside from backing Capitol Hill action on the Kennedy tax-cut proposals and a farm support bill, he insisted all else be held in abeyance until the civil rights bill was dealt with in the Congress. "This level of Presidential support," wrote Humphrey's aide John Stewart, "proved vital in sustaining an effort which otherwise might have fallen victim to the normal Senatorial pressures for concession and compromise."[86]

The spring of 1964 was not the time for normal pressures. On April 7, less than two weeks after the Senate debate formally began, Wisconsin held its presidential primary; George Wallace of Alabama won 264,000 (34 percent) of the Democratic votes. Wallace won 29.8 percent of Indiana's Democratic presidential primary votes, and on May 19 he carried over 42.7 percent of the Democratic vote in Maryland.[87] Wallace's pledge to "make race the basis of politics in this country" was becoming reality.[88] His notorious racism found a niche in the North as white reaction to black demonstrations mounted. White backlash, the white, predominantly blue-collar anger or fear surfacing as antiblack politics; became a common term of use by journalists and politicians.[89] Southern senators were hopeful that the Wallace campaign would move uncommitted senators their way in response to their constituents' pressures.[90] Members of the White House staff, mindful of this possibility, expressed their concern to Johnson that he play a role, privately and publicly, to keep the black demonstrations under control. Richard Goodwin wrote: "I believe this is worth an awful lot of energy and foresight since it is an issue which could dominate the campaign."[91] The White House funneled staff support and Democratic National Committee funds to aid Senator Daniel B. Brewster of Maryland in his stand-in campaign against Wallace.[92] Yet Wallace's message was well received by many Democrats, even if he did not win any primary elections.

Wallace's triumphs did not panic the liberal forces. After the Alabaman completed his primary run, Clarence Mitchell wrote to his boss: "In Washington there is a lot of talk about what Alabama's George Wallace is doing in the North. However," he continued, "there is no evidence here that his activities have caused us to lose a single vote in the Senate."[93] The liberals were not interested in pressing their luck with more white reaction to black demonstrations. Humphrey and Kuchel issued a joint statement that argued, "Civil disobedience does not bring equal protection under the law." On the same day, Johnson asked for "moderation." When asked about his reaction to a black sit-in demonstration that took place as he attended the opening of the New York World's Fair, Johnson called for understanding and congressional action on the bill. And LBJ went into the

South and told a small-town Georgia audience, "The Constitution of the United States applies to every American."[94] He stuck by his message of morality and civil rights even as he spoke to the Georgia legislature.

LBJ believed that the major consequence of the Wallace campaign was that it "stiffened the will of the Southerners to keep on fighting the civil rights measure."[95] LBJ, in turn, stiffened the pro–civil rights forces. In mid April he told the nation's leading newspaper editors, "Our nation will live in torment . . . until the civil rights bill now being considered is written into law." He continued, "The question is no longer, 'Shall it be passed?' The question is 'When, when will it be passed?'"[96]

Everett Dirksen started to hold meetings with the Senate Republicans in early April to lay out his proposed amendments to the civil rights bill and to solidify his party's position. In mid April he began to negotiate with both the Senate civil rights leaders and the Justice Department leadership to determine what he could get to meet his needs on the bill. When he met with the president at the end of the month, he found out there was very little to be negotiated. LBJ remained inflexible—the House bill had to set the parameters for the Senate bill.[97] At a May 5 meeting of administration and bipartisan Senate leaders in Humphrey's office, Dirksen let it be known that he would propose more than seventy amendments to the bill.[98] The liberal team was flabbergasted; they had never expected such extensive proposals. The next day LBJ told a news conference that he expected the Senate to act on civil rights by early June, "and then we can go on with our food stamp plan in the Senate, our poverty program, our Appalachia program and our medical aid bill." The president told the reporters that if the filibuster continued, "I will seriously consider calling them back [after the national conventions] until they vote the bills up or down."[99]

On May 12 Humphrey, Mansfield, Kuchel, and Justice Department leaders concluded that the Illinois senator *had* to go along with the bill— he had little choice to do otherwise given the GOP's need for support in the industrial states. Stephen Horn, Kuchel's chief aide, emphasizes that by this point Dirksen had established a common ground on which most of the GOP senators could agree. "Dirksen had [also] been watching," recalled another staffer, "to see just how serious the Democrats were in support for the bill and he therefore offered a series of amendments to see how much maneuvering room he had. He learned the Democrats were serious about the bill and the Republicans had to stick together."[100] When Dirksen joined this meeting, Humphrey bluntly told the GOP leader that he had to support cloture on the entire bill or everything would remain at an impasse. The GOP leader was ready to move on civil rights. By the end of the session his recommendations were transformed into a substitute proposal for the House bill.[101] Richard Russell was melancholy as he accused Dirksen of selling out the Republicans' position of support for a restrained federal government.[102] But the liberal forces were delighted because the Dirksen substitute did not essentially alter the original bill.

The critical hurdle had been successfully negotiated. Robert Kennedy announced, "There is an understanding between all who participated. We are going back now and consult all who are interested in passing civil rights legislation."[103] "A dramatic development has occurred," reported a delighted Clarence Mitchell. "Senator Dirksen . . . has pledged to make a fight for cloture on a bill which includes enforcement powers in the Public Accommodations and FEPC Titles." Mitchell realized that Dirksen's "change of position will undoubtedly bolster our chances for limiting the filibuster." As Mitchell later recalled in an interview, "We hadn't votes to invoke cloture in the Senate without Dirksen. So, Humphrey . . . made it possible for the bill to be theoretically rewritten by Dirksen." The NAACP lobbyist concluded, "Dirksen genuinely believed it was his bill. But if you look at it carefully you'll see it wasn't very different from what Senator Humphrey was supporting in the first place."[104] The last obstacles were ready to be overcome.

The "Dirksen package" or the "Dirksen formula" as it was labeled in Washington was ready for the Senate floor.[105] Mike Manatos, the administration's Senate liaison, concluded, both "party caucuses have developed surprising support for the civil rights package worked out with the bi-partisan Leadership and the Department of Justice."[106] Even former president Dwight Eisenhower, who had remained silent about the proposed legislation, now joined the chorus of support for the measure. "We

Republicans have a particular obligation to be vigorous in the furtherance of civil rights. In this critical area," he emphasized, "I have been especially proud of the dramatic leadership given by the Republicans in Congress these past two years."[107] On May 26 the Senate minority leader and the majority leader jointly brought the new civil rights proposal to the floor as a substitute for the House bill.

The minority leader and the majority leader jointly sponsored a substitute for the pending bill, but there was general agreement that the liberal forces had only fifty-five of the sixty-seven votes needed for cloture in the event that the entire Senate participated in this vote. By early June there were a solid sixty-six votes counted for cloture.[108] Johnson joined Humphrey and the LCCR, especially the union elements, to line up the last vote and then some for a cushion.[109] On June 8 the White House count showed seventy-one votes for cloture.[110] The vote was taken on June 10. Forty-four Democrats voted in the affirmative. Except for Texas's liberal Ralph Yarborough, all of the southern Democrats were in opposition. Dirksen had twelve liberal Republicans lined up, and in the end he added fifteen of the twenty-one moderate and conservative Republicans to the aye column. Barry Goldwater, the leading candidate for the GOP presidential nomination, voted against cloture. The last speaker on the floor prior to the vote was Everett Dirksen. "Stronger than all the armies is an idea whose time has come," he declaimed. "The time has come for equality of opportunity. . . . It will not be stayed or denied. It is here."[111] The longest Senate filibuster in history—fifty-seven days—was ended.[112] This was the first successful cloture vote with a civil rights bill pending.

The civil rights forces had won a resounding victory. They did it by finessing the opposition as well as overwhelming it. For example, Humphrey and Mansfield agreed to set the cloture vote for June 10, after the June 2 California primary was held. This avoided forcing five Republicans who supported Barry Goldwater's presidential bid from having to take a position that differed from him on this critical issue.[113] In another instance several conservative Republicans felt that Dirksen had unduly manipulated the GOP Senate caucus. They were also somewhat jealous of the attention that had been showered on Dirksen. As Bourke Hickenlooper of Iowa told Humphrey, "All we want is the chance to show that Dirksen wasn't the only Republican on the floor."[114] Humphrey agreed to let them have the Senate floor to put forward amendments they believed were important. All of the amendments failed, but the threatened defection was averted. Humphrey noted, "Senator Russell [was] complaining quite bitterly that we hadn't cooperated with him when he wanted to vote, and I said to him, somewhat in jest, but also in truth, 'Well, Dick, you haven't any votes to give us in cloture and these fellows do.'"[115] The pro–civil rights forces had the votes, and they used them forcefully and skillfully to control the floor.

Once cloture was invoked, the administration and the Senate rights leaders agreed, "Nothing will move in the Senate until after civil rights" clears the floor.[116] On June 19 almost as an anticlimax, the Senate voted seventy-three to twenty-seven to pass the Dirksen-Mansfield substitute. The day before the vote, Barry Goldwater announced he could not support the bill. The Arizona conservative was joined by four other Republicans, all from states with relatively small black populations—Iowa, New Hampshire, New Mexico, and Wyoming—and John Tower of Texas, the lone Republican from Dixie.[117] On the Democratic side of the aisle, the southern opposition was joined only by Robert C. Byrd of West Virginia. Russell forlornly wrote his constituents: "Our little band of southern constitutionalists put everything we had into the fight . . . but our ranks were too thin and our resources too scanty. In the end we were gagged and overwhelmed."[118] Few could debate these words.

The House leadership agreed to accept the Senate substitute. The need for a conference committee and another Senate floor battle that would have followed if any changes had been made in the bill, was sidetracked. In addition, Chairman Smith yielded to pressure and scheduled a Rules Committee meeting to provide a rule for prompt House floor consideration. On July 2 the House voted, 289 to 126, to pass the Dirksen-Mansfield substitute. Congressman McCulloch received a standing ovation from the House for his dedicated work on behalf of the cause.[119] On July 2, 1964, within hours of the House vote,

Lyndon Johnson signed the Civil Rights Act of 1964 into law.[120] The ceremony in the White House was attended by the congressional leadership and the myriad of black leaders and liberal leaders who had struggled for the bill. LBJ was at his exuberant best, and he said a special thank-you to Martin Luther King, Jr., and other civil rights leaders. At this time, King wrote about Johnson's civil rights leadership: his "emotional and intellectual involvement were genuine and devoid of adornment."[121] LBJ was obviously delighted at the signing ceremony. Quietly, as he signed the bill, Johnson turned to Nicholas Katzenbach and asked, "What are we going to do next year in civil rights?" Incredulous, Katzenbach responded, "Jesus Christ, Mr. President, we just spent two years on this bill and practically nothing else happened." LBJ shot back, "What are we going to do? Let's get a bill. Let's get a voting rights bill."[122]

Johnson played a crucial role in the fight to achieve a strong civil rights bill. Behind the scenes he helped secure several critical votes for cloture and kept pressing the civil rights forces to maintain the integrity of the House proposal.[123] Most important, Katzenbach recalls, was "the very courageous public attitude for a man who was not really persuaded that cloture could be gotten, but who was willing to put his neck right out. . . . I think it was basically the reason that we got it, because they all thought that he knew the Senate."[124] Johnson wrote, "I gave to this fight everything I had."[125]

The legislative struggle had paid off with a tougher bill than anyone had imagined possible the previous year.[126] It paid off with many in the South conceding that the nation was now behind the federal courts' call for equality. Senator Allen J. Ellender of Louisiana told his constituents that although he had fought against passage of the bill, "the laws enacted by Congress must be respected." Senator William J. Fulbright of Arkansas told his constituents, "Now that the bill is law it is time for calmness, reflection and adjustment."[127] Congressman Charles Weltner of Atlanta told his constituents, "We can offer resistance and defiance. . . . Or we can acknowledge this measure as the law of the land. We can accept the verdict of the nation." He concluded, "We must not remain forever bound to another lost cause."[128] In a widely reported speech that he gave in Rome, Georgia, in mid July, Richard Russell told his audience that the Civil Rights Act of 1964 was now the law of the land: "As long as it is there it must be obeyed." There was widespread, immediate compliance with the act across much of the South. Ramsey Clark of the Justice Department remarked, "Almost overnight, as if by magic," there was compliance. "It certainly surprised and relieved many of us."[129] Lawsuits and federal intervention to assure compliance with sections of the act would become commonplace across the nation, but the immediate nonviolent southern acquiescence to the act as legitimate provided balm to the nation's leaders.

The successful conclusion of the legislative battle paid off for LBJ in his emergence as a certified liberal. Martin Luther King, Jr., for example, was now convinced that Johnson's "emotional and intellectual involvement [in civil rights] were genuine and devoid of adornment."[130] TRB of the liberal *New Republic* wrote: "LBJ has been hurling himself about Washington like an elemental force. To be plain about it, he has won our admiration in the last fortnight."[131] Lyndon Johnson was now the heir to the liberal Democratic party mantle. The theme he chose for his nominating convention that August was Let Us Continue.

7

Forging the
Election Coalition

WITH THE PASSAGE of the Civil Rights Act, Johnson looked forward to getting on with the more usual business of politics. The national party conventions were coming up during the summer. Barry Goldwater was destined to be the GOP standard bearer, and the celebration of LBJ's accession to command was scheduled to be the Democrats' order of the day. Much like his predecessor, LBJ believed that Goldwater would be the perfect opponent around whom to organize his own campaign. Goldwater's narrow right-wing perspective could provide Johnson with the opportunity to redefine the political center as liberal, and the possibility of an overwhelming electoral victory could enable him to bring a liberal majority into Congress on his coattails. In the spring of 1964 Johnson began to plan for the Great Society with its myriad social programs for the cities, the poor, the elderly, and education.[1] Civil rights and civil disorder, however, continued intruding into the nation's normal course of politics, and white reaction to these disorders threatened Johnson's dream of a great election victory. From the fall of 1963 through the spring of 1965, the civil rights issue almost consistently remained the number one concern of most Americans.[2]

In April of 1964, while the southern filibuster of the civil rights bill was in full force, a group of black leaders operating under the banner of the Council of Federated Organizations (COFO), met in Jackson, Mississippi, to form the Mississippi Freedom Democratic party (MFDP).[3] The MFDP planned to send delegates to the 1964 Democratic National Convention to challenge the credentials of the all-white Mississippi state Democratic party delegation. This created a major problem for Johnson: how to keep the MFDP challenge from disrupting the convention. In addition, violence befell white students who were brought into Mississippi to help in a COFO-organized voter-registration project. This created a second problem for the administration: how to keep black reaction to white violence under control. The latter problem was the first that the administration faced.

Robert Moses, the highly respected director of COFO, had convinced his colleagues that there was a need for a biracial voter-registration project in Mississippi. Potential black voters would be brought to the county courthouses in massive numbers and instructed on how to fill out the registration forms. White and black students would go door to door to encourage participation in the registration process and to sign up MFDP members. Some of them would also teach in COFO-sponsored Freedom Schools. This was to be the Mississippi Summer Project, or Freedom Summer. Initially, the COFO staff was opposed to bringing in whites, but Moses argued, "I'm not gonna be a part of anything all-black. We're gonna have the Summer Project. We need it." Dave Dennis, who developed the project with Moses, recalls a major reason why white students were crucial to its success: "We knew that if we brought in a thousand blacks, the country would have watched them slaughtered without doing anything about it. Bring a thousand whites and the country is going to react to that. . . . The death of a white college student would bring on more attention to what was going on than for a black college student getting it."[4]

During the Kennedy administration, Bob Moses was among the young black leaders who went into the Deep South to register voters. These idealists believed that the southern white violence that was bound to be employed against them would force the federal government to come into these states. They were wrong. Criminal cases were, by and large, state cases. Even the murder and maiming of individuals because they were attempting to register to vote were regarded as state matters. The federal government, aside from FBI agents occasionally being present to take notes on the mayhem as it happened, stayed out of the registration process and the violence that swirled around it. The Freedom Summer project was going to test whether or not the federal government would hold to this position if white middle-class students from the best colleges and universities were the targets of southern violence.[5]

James Forman, another black leader in the Freedom Summer project, extended the argument put forward by Dave Dennis. "We could not bring all of white America to Mississippi, but by bringing in some of its children as volunteer workers, a new consciousness would feed back . . . as they worried about their sons and daughters confronting the 'jungle of Mississippi.'" Forman was convinced "any horror that might be brought into the homes of white America would be acted out in the nation's political arena."[6] On June 13, 1964, the first few hundred of what became nine hundred white volunteers arrived in Oxford, Ohio, to train for Freedom Summer.[7] They had to be acclimated to the Mississippi environment, and they had to learn to be nonviolent. John Doar, an attorney in the Justice Department's Civil Rights Division, visited the trainees and told them, "Maintaining law and order is a state responsibility." He reminded them that the federal government would be powerless if violence befell their efforts.[8] They were determined to make Americans pay attention to the tragedy of blacks in Mississippi.

The Johnson White House grew more concerned as it learned more about the plans for Freedom Summer. On May 21 the deputy attorney general wrote a memorandum to the president to inform him that "in Mississippi an organization called the Council of Federated Organizations (COFO) has been formed for the purpose of recruiting students to do voter registration and adult education work this summer." The deputy attorney general continued: "Our information at present is that COFO has recruited several hundred students from northern university campuses for this purpose."[9] Robert Kennedy wrote to the president in early June about a well-known reality of southern police officialdom: Mississippi "law enforcement officials are widely believed to be linked to extremist anti-Negro activity, or at the very least to tolerate it."[10] RFK's concern was that now the law and the Klan were going to go after northern white students, and again a presidential administration was going to be embarrassed unless something was done to prevent it. The administration explored alternative responses to the inevitable violence. But associate counsel Lee White wrote the president there was little that could be done for these students who were "voluntarily sticking their head into the lion's mouth."[11]

On June 21, four days after White sent the latter memorandum to the president, three civil rights workers did not return from their trip to investigate a church burning in Meridian, Mississippi. James Chaney, a black Mississippi CORE staffer; Michael Schwerner, a white New York CORE staffer assigned to Mississippi; and Andrew Goodman, a white Queens College student volunteer had disappeared. On June 22 the story of the missing civil rights workers made page one of the *New York Times*. Chaney, Schwerner, and Goodman became household names as the search for them grabbed the nation's attention.[12] At his June 23 news conference, Johnson was asked if he had "any information about those three kids that disappeared in Mississippi?" LBJ responded, "The FBI has a substantial number of men who are closely studying and investigating the entire situation." While he had nothing substantial to report on the whereabouts of the three, Johnson let it be known that "several weeks ago I had asked [the FBI] to anticipate the problems that would come from [Freedom Summer], and to send extra FBI personnel into the area."[13] That evening the president asked Allen W. Dulles, a former director of the Central Intelligence Agency, to fly to Mississippi to "evaluate the situation."[14]

Dulles spent twenty-four hours in the state, meeting with Governor Paul B. Johnson and various black and white leaders. On June 26 he returned to Washington and met with the president, Katzenbach, and Marshall. He was pessimistic about the conditions in Mississippi. The whites were totally opposed to any change in the status of the blacks. "There is no progress in any direction or substantial attempt at progress." The white students were "invaders. . . . This term is universally applied to them in the State." Dulles added, "The state government is enraged at this [voter-registration] project." He also informed the president of a finding that should not have surprised him: "The Radical Negro groups secretly desire to bring about federal intervention by provoking incidents."[15] In sum, the lines in Mississippi were drawn and were not about to be altered by either of the major combatant groups. On the same day that Dulles reported to LBJ, the NAACP Board of Directors requested the president "to take such . . . steps under Federal law as may be needed to restore law and order and protect the life and liberties of all citizens of Mississippi."[16] The president ordered more FBI agents into Mississippi.

The administration continued to consider the need for more of a federal presence in Mississippi. Katzenbach informed the president that he could find "no specific legal objection to sending federal civilian personnel to guard against possible violations of federal law." He noted, however, that local law enforcement personnel are "most crucial . . . in maintaining law and order in a community gripped by racial crisis."[17] The public, while opposed to student involvement in Mississippi, was strongly in favor of the president sending troops to the state "to restore peace if violence breaks out."[18] On July 10 Johnson told the press that J. Edgar Hoover was going to Mississippi to bring in additional FBI agents and to establish a new FBI office in the state.[19] One hundred and fifty-three agents were sent into the state—ten times the usual number assigned there. "Getting Mr. Hoover to go down to Jackson, Mississippi, to open that office was quite a feat," recalls Ramsey Clark. "I wouldn't have bet much on being able to talk him into doing it but he [LBJ] did."[20] Hoover had always previously avoided being brought into the civil rights situation. But now the president left him little choice.

Johnson wanted national attention to move away from Mississippi, but the violence continued there despite the increased federal presence. Although Mississippi law enforcement agents arrested more than a thousand Freedom Summer participants on a variety of charges ranging from traffic violations to illegal marches, they never found any of the white perpetrators of a series of violent crimes that spewed across the state. During Freedom Summer, eighty of the COFO workers and their supporters were beaten; thirty-five were shot at or wounded; thirty of their homes and businesses were bombed; and six were murdered.[21] On August 4 the bodies of Chaney, Schwerner, and

Goodman were found by federal forces, buried beneath an earthen dam. The two white men had been shot one time through the head. The black civil rights worker had been severely beaten and then shot three times. The state of Mississippi never convicted anyone of these murders.[22] On August 19, five days prior to the meeting of the Democratic National Convention, John Lewis wrote to the president of "the need for increased Federal action in this state."[23] He never received a reply. In the Jackson headquarters of the MFDP, there hung a sign that read: There's a Town in Mississippi Called Liberty, There's a Department in Washington Called Justice.[24]

Freedom Summer had its political successes. Mississippi was enveloped in national attention. A sense of the violence and deprivation that was a daily occurrence in the lives of its black citizens was brought into Americans homes in television broadcasts and newspaper reports. In addition, the COFO leaders believed they achieved an important symbolic victory by having more than 17,000 age-eligible blacks walk into county registrar offices and complete the voter registration forms. County registrars rejected more than 15,400 applicants on various grounds, but 1,600 actually were registered to vote. This occurred in a state where in 1962 only 5.3 percent, or 23,920, of the 514,589 age-eligible blacks were registered to vote.[25] The new registrants did not alter the political balance of power in Mississippi, but a new black political consciousness was being fostered. One indicator of this new awareness is that more than fifty thousand black Mississippians signed up as MFDP members. Further, when the regular state Democratic party barred blacks from participating in its national convention delegate-selection process, the MFDP held a series of precinct and county convention meetings across most of the state, culminating in an August 4 state party convention held in Jackson, Mississippi. The state convention elected forty-four delegates and twenty-two alternates, which included four whites—one of whom was a sailor stationed in Biloxi and another was a New York City school teacher temporarily working in Mississippi—to attend the Democratic National Convention and challenge the all-white Mississippi state Democratic party for the right to be seated as Mississippi national convention delegates.[26] This did not portend good tidings for Lyndon Johnson. He did not want a party rent by a southern walkout because of civil rights. He wanted a party and a nation ready to be bedazzled at the forthcoming Democratic National Convention, and racial bedlam in Mississippi and party strife at the convention were not on his agenda.

The Republican National Convention was scheduled to begin on July 13, prior to the Democratic conclave, and the moderates of both political parties were dismayed at what was about to transpire. Barry Goldwater, the leading GOP contender of 1963, successfully ran a gamut of primaries in 1964 that, according to journalist Theodore White, "exceed[ed] in savagery and significance any other in modern politics."[27] GOP primary elections were bitterly fought in three states: New Hampshire (March 10), Oregon (May 15), and California (June 2). Governor Nelson Rockefeller of New York, Ambassador to Vietnam Henry Cabot Lodge, and Governor William W. Scranton of Pennsylvania all challenged Goldwater's extremism. The conservative leader was defeated by a write-in vote for Henry Cabot Lodge in New Hampshire, and he conceded Oregon to Nelson Rockefeller; but he won a narrow victory for California's eighty-six delegates, and this win sealed his nomination. The moderates were outorganized in almost every convention state; and quietly but surely, the Goldwater forces sewed up these delegations. Beginning in 1961 the GOP right wing and its allies were mobilized on Goldwater's behalf, and their efforts paid off.[28] Theodore White's chronicle of this campaign notes: "Their forces were more useful, more determined, and earlier begun than that of any previous presidential campaign."[29]

Goldwater articulated his conservative view in his two books, *The Conscience of a Conservative* and *Why Not Victory?* Both are statements of ideological purity. He denounced the establishment of the liberal welfare state and federal intrusion into the states. His position on the federal effort to integrate education was forthright—and appalling to the civil rights community. "The Federal Constitution," he maintained, "does not require the states to maintain racially mixed schools. Despite the recent holding of the Supreme Court, I am firmly convinced—not only that integrated schools are not required—but that the Constitution does not permit any interference whatsoever by the federal government in the field of education." The second book argued for complete victory over immoral international communism and denounced the Democrats for not adequately supporting American military forces.[30] He was "Mr. Conservative."

The Goldwater campaign strategy throughout the year was to "go hunting where the ducks are." He publicly argued, "The Republicans do not have the Negro vote. It is our own fault. We lost it in the thirties. I think we will lose the vote in the big cities, and I don't think we can change it this year."[31] The East Coast, as far as Goldwater was concerned, "could be sliced off and set adrift."[32] Its social-welfare beliefs and softness on defense represented all that was destroying the moral fiber of the country. The eastern establishment was a special target of his ire as one after another of its leaders fell before his juggernaut. The South and the West were his base. His strong posture on defense, his economic conservatism, and his rugged individualism won him adherents across these states. His advocacy of states' rights and his explicit decision not to go after black votes won him special favor in the South. Despite Everett Dirksen's personal plea, "You just can't do it. You can't do it to yourself and you can't do it to the party," Goldwater voted against the 1964 Civil Rights Act.[33] Time and again Goldwater argued that states' rights demanded that civil rights could not be tampered with by the federal government. The white ducks in the South were his targets.

In San Francisco's Cow Palace that July, the Republican right wing controlled the GOP National Convention. They brooked no dissent as they flaunted their triumph. Liberals were booed when they mounted the convention podium. Catcalls echoed off the walls of the Cow Palace when some leaders argued the case for moderation. The convention hall reverberated with chants of "We want Barry. We want Barry," and he was theirs when South Carolina cast the votes that secured his nomination.[34] Goldwater swept 271 of the 278 votes cast by southern delegates. On the other hand, he won only 46 of the 294 votes in the states that extend from Maryland to Pennsylvania, up through New Jersey, New York, and New England.[35] For the second spot on the ticket, Goldwater chose William E. Miller, a nondescript national party chairman and conservative congressman from upstate New York.

On July 16 Barry Goldwater mounted the convention podium to a tumultuous roar. He was Galahad, and his acceptance speech reflected the purity of his vision. "Extremism in the defense of liberty is no vice," he declaimed. "Moderation in the pursuit of justice is no virtue."[36] As the nominee gave his address, a reporter turned to Theodore White and marveled, "My God he's going to run as Barry Goldwater."[37] "I'd rather be right than President," Goldwater commented time and again. And he was going to be right, if only by his own light; but he was not going to be president. He told his senior campaign staff, before he made his public announcement of candidacy, "I want you all to know from the start I believe it's a lost cause." But he continued, "There are a lot of people out there [who believe in our cause]. We can't let them down. Some day they are going to pick up where we left off." He closed by reminding his staff, "First let's take over the party, then we'll go from there."[38] His battle was for the future direction of the Republican party, not for the presidency. His candidacy drew thousands of young, ideologically committed activists into the ranks of the GOP, especially in the South.[39] Nothing at the GOP convention detracted from the message of pure conservatism; nothing at this convention detracted from Johnson's vision of a perfect fall campaign.

Goldwater's general election campaign was remarkable for its lack of political dissembling. In St. Petersburg, Florida, he told the elderly that social security needed a major change. In the heart of the Tennessee Valley he told an audience whose livelihood depended on the great government projects in the area, that it needed to be sold off. Time and again, fidelity to the truth, as he saw it, was more important to Goldwater than the reality of political campaigning. There would be no compromise—he conceded the middle ground and the liberals to Johnson. It was a campaign based on the argument that the major parties did not differ much over issues: they both had accepted the liberal welfare state. "A choice, not an echo," became a Goldwater theme, echoed by another theme, "In your heart, you know he is right." George Wallace, who repeatedly had stated, "There is not a dime's worth of difference between the two parties," now found a difference. Within days of Goldwater's nomination, the Alabama governor publicly withdrew from his effort to make a third-party run for the presidency and endorsed the states' rights Republican.[40]

The Goldwater nomination met with a chorus of excoriation from the mainstream white and black leadership. The moderate white leadership feared the GOP abandonment of the center. "With the nomination of Barry Goldwater for the Presidency of the United States," the *New York Times* editorialized, "the right wing of the Republican Party has won a great victory. . . . It has succeeded in naming as leader of the party and standard-bearer in the national election a man who is the very symbol of radical reaction."[41] The civil rights forces feared that if Goldwater became president the end of the Second Reconstruction could be at hand and much, if not all, of their recent gains would be lost. The black leadership, for the first time in the history of its major organizations, openly opposed a major party nominee. "It is both unfortunate and disastrous," Martin Luther King, Jr., told the press, "that the Republican Party has nominated Senator Barry Goldwater as its candidate for the Presidency of the United States. I have no alternative," he continued, "but to urge every Negro and white person of good will to vote against Mr. Goldwater and to withdraw support from any Republican candidate that does not disassociate himself from Senator Goldwater and his philosophy."[42] In this matter the black community was virtually unanimous.

Within days of Goldwater's nomination, black riots broke out—first in New York City's Harlem, and then in Bedford Stuyvesant after a black teenager was shot and killed by a white police officer. Black rioting then shook areas of Rochester, New York; Philadelphia; the Chicago suburb of Dixmoor; and several cities in New Jersey.[43] As the rioting spread and the demonstrations across the South continued, the White House grew more concerned about the specter of white backlash. There were some White House aides who were anxious about the election. Political advisor Henry Hall Wilson wrote to Lawrence O'Brien: "I suggest it is time someone said to the President what apparently no one has yet said to him— that he could lose this election."[44] The president was aware of the seriousness of the situation. He met at the White House with Barry Goldwater to discuss the riots and the fall campaign. Goldwater told LBJ it was wrong to play to people's racial fears, and he did what politicians rarely do: he gave up using a politically advantaged position because he believed it was wrong to use it. The two candidates did not mention this issue during the campaign.[45] But both the White House and the black leadership recognized that continued riots or demonstrations would provide aid and comfort to the Goldwater campaign.

The administration and most of the black leadership converged on a common strategy: demonstrations and riots had to be halted. Hobart Taylor, Jr., now a White House aide, wrote LBJ, "I am disturbed about the continued demonstrations and what I see on radio and television." He urged that black leaders be contacted and that the White House "make a major and organized effort to direct their thinking along a proper course. . . . Demonstrations and picketing can be avoided through personal contact and explanations of the seriousness of the problem."[46] The black leaders were already getting organized to deal with this concern. "It is of [the] highest importance," Roy Wilkins telegraphed the leaders of the major black organizations on July 22, that "we take counsel at [the] earliest moment . . . to ensure we do nothing to produce votes for Goldwater."[47]

Dwight Eisenhower, who never publicly spoke against Goldwater as the Republican standard-bearer, privately wrote to his brother, Milton, on July 27 that he did not understand "why some responsible persons don't call [the] leaders of [the] civil rights movement and tell them they are playing into Goldwater's hands."[48] In fact, immediately after he signed the Civil Rights Act, LBJ privately told the civil rights leaders this law made "demonstrations unnecessary and possibly even self-defeating."[49] The president repeatedly called the black leaders to let them know of his concern over the disorders and his belief that they would hurt the implementation of the Civil Rights Act and weaken his campaign against Goldwater.[50] In addition, Johnson had a lengthy telephone conversation with Wilkins on

July 27 and called him again on July 28, the day before the black leaders convened in response to Wilkins's telegram.[51]

James Farmer saw LBJ's hand behind the discussion that ensued at the meeting. The better part of the dialogue centered on bringing demonstrations to a close until the presidential campaign ended. But the foundation of James Farmer's organization, CORE, and John Lewis's organization, SNCC, was embedded in mass-action projects and demonstrations. Farmer and Lewis would not go along with this proposal.[52] CORE was committed to demonstrating in favor of the MFDP at the Democratic convention, and SNCC was bound up with the MFDP. Wilkins, Randolph, King, and Whitney Young, however, agreed to issue a statement urging that "the major energy of the civil rights forces should be used to encourage the Negro people, North and South, to register and to vote." They "call[ed] upon our members to voluntarily observe a broad curtailment, if not total moratorium, of all mass marches, mass picketing and mass demonstrations until after Election Day, November 3." The demonstrations had to be halted. "We see the whole climate of liberal democracy in the United States threatened."[53] Three days after the call for a moratorium, the New York Times headlined an article: "Campaign—Major Issues Are Coming into Focus, Civil Rights Held Major Factor."[54]

The Gallup Polls never showed Johnson's election to be threatened by Goldwater or the civil rights issue. To the contrary, they indicated strong public approval—57 percent to 21 percent outside of the South—for LBJ's civil rights policy, and a consistent 70 percent to 30 percent majority who would vote for the president over Goldwater. In the South, Goldwater was slightly favored over Johnson in the early summer, but by August even that support had withered.[55] Johnson was going into the Democratic National Convention with a totally free hand to control the party platform and to name his running mate. But the MFDP challenge loomed as a spoiler on the president's horizon.

On August 6 the MFDP held its state convention and selected delegates for the trip to Atlantic City. Johnson's thinking about the Freedom party challenge changed at that time. John Stewart, who became intimately involved in this conflict as one of Humphrey's closest aides, recalled that "Johnson of course had figured: 'For God's sake, how could all of these people come making all this trouble when I've been the President who got this historic bill through?' He saw it as ingratitude." When he realized they were coming to challenge the regular Democrats, LBJ understood that chaos could ensue and that the southern white delegates could leave the convention as their predecessors had done in 1948. Furthermore, Joe Rauh, one of the players who had instigated the liberal civil rights plank that caused the 1948 walkout, was the MFDP's attorney for this challenge. Stewart's recollection continues, "LBJ's old nemesis, Joe Rauh, was going to be leading the charge, and it was going to be on T.V., and it was going to be just awful. It was going to ruin LBJ's convention."[56]

In May of 1964 the MFDP established an office in Washington, D.C., and sent out representatives to line up support for the convention challenge.[57] Convention delegations in California, Colorado, Massachusetts, Michigan, Minnesota, New York, Oregon, Wisconsin, and Washington, D.C., passed resolutions of support for the MFDP.[58] By early June the Mississippi dissidents had lined up enough members of the convention Credentials Committee that they believed they could force a minority report to be brought to the convention floor. White House pressure to stop the challenge began to be applied, especially on Rauh. But the party forces were fighting a believer who felt he had little to lose and much to gain simply by taking on the mighty. Rauh fondly recalls, "Everyone says that [to continue this battle] took a lot of courage and principle, but I don't think anybody realized how much fun this was to really get into a real battle like this, to have troops and to have a real fight with all the power. You had the whole Democratic political machine, the President . . . and the whole labor movement trying to stop a few little Mississippi Negroes and me from making a little stink at the Democratic Convention."[59]

For Johnson, this was no "little stink." He had the FBI place an electronic surveillance on the MFDP's Atlantic City convention office, and the bureau kept him informed of the Freedom party's activities.[60] Johnson's convention was not going to be disrupted or possibly destroyed by this radical band if he could prevent it from occurring. On August 7 LBJ called in Governor Pat Brown of California and stormed at him over his delegation's support for the challenge. Brown returned to his state delegation and asked them to reconsider their position. Rauh released the story to the *Los Angeles Times*, and the governor retreated as public reaction backed the black challenge.[61]

At the end of the first week in August, Johnson ordered the national convention Credentials Committee chair, Governor David Lawrence of Pennsylvania, to get to work on a solution to the MFDP problem. Lawrence conferred with the national party chairman, John Bailey, who in turn contacted Harold Leventhal, the national party attorney; Jack Conway, the deputy director of the Office of Economic Opportunity; and Joe Rauh to set up a meeting of this group at Lawrence's office. Conway had been the executive director of the Industrial Union Department of the AFL-CIO when Walter Reuther was the president of the department. He and Reuther had gone to bat time and again for the civil rights movement, and they had arranged for the department to finance the Washington headquarters staff and office lease expenses of the LCCR. In his job at the Office of Economic Opportunity, Conway helped secure funding for the Freedom School project. Now Conway was to be one of the administration's point men during the MFDP battle.[62]

The preliminary plans for the convention's Credentials Committee to handle the MFDP challenge hearing were discussed at this meeting. Everyone agreed that the MFDP would be given committee hearing time. Conway, who had been associated with Rauh's causes in the past, made it clear that this time he was likely to part company with the MFDP counsel. Lawrence reiterated that the president wanted a solution to the problem that did not cause undue disturbance within the party. Rauh, in turn, made it clear to the other three leaders that the MFDP challenge was not just going to disappear. After this meeting Conway took a leave of absence from his government position to work on the MFDP conundrum at the convention.

On August 11 Lee White told Rauh that LBJ wanted to know what the MFDP was willing to settle for to resolve the dispute. Rauh told him that the MFDP would consider accepting the compromise seating of both Mississippi delegations. This appeared to be agreeable to the president's counsel. John Bailey and David Lawrence also agreed that this was a reasonable solution. After all, as Rauh noted in the appendix of his forthcoming remarks before the Credentials Committee, this was consistent with the resolution of most previous settlements of convention seating challenges, including the 1944 seating of both the Texas Regulars, the official state party–supported delegation opposed to FDR, and the Texas Loyalists, who supported FDR. Congressman Lyndon Johnson was a member of the upstart Texas Loyalist delegation.[63] But the Mississippi delegation was determined to leave the convention if an insurgent, black-dominated delegation was seated under their state banner, and LBJ feared the other southern states would also walk out if the MFDP delegates were seated under the Mississippi standard. On August 12 the president told Mississippi's Governor Johnson that his lily-white delegation was going to represent Mississippi at the convention.[64]

The president's men were scrambling. "There were so many Hatchet men," recalls Rauh, "that you had to stand with your back to the wall." On August 14 another presidential envoy spoke with Rauh, and another element was added to the quarrel. Walter Reuther, the president of the United Auto Workers and a longtime liberal ally who employed Rauh as the UAW's general counsel, told Rauh of LBJ's repeated threats to keep Humphrey off of the ticket if the challenge continued. Reuther warned Rauh, "The Hubert [Humphrey] vice-presidency rode on the settling of the Mississippi thing to the satisfaction of the President." Rauh recalls Reuther telling him, "I would have Hubert's blood on my hands, if I did not stop this thing." On the same day as Reuther spoke to the MFDP counsel, Hubert Humphrey met with Rauh; they agreed that the seating of both delegations made sense. Humphrey had not yet gotten the word from the president that this was unacceptable. The *New York Times* called for the seating of both delegations, with the state's vote to be split equally between them.[65] As the convention date approached, Humphrey was drawn deeply into this fight.

Humphrey was called to the White House. He already knew that he was high on Johnson's list of potential running mates and that background checks had been done on him. Almost all of the president's advisors favored Hubert Humphrey for the vice-presidential slot. After the president publicly removed Robert Kennedy from consideration as his running mate on July 29, Humphrey was the liberal choice for the position. He was the happy warrior of the liberal-labor alliance and a mainstay of the agricultural Democrats. On July 19, the day before Humphrey's appointment, Johnson met with a group of moderate black leaders, who told him the White House had to make concessions to the MFDP's challenge. Johnson lectured them on the need to stop the MFDP demonstrations and the need to abort the credentials fight.[66] They maintained their support for the MFDP challenge.[67] When Humphrey visited the White House the next day, LBJ told him that he had to go to the convention and find a solution to the MFDP problem that would keep his civil rights friends happy and not send the South bolting out of the party. His liberal friends had to stay with the president on this one, or the vice-presidency would go to someone else.[68]

The Johnson-Humphrey relationship went back to the early 1950s, and although the two men were sometimes at odds on the issues, they were also often allies both in the Senate and in the party. Humphrey had tied himself to the Johnson forces in a stop-Kennedy movement at the 1960 convention. And Johnson was instrumental in Humphrey's selection as the Democratic Senate whip in 1961.[69] "Lyndon Johnson had tremendous love and affection for Hubert Humphrey," recalls Harry McPherson. "He had immense admiration for his heart and for his brains. He had a rather low estimate of his judgment and felt . . . that he was not tough enough."[70] Now Johnson was going to see if Humphrey was "tough enough." John Stewart remembered his boss's words as he returned from the White House, "Now we've got this one to work out, too. They finally accept the fact that there's a problem, and the President has said I'm to work it out—so get going."[71] Humphrey later wrote, "Johnson was testing me one more time."[72] It was one of the toughest jobs Humphrey ever faced. His cause was civil rights. Now, in order to fulfill his ambitions he had to find a safe passage between the needs of his longtime comrades-in-arms and the demands of Lyndon Johnson.

On August 22 the Freedom party presented its case before a nationally broadcast session of the Credentials Committee. Rauh's remarks emphasized the publicly announced intention of the Mississippi regulars to support Goldwater in the fall election. He also spoke of the refusal of the Mississippi regulars to allow black Mississippians to participate in their party processes. Finally, he introduced the testimony of brutality and vote fraud that was to be presented that afternoon.[73] The nation sat transfixed as witnesses provided details of police cruelty and state repression.

The hearing reached a peak of intensity as Fannie Lou Hamer told of the ordeal she faced following her arrest for aiding voter-registration efforts. She was taken from her jail cell, and on the orders of a Mississippi state highway patrol officer a male prisoner hit her. "The first Negro began to beat and I was beat. . . . After the first Negro was exhausted the State Highway Patrolman ordered the second Negro to take the blackjack. The second Negro began to beat . . . I began to scream and one white man got up and began to hit me on the head and tell me to 'hush.'" Hamer's testimony continued. "All of this on account we want to register, to become first-class citizens, and if the Freedom Party is not seated now, I question America." Theodore White recalled, "As her fine mellow voice rose, it began to chant, with the grief and sobbing that are the source of all the blues in the world. The hot, muggy room was electrified."[74] The president called a televised news conference in the middle of Hamer's testimony, but the networks rebroadcast her tragic account of Mississippi justice before the evening news audience. Telegrams and telephone calls of support for the MFDP inundated Atlantic City and Washington. The morality play now had the spotlight, and the president's forces pressed to find a solution.

As the convention began on Monday morning, Humphrey met with the MFDP leadership and the leaders of the other major black organizations. While Humphrey discussed possible compromises, the Mississippi group did not alter its position. The liberal firebrand of the 1940s and 1950s could not bring the radicals of the 1960s to relent on their demand to be seated in the Mississippi delegation's seats. "The meeting was a total flop," recalls Rauh. "Everyone was disappointed. No one budged on their positions."[75]

Humphrey could not press hard enough, and as Jack Conway saw it, he never had a chance. He did not have the power to make a bargain. "That Hubert Humphrey meeting was a disaster," recalls Conway. "Everyone was mad. Hubert was sitting there talking, but he could not say anything. It was a vacuum. The whole objective was to get this challenge thing dealt with," recalls the union leader, "but there was no one to talk to. The thing that struck me was that there was no one representing Lyndon Johnson that you could talk to and say, 'Will you take this?' I needed someone who could communicate with the President." The president did not trust Humphrey to do the job even though he gave him the job. LBJ needed someone there whom he could trust.[76]

Word about Humphrey's meeting filtered back to the White House. LBJ called Walter Reuther, who was in the midst of contract negotiations with the president of General Motors. Johnson demanded that Reuther go to the convention and bring his civil rights friends into line. Reuther halted negotiations with General Motors and flew to Atlantic City that evening to help bring LBJ's convention back into order.[77]

The Reuther-Johnson relationship went back to the days when LBJ was a young congressman. President Franklin Roosevelt arranged a meeting between the two young men and suggested they stay in touch with one another. Although Johnson seldom went along with Reuther on labor issues, they did become friends. When Reuther had to go to Washington during World War II and the hotels were booked, he occasionally spent his nights on the Johnson family couch. Reuther repeatedly told his allies to stay in touch with the Texan despite their differences with him. "Roy Reuther and I used to tear our hair out because we could never get anything out of Johnson," recalls Conway. "Yet Walter stayed the course with him."[78] Now Johnson turned to this trusted, longtime associate and tough negotiator. He could bargain for LBJ and get back to him as the situation demanded.

Reuther, Rauh, and Humphrey were old political allies. They were among the founders of the Americans for Democratic Action after World War II. Reuther ensured that Humphrey's 1960 campaign debt was paid off. Reuther, often with Humphrey's and Rauh's advice, helped secure financing for many of the civil rights activities of the 1960s. The UAW leader went to the convention because Johnson demanded it and because he secured the president's assurance that Humphrey would get the nomination if the MFDP imbroglio was settled in accordance with Johnson's needs.[79] Now he was going to secure the movement's compliance with Johnson's wishes and help Humphrey achieve the vice-presidency.

Rauh stopped by Humphrey's headquarters that first evening of the convention, much as he would each evening the convention met, and he asked his friend how his vice-presidential campaign was coming. Humphrey told Rauh, "At this stage, honestly, I'm so tired of it, I honestly don't care too much anymore. I'm so tired of it all. I'm never at ease." Rauh responded, "Hubert, you got to give us some more. You got to give it some more if you don't want to get beat."[80] Humphrey never asked Rauh "for a single concession to help him win" the vice-presidency. He would not let his friendship serve this end.[81] But the Minnesota Warrior was dispirited.

That night and on into the next day, the president's forces, now joined by Reuther, continued their search for a solution. Early Tuesday morning Reuther, Humphrey, Conway, and Walter Mondale, a young political ally of Humphrey's, met to discuss strategy. The general idea, "to balance the unbalanceable," as Walter Mondale recalls, "grew out of discussions and debates and sort of evolved over the few days before the convention and into the beginning day or two of the convention." There were repeated telephone calls between the White House and its agents at the convention as the compromise proposal was worked out.[82]

There was no doubt about "the clear moral credibility and strength of the Freedom Democrats' charges. But," Mondale noted, "the Freedom Democrats were not a political party. They were a collection of people who came up to the convention to make this case. For symbolic purposes we chose to seat the two MFDP representatives." Seating only two MFDP delegates was one important element in the final administration proposal. Another important element was that the Mississippi state Democrats would pledge their support to the national Democratic ticket. A final critical part of the proposal was that future state party delegations to national conventions could not be chosen in a racially biased manner. The national Democratic party would establish a committee to ensure that this provision was carried out. This was central to Mondale's thinking, and it became the basis for a key provision in the compromise. "I really wanted to make certain that when these rules went into effect there would be energetic enforcement of them. I wanted to make sure the door would be held open for black delegates." The Minnesota liberal recalls, "These rules contemplated affirmative participation by minorities." As for the broader implications of the creation of a national party committee to set the standards for the selection of state delegates, Mondale recalls, "I don't think we spent much time on that."[83]

Jack Conway left the meeting before the specifics of the proposal were worked out, but his job was to line up the delegates for it. Loyalty to the administration and the reasonableness of the proposal would be his watchwords to the delegates. "We bowed to Lyndon Johnson's will. There had to be a compromise to him: that he have the southerners in the party, and yet the liberals had to be there, too." This was the key to the solution, as Conway remembers. "There was a lot of discussion about the importance of a loyalty oath, but there was no discussion about the ramifications of the agreement for the party. We had a job to do. There was a convention to get in order and a campaign to get under way. We just did what we had to do to get a solution for what was confronting us." Mondale worked out the details of the proposal, referred to afterward as the Mondale compromise, and Reuther secured the president's agreement.[84] Now it was time for Reuther and Humphrey to bring the civil rights groups into the fold. The problem of the moment was finessed.

On Tuesday afternoon the Credentials Committee was about to meet to consider a recommendation to be brought before it by the subcommittee dealing with the MFDP challenge. Rauh was waiting for the meeting to begin when a committee member, Congressman Charles Diggs of Michigan, approached him: "Joe, you are to call this [telephone] number. Walter Reuther." Lawrence, the Credentials Committee chair, agreed to hold off on beginning the meeting until Rauh and the president's man had spoken. Reuther told the MFDP counsel, "This is the decision: they are going to exclude the [white] Mississippi people unless they take an oath which they said they won't take. So they're going to be excluded. They're going to give you two delegates, so you've won that. They're going to give you a pledge they'll never seat lily-white delegates again. The party will set up a committee to insure that this promise is carried out." The UAW leader concluded, "This is a tremendous victory. And I want you to take this. The convention has made its decision."[85] Of course, the convention had not made any decision as yet; but Johnson, after consulting with Reuther, had made his decision, and this was his convention.

Although Rauh thought this was a great victory for the Freedom party, he could not accept the proposal on the spot. He had agreed with Aaron Henry, the MFDP chair and the NAACP state chair, that neither of them would make a decision without the consent of the other. In addition, Rauh knew the administration had made a terrible blunder by not allowing the MFDP to select its own floor representatives. The White House chose two MFDP members as delegates-at-large: Aaron Henry and the Reverend Edwin King. The Mississippians wanted to choose their own people for their own positions. The MFDP represented the dispossessed and the sharecroppers, like Fannie Lou Hamer, and they would not accept a middle-class pharmacist, Aaron Henry, and a white professor, Edwin King, to be their sole representatives. Rauh asked Reuther to have the committee hold up its meeting, "then I can come back and make the proposal to make it unanimous after Aaron Henry tells me he agrees with it." He needed time to talk with Henry and get a little more movement from the White House. As he walked the convention floor the previous evening, Rauh had realized the White House had gotten to some of his allies. Even Senator Paul Douglas of Illinois, a bulwark of liberalism, begged off when Rauh asked him to take to the floor on behalf of the challenge. "I'm tired, Joe," he responded, "and I have an election coming up. Let me pass on this one."[86] Rauh knew he had a weak hand at this point.

The White House would not give Rauh the time he needed. The Johnson people were not interested in giving him or the MFDP anything more. They had been reasonable, and they wanted to get away from the battling and on with the celebration. Rauh knew "they had given enough now so that from now on we looked like the greedy [ones]."[87] The moderates and liberals would support the administration offer. The White House allies prowled the halls to ensure acceptance of their proposal. Sixty-four of the sixty-eight Mississippi regulars left the convention that day rather than pledge support for the national ticket. The Alabama delegation also left. But all of the other southerners remained with LBJ's forces.[88]

The Credentials Committee convened and voted to recommend the Mondale amendment to the convention as part of its report. Rauh, a voting member of the committee as a Washington, D.C., delegate, and six others were opposed. On Tuesday afternoon, as the Credentials Committee met, Reuther and Humphrey spoke with the MFDP leaders and the mainstream black organization leaders. Aaron Henry was at this meeting, while Rauh was at the Credentials Committee meeting.[89] Humphrey was talking with Bob Moses when they heard that the Mondale amendment was accepted by the Credentials Committee. The MFDP leader was infuriated. He believed he was bargaining in good faith with the Johnson forces, and now he learned that the outcome of the bargaining had been decided elsewhere. Aaron Henry and Fannie Lou Hamer, the MFDP vice-chair, were also adamant as Humphrey tried to persuade them to go with the administration offer.[90]

Walter Reuther was more persuasive with the moderate black leaders who were not part of the MFDP. He argued with Martin Luther King, Jr., Roy Wilkins, and Bayard Rustin that they had to accept the administration proposal. "After all," the president's man said, "we helped you in the past, and if you want our help in the future you have got to help us out now." Financial support for the movement, he noted, was not as likely to be forthcoming from his liberal friends as it had in the past. They agreed to help him try to bring the MFDP leaders to accept the White House offer. They believed it was a reasonable compromise solution.[91] Reuther returned to Detroit soon after this meeting ended. His job was done. He knew the Mondale compromise would be broadly accepted and that Humphrey had the vice-presidential nomination.

The next day, August 26, Rauh, Martin Luther King, Jr., Bayard Rustin, and James Farmer met with the MFDP delegation; and all of them spoke in favor of the compromise. Both Rustin and Wilkins were asked by Humphrey to attend the meeting and help get the compromise accepted.[92] King said he believed it was a fair deal, but he would not tell the delegates how to vote. Rustin, in evident allusion to Reuther's words, urged the delegates to "think of our friends in organized labor, Walter Reuther and others, who have gone to bat for us. If we reject this compromise we would be saying to them that we didn't want their help."[93]

The Freedom delegates were angry. They were believers, not compromisers. James Forman told the Freedom delegates, "There may be a difference between protest and politics, but . . . we must try to bring morality into politics." As another MFDP member saw it, the outside supporters of the deal, including the counsel, Joseph Rauh, were dealt with by the MFDP leaders "as if they were the archenemies of the Freedom Democrats."[94] There never was any serious consideration by the MFDP leaders to take the deal.[95] Aaron Henry and Edwin King officially turned the deal down on behalf of the MFDP.[96] The challenge was over, and the seats in the Mississippi delegation area were removed from the convention floor after a brief MFDP sit-in.

On August 29 Aaron Henry wrote: "We went to this Convention armed with the greatest might one could have on his side—the might of truth! We presented the truth. . . . It took the personal hand of President Lyndon Johnson to keep this vote from our grasp." The MFDP chairman continued his argument: "It was not that the President was against us, however, he took the position that he would lose the states of [the South] . . . if the Convention voted to seat us, we of the Mississippi Democratic Freedom Party. Thus," he concluded, "the issue within the Administration was purely political. Our victory on moral and legal grounds was overwhelming."[97] He later remarked, "Lyndon made the typical white man's mistake. Not only did he say you've got two votes, which was too little, but he told us to whom the two votes would go."[98]

While a good number of the Freedom Democrats remained active in Democratic party politics after the convention, for others this marked the end of their faith in liberalism and institutional politics. The spiral of black nationalism and alienation moved upwards.[99] An increasingly cynical view of liberalism, politics, and LBJ set in among many of the younger black activists and their young white allies, as well as some of their more radical elders. Liberalism meant compromise, even of basic values and integrity. Liberals would not fight for principle when they could get a deal. Johnson chose to make sure he was president, rather than be right on the issue. Rauh, who but recently had been given access to the Johnson White House, now found the relationship with Johnson ended. "I really trace the end of it pretty much to the '64 Mississippi thing. After that it was never the same," he recalled. "It was really back to pushing for things from the outside."[100]

For most mainstream liberals, the avoidance of a floor fight with a reasonable compromise that gave their champion the vice-presidency was a victory.[101] On July 26 Johnson flew to the convention with Humphrey to display his running mate. The Democratic platform sang the praises of the liberal welfare state. Its opening sentences summarized the rest of the document's intent: "America is *One Nation, One People*. The welfare, security and survival of each of us reside in the common good—the sharing of responsibilities as well as benefits by all the people."[102] The Johnson-Humphrey ticket was acclaimed by the convention delegates. A great eulogy for John F. Kennedy on August 26 was followed by a grandiose birthday party for Lyndon Baines Johnson on August 27. On Labor Day, LBJ officially kicked off his election campaign in Detroit. At his side was Walter Reuther.

8

The Second Great Emancipator

THE 1964 GENERAL ELECTION campaign went according to LBJ's script. "From the beginning," White House aide Richard Goodwin recalls, "the only issue was not victory or defeat but the size of the inevitable triumph."[1] Johnson seized the middle ground, and the Democrats won an overwhelming victory for both the presidency and the Congress. LBJ commented on election eve, "It seems to me tonight . . . that I have spent my whole life getting ready for this moment."[2] Goldwater only carried the five Deep South states of Alabama, Georgia, Louisiana, Mississippi, and South Carolina and his home state of Arizona. Johnson carried 375 of the nation's 435 congressional districts. The Democrats gained two seats in the Senate, providing them with a 68 to 32 seat margin, and 37 seats in the House, providing them with a 295 to 140 seat margin. LBJ would not have to depend on the South in Congress the way his Democratic predecessors had. Journalist Richard Rovere concluded in his review of the 1964 election results: "Johnson's power base is far more secure than Roosevelt's ever was."[3] Roosevelt could have carried the nation without the South in the Democratic column, but as Harry Truman's surprise victory of 1948 reminded the Democrats, having the South in the fold made things a lot easier. What Johnson did have that Roosevelt and his successors often lacked, was a working, liberal majority in both houses of Congress.

LBJ recognized the importance of the gift that Goldwater gave him. "Johnson called me twice on election night," Larry O'Brien recalls, "elated by his electoral landslide and the huge new Democratic majorities in the House and Senate." LBJ told O'Brien, who served as the chief White House liaison to the Congress, "We can pass it all now."[4] Despite Johnson's great victory, the 1964 election held menacing tidings for the Democratic party.

The political alignment of a generation was altered. Johnson lost the southern popular vote to Goldwater—49 percent to 48.9 percent, and he lost a majority of the white vote in every former Confederate state except Texas.[5] Black voters, for the first time in history, actually provided the Democratic party candidate with the margin of victory in four southern states, Arkansas, Florida, Tennessee, and Virginia, and most likely a fifth state, North Carolina. But the white vote, especially in the rural South, was in revolt against the national Democratic party. Goldwater carried Mississippi with 87 percent of the popular vote; 69.5 percent in Alabama; 57 percent in South Carolina and in Louisiana; and 54 percent in Georgia. Across the South, counties carried by the Dixiecrats in 1948 were swept by the GOP in 1964.[6] Senator Strom Thurmond of South Carolina switched parties during the 1964 campaign and joined Texas's John Tower as the South's second Republican member of the United States Senate. On the House side, Alabama elected five new Republican members, and Georgia and Mississippi each elected their first GOP congressman in the twentieth century.

One more ominous result for the Democrats was tied to the congressional election results. Democratic congressmen John Bell Williams of Mississippi and Albert W. Watson of South Carolina had both openly endorsed Goldwater during the 1964 campaign. Both congressmen were reelected as Democrats, and a brief intraparty and interregional struggle ensued in the House Democratic caucus concerning the privileges and rights these individuals were entitled to as Democratic congressmen. Thomas "Tip" O'Neil wrote to his "Dear Friend" Martin Luther King, Jr.: "I am more than happy to inform you that in the Democratic Caucus held on Saturday, January 2nd, we were successful in our efforts to strip seniority from" both congressmen.[7] To many southern Democrats this was not a happy event. It was one more indication of the growing inhospitality of the

Democratic party to them and their region. The 1964 election reflected this southern upheaval.

Ineluctably the ties that had held the New Deal together were coming undone. In the fall of 1964 Larry O'Brien, Johnson's top political operative, took a six-week trip across the country to assess the state of both the Democratic party and the presidential campaign. One result of this trip was a memorandum drawn up for the president on the "Negro Vote in the South."[8] Evans and Novak, whose chronicle of LBJ is considered a standard in the field, wrote: "To the President . . . the O'Brien reports became The Word."[9] The report on the South, in particular, as Bill Moyers recalls, became "critical" to LBJ's political thinking.[10]

The O'Brien memorandum was prescient in its understanding of the changing political South; its prescription for the Democratic party's course of action in reaction to that change was radical and yet borne out by the course of events over the decades that followed. O'Brien believed that LBJ's victory in at least six of the southern states "hinges upon the percentage of Negro voters who go to the polls on Nov. 3. . . . In the South as well as in the rest of the country," he told Johnson, "you will get about 90 percent of their vote—*if they vote*." In almost a parody of understatement, O'Brien continued, "Dependence upon the Negro vote is a new experience for most regular Democratic leaders in the South. Before this year they never have encouraged the Negro to vote—or particularly wanted him to vote." O'Brien noted that there had been exceptions to this general rule, particularly in a few cities, but these were rare exceptions. The southern Democratic leadership had to catch up with changed realities. Black attitudes had already changed due to "Negro recognition of your role in the civil rights struggle, coupled with their fear of Goldwater." White southern Democratic leaders, having rarely worked with blacks, "are awkward in their attempts to establish the desired rapport" with them. "Negro leaders (and rank and file), on the other hand, distrust many Southern Democratic leaders. After being ignored and in some areas intimidated for years, Negroes are somewhat suspicious of joining in a love-fest with Southern white political leaders."

O'Brien pointed out to his chief that in eight states of the South, all except Arkansas, Texas, and Louisiana, the white Democratic leaders "have established no effective get-out-the-vote apparatus for Negro voters. In almost every case the comment was, 'the Negroes are taking care of themselves.'" But "approximately 625,000 new Negro voters have been registered in Southern states, bringing total Negro registration in the South to approximately 2.1 million," and this vote has to be gotten to the polls. The Democratic National Committee, O'Brien reported, "is distributing directly to Negro leaders in nine [southern] states a total of $69,800 for get-out-the-vote activities." The state Democratic organizations, out of necessity, were being bypassed.

Louis Martin, the publisher of the *Chicago Defender* and a member of the Democratic National Committee, was coordinating this effort. Martin was working with twelve different black organizations to get blacks to the polls. "The regular party organizations," O'Brien noted, "gave the National Committee little help in Negro voter registration drives, and Martin is apprehensive, with cause, about letting them in on . . . efforts to make sure the Negro vote gets to the polls." Yet Martin told O'Brien, these efforts "are better than they have ever been, and better than we ever thought they would be." Martin conveyed to O'Brien "one suggestion which I consider very important: If white Democratic leaders would assure Negroes that they really *want* them to vote . . . it would go a long way toward relieving some Negroes of deep-rooted fears about the possible consequences of voting in this election. Obviously we must see this is done by passing the word without fanfare to avoid further [white] backlash."

O'Brien believed that it was in the interest of the southern white leadership to help the blacks get to the polls. "Frankly, I think party leaders in the South are sophisticated enough to realize they need the Negro vote and want the Negro vote, but I am not sure they have adequately communicated this feeling to the Negro." The national party, was already taking steps to help the southern white leaders accomplish this task. "For example, contact has been made today with Governor Faubus and his people to send a task force into Arkansas to work quietly and cooperatively." Furthermore, "The DNC [Democratic National Committee] has assisted in creating Election Day organizations aimed specifically at the Negro vote in every major city in the South. Field representatives from the DNC are touring these cities now, putting together the nuts and bolts of the operation." O'Brien concluded his memorandum by telling LBJ, "If the Negro vote comes through as we anticipate, you can win every state in the South except Alabama and Mississippi."

When O'Brien returned to the White House from his campaign evaluation tour, he was struck by how seriously Johnson took his memorandum on the South. "It just hit him between the eyes," recalls O'Brien. "He thought it really targeted the political problems. It really projected the problems we faced in the future with party realignment. He had the South in '64. We knew that. But the future was what he was seeing." The president's scout continues, "It's almost like, to Johnson, I went out and found some key to some lock. To me it was a statement of fact. To him, O'Brien had put in some coherent form something that was absolutely pivotal to the Democrats and to him. To me, it was no surprise."[11] Johnson had been the operator on Capitol Hill. He was not a national political campaigner. His 1960 presidential bid had been tied to insiders and political alliances at the top, and it failed miserably. O'Brien gave Johnson his first intimate view of the changing American political landscape.[12] The 1964 election results conveyed to LBJ the reality of O'Brien's analysis.

The southern black vote was now critically important to the Democratic presidential election effort in the South. O'Brien suggested it was also important to at least some state and local southern Democratic campaigns. Increasingly, the white South was abandoning its ties to the Democratic alignment. National party leaders hoped that a coalition of southern blacks combined with a substantial remnant of southern whites could be put together to hold the South for the Democratic party.

A postelection analysis by the nonpartisan Southern Regional Council noted the "'lily-white' conversion of the party of Lincoln." The council also noted that Johnson only "failed to carry those states with less than 45 percent of [age] eligible Negroes registered."[13] Within the administration there ensued a flurry of memo writing concerning the political situation in the

South and the southern black voter. There was also a focus on the strategy to be pursued in order to bring southern Democrats into the Democratic presidential column.

On November 17, 1964, exactly two weeks after election day, Louis Martin proposed to John Bailey that a black voter–registration drive be undertaken by the party and by other groups in the five southern states carried by Goldwater. In this memorandum, entitled "Operation Dixie, 1964–1965," he also suggested that the Justice Department press voting suits more vigorously in the South and that legislation to aid black voting and registration should be considered.[14] The next day, Lee White advised the president that the nation needed time to absorb the 1964 Civil Rights Act, and no new voting legislation was needed.[15] Yet in June of 1964 the administration's Task Force on Civil Rights had expressed "doubt whether the pending [civil rights] bill provides the gains expected by Negroes in the area of voting. Strong moves to assure the speediest possible accession of Negroes to voting rolls, particularly in the South, are essential." The task force concluded, "This may require some form of direct federal intervention either administratively or legislatively."[16] White's focus and the task force focus was on civil rights, but others in the administration were paying attention to the party politics of the issue.

On November 27 Hobart Taylor, Jr., who had served as Johnson's chief staff appointee on JFK's Committee on Employment, suggested to LBJ that the Republicans would now move to the middle ground after the Goldwater debacle, and the Democrats would have to renew their efforts on behalf of blacks. Less emphasis had to be placed on civil rights issues, LBJ's black ally argued, "while placing more emphasis on Negro participation in the management of the party and Negro candidates for state and local office."[17] In December, Matthew A. Reese, Jr., director of operations for the Democratic National Committee, gave the White House a confidential report on registration and election law reform. The central theme of the report was that "it should be recognized that the first step toward getting out a big Democratic vote is to increase registration."[18] Black registration and participation were viewed as key elements in the future of the national Democratic party.

Outside of the White House, civil rights forces were shaping up to push for voting legislation almost before the ink was dry on the 1964 measure. Clarence Mitchell noted right after passage of the 1964 act, "It was immediately apparent that we had to do something in the area of voting."[19] While Title I of the 1964 act focused on voting rights, everyone agreed it did little to improve the dismal record of racially based voter discrimination in the South.[20] More than half of the southern black population remained disfranchised, and in the Deep South there were more than one hundred counties with less than 25 percent of the age-eligible black population registered to vote. In this region little had changed since the turn of the century.[21]

On November 4, the day after the presidential election was held, Martin Luther King, Jr., told a *New York Times* reporter, "We will probably have demonstrations in the very near future in Alabama and Mississippi based around the right to vote."[22] On December 18, upon his return from Sweden, where he had just received the Nobel Peace Prize, King talked to the president. Voting rights and demonstrations were topics on the agenda.[23]

King had already committed himself and the SCLC to a major voting campaign in Selma, Alabama, and the president was aware of King's plans. The Selma director of public safety, Wilson Baker, had obtained a copy of King's planning papers in October of 1964 and talked with Burke Marshall about the possibility of the administration pressuring King to call off the demonstrations while a new, more moderate Selma city administration came into power. Marshall told him this was impossible.[24] When King asked the president for voting legislation, Johnson responded, "I can't get a voting rights bill through in this next session of Congress." The president told the Nobel laureate he needed southern votes to get the Great Society program through Congress, and these votes would be lost if he pressed for voting rights legislation. LBJ assured King that he would support such a measure in the future.[25]

Johnson had not yet made up his mind about when to move forward with a voting rights bill, but voting rights legislation was actively discussed in the administration.[26] O'Brien, LBJ's top legislative liaison, recalls, "There was never any indication given to me by Johnson of any planned delay on voting rights.

It was coming right after the 1964 act, and the election pushed it further. He was hell-bent to get every piece of civil rights legislation he could get."[27] At the signing ceremony for the 1964 Civil Rights Act, after Acting Attorney General Katzenbach suggested to the president that the legislative agenda could now move to matters other than civil rights, Johnson responded, "Let's get a bill. Let's get a voting rights bill."[28] Jack Valenti, another close Johnson aide, remarked, "It was his judgement, I know that he spoke to me before he became President, that the key to all the Negroes' future free movement and power in the United States had to do with the vote."[29]

While LBJ may indeed have had altruistic motives, the Democratic party was also at issue. The 1964 election demonstrated the pivotal importance of southern blacks for the Democratic party, and Johnson was the party's chief steward. Lyndon Johnson believed, much as he had maintained in the struggle over the 1957 Civil Rights Act, that black voting was a significant key to black freedom; and he now argued fervently on the need for the black citizen to be free if the South and the nation were to make progress. Again, as in 1964, there was a convergence of political necessity and idealism for Lyndon Johnson.

On December 28 Acting Attorney General Katzenbach forwarded to the president a memorandum with three alternative "major legislative proposals" dealing with voting.[30] Two days later Lee White sent a memorandum to White House aide Bill Moyers stating the marching orders on voting legislation: "The President has indicated a desire to move forward early next year with a legislative proposal authorizing a Commission to appoint federal officers to serve as registrars for the purpose of registering individuals for federal elections."[31]

King pushed the White House further in this matter as he moved forward with his plans for a voting rights campaign in Selma, Alabama.[32] Selma represented a perfect target of opportunity for the black rights movement to maintain its momentum and add voting rights to the legislative record. Selma was located in Dallas County. Sheriff James G. Clark, Jr., was a model of southern bigotry, easily driven to violence when it came to black demonstrators. Dallas County's treatment of black voter applicants was a model for the reactionary Deep

South: many blacks applied but few were registered. Only 335 of Dallas County's 15,000 age-eligible blacks were registered to vote, while 70 percent of the county's age-eligible whites were registered. The local judiciary and courthouse crowd rounded out this exhibit of a Deep South county and its populace. Since 1961 the Justice Department had pursued voting cases in the county, but not one black was added to the voter rolls as the courts delayed and circumvented and frustrated the legal process.[33] For the South as a whole, Acting Attorney General Katzenbach pointed out to LBJ in early January 1965, while sixty-seven voting rights cases had been filed the previous year only sixteen had actually been brought to trial. Obstruction and delay was the southern judicial order of the day in these matters.[34]

The aim of the Selma campaign was to arouse the national conscience and to convince the federal government that it had a legislative responsibility to ensure the franchise for southern blacks.[35] Over 95 percent of the public believed that a "voting rights measure for Negroes" ought to be enacted.[36] Moving that support into executive and congressional action was the black strategic concern at hand. The president's staff began to draw up a voting proposal as the demonstrations and public outcry pushed the black voting issue to the head of the legislative line. Selma would be an opportunity seized by Johnson to move forward with black voting rights legislation and to add black Democrats to the voting rolls to offset southern white defections.

The franchise for southern blacks was going to be achieved without further delay if the civil rights forces had their way. On December 29 the *New York Times* ran a story on the planned January 2 opening of King's Selma campaign. And on January 2 at Brown Chapel in Selma, King told his followers that they were now beginning a "determined, organized, mobilized campaign to get the right to vote everywhere in Alabama." If Alabama did not respond to their efforts then, the SCLC leader noted, "We will seek to arouse the Federal government by marching by the thousands to the places of registration. We must be willing to go to jail by the thousands." Andrew Young, one of King's key aides, told a reporter, "We want to establish in the mind of the nation that a lot of people who want to register are prevented from doing so. We hope this will lead to a revision of the voter registration laws." Selma's blacks marched to the courthouse by the hundreds to line up and register to vote. They were then marched off to the county jail and charged with unlawful assembly, parading without a permit, disorderly conduct, and a variety of other counts.[37] Events in the nation and within the White House were again converging toward a flashpoint.

The president's State of the Union message addressed the voting rights issue. "I propose," he declared, "that we eliminate every remaining obstacle to the right to vote."[38] How this was to be accomplished was not stated by Johnson. But at a confidential background news conference for attribution only to White House officials, Bill Moyers told reporters the administration would "make proposals to deal with arbitrary restrictions to the exercise of the vote on the part of people who are eligible to vote. . . . The basic decision has been made by the President to do something about these particular areas and to make a recommendation to Congress in this session." A reporter followed up with a question as to the type of restrictions the president was talking about. Moyers answered, "Absurd literacy tests and unreasonable residential requirements. Those are the two most obvious ones." Another question followed, "Either one would require legislative action wouldn't they?" Moyers again answered directly, "Both of them require legislative action."[39]

The legislative allies of the movement had word by early January that the White House would "likely" propose "a bill authorizing the Presidential appointment of Federal registrars, in areas of the Deep South where voting discrimination is evident, to enroll Negro applicants."[40] The Civil Rights Commission had made such a recommendation back in 1959, and it had been given strong support by King and other black leaders.[41] Now it was finally being given consideration by the Justice Department drafters of the voting rights legislation. In addition, the administration was considering proposing a constitutional amendment to prohibit literacy tests.[42]

On January 28 King and 265 fellow marchers were arrested for violating a local ordinance restricting public parades. That afternoon 500 schoolchildren were arrested, and they joined the adults in jail. By February 3 more than 2,600 Selma residents were in jail because they marched to the courthouse to support the right to vote.[43] Telegrams and letters from major black and liberal leaders poured into the White House protesting the mass arrests and the police brutality.[44]

A letter dated February 1, which appeared as a large advertisement in the *New York Times* of February 5, was titled, "A Letter from MARTIN LUTHER KING from a Selma, Alabama Jail." "Why are we in Jail?" King asked rhetorically. "Have you ever been required to answer 100 questions on government, some abstruse even to a political science specialist, merely to vote? Have you ever stood in line with over a hundred others and after waiting an entire day seen less than ten given the qualifying test? THIS IS SELMA ALABAMA THERE ARE MORE NEGROES IN JAIL WITH ME THAN THERE ARE ON THE VOTING ROLLS." The black leader wanted the nation to know that it was more than voting that he was concerned about. He continued: "Merely to be a person in Selma is not easy. When reporters asked Sheriff Clark if a woman defendant was married, he replied, 'She's a nigger woman and she hasn't got a Miss or Mrs. in front of her name.' This is the U.S.A. in 1965," the Nobel laureate wrote. "We are in jail simply because we cannot tolerate these conditions for ourselves or our nation." This was King's public plea for moral, political, and financial support.

On February 2 King gave Andrew Young a set of written instructions on what needed to be done to move the cause forward while he remained in jail. The first three points involved making sure that the federal government got directly involved in the Selma situation. He wanted Young personally to contact the president to urge him to intervene. He also wanted former Florida governor LeRoy Collins, the head of the newly established Community Relations Service, to be contacted and brought into the situation and to "follow through on suggestion of having a congressional delegation to come in for personal investigation." He also wanted Young to be sure to keep up the daily activities and the marches and to bring in national celebrities to keep attention focused on the Selma project.[45]

King's moves brought a quick response from the executive and legislative branches. Immediately after Young informed Lee White of King's requests, White wrote the president that the jailed black leader wanted the White House to send an emissary to Selma to report on the problem; he wanted a statement supporting the right of Selma's blacks to register and vote; and he wanted federal legislative action to secure the vote for southern blacks.[46] The next day, February 4, Johnson told reporters, "I should like to say that all Americans should be indignant when one American is denied the right to vote. The loss of that right to a single citizen undermines the freedom of every citizen. The basic problem in Selma is the slow pace of voting registration for Negroes who are qualified to vote." The president concluded, "I hope that all Americans will join with me in expressing their concern over the loss of any American's right to vote. . . . I intend to see that right is secured for all our citizens."[47] Governor Collins would go to Selma later, but Johnson withheld this commitment for the moment. On February 6 presidential press secretary George Reedy announced that the president would make a "strong" voting rights recommendation to Congress in the future. The *New York Times* noted that this was the "first official confirmation of reports that President Johnson would definitely press" for voting legislation.[48] But the future date was left unspecified.

After being released from jail, on February 7 King publicly requested new federal voting legislation as he pointed out the weaknesses of earlier federal legislation in this area.[49] He also arranged to meet with Katzenbach and Johnson on February 9.[50] Although the president would still not make a firm commitment of when voting rights legislation would emerge from his administration, he reassured King of the direction the legislation would take and that it would be forthcoming in a reasonable time. As he left the White House, the minister publicly praised Johnson's "deep commitment to obtaining the right to vote for all Americans."[51]

In the Congress, House liberals were already planning their legislative floor strategy for new voting rights legislation when King's pleas moved them to public action.[52] On February 4, in response to a letter from King to House Judiciary Committee chairman Emanuel Celler and telegrams sent to other liberal congressmen, a group of fifteen congressmen announced their plans to visit Selma on February 5. After returning from their visit, five of the congressmen filed voting rights bills, as did New York's Republican John Lindsay.[53] Fourteen members of the congressional delegation that went to Selma telegraphed the president: "Local authorities [in Selma] will not act in good faith to protect the right of franchise. Further legislation is necessary to insure the right to vote. . . . A comprehensive set of proposals must be developed and enacted to eliminate once and for all racial restrictions on the right to vote."[54] Johnson told Katzenbach, "I want you to write the goddamndest, toughest voting rights bill that you can devise."[55] By mid February, the Justice Department had rejected the idea of trying to propose a constitutional amendment and was busily drafting a voting bill along the lines suggested by King.[56] A general sense of the administration position is reflected in the line of reasoning now taken by Attorney General Katzenbach: "We brought the voting [suits] case by case. It was just an impossible system of law enforcement. So this coupled with the voting demonstrations and Dr. King's march at Selma and all that great public pressure . . . really required a legislative solution."[57]

The federal government was moving on voting rights, but events in Mississippi kept prodding the political leadership to move faster. During the week of February 16–20, the United States Commission on Civil Rights held hearings on the denial of black voting rights in Jackson, Mississippi.[58] Cases of voter intimidation and the jailing of individuals on trivial charges after they attempted to register to vote captured the nation's attention. In the midst of the hearings on February 18, Jimmie Lee Jackson, a black youth, was mortally wounded by sheriff's deputies when he came to the aid of his mother, who was being beaten as she participated in a demonstration. The Jackson killing incited outrage among blacks; at the young man's funeral, King spoke of the "timidity of a federal government that is willing to spend millions of dollars a day to defend freedom in Vietnam, but cannot protect the rights of its citizens at home." The White House let it be known that "the Justice Department had barely completed the draft of the bill and that it would go to Congress in a few days."[59] Actually, the draft was not finished, but on March 1 O'Brien informed Johnson that the Justice Department would have one ready for "submission to the White House" later in the week.[60]

Johnson wanted his administration to move faster. He wanted a voting bill ready for congressional action before King's demonstration got out of hand and either created a backlash or made it appear that the administration was not moving fast enough to stay in control of events. "In early 1965," Assistant Attorney General Ramsey Clark recalled, "he was the one who was prodding us to get a voting rights act out, and he was angry that we had been unable to develop the formulas we needed."[61] On March 5 the Justice Department's draft of a voting bill was completed under the direction of Katzenbach, Marshall, and Ramsey Clark.[62] Clark's assistant, Harold Barefoot Sanders, explained, "The instructions, as I understood them from the White House . . . [were] just, 'get a bill up here that will work,' because what we had wasn't working." It was not working, Sanders continued, "because you had to litigate every lawsuit. What you had to have was something, a formula, which would by-pass the litigation, in effect, and put the presumption in favor of the voter. In other words, which would say that everybody can vote if he fulfills certain minimum requirements."[63]

The Justice Department bill contained an automatic triggering mechanism that suspended literacy tests and permitted voter registration by federal registrars if voter registration or voter turnout fell below 50 percent of the voting-age population in 1964.[64] This covered the states of Alabama, Georgia, Louisiana, Mississippi, South Carolina, Virginia, and sections of North Carolina. It was a tough Reconstruction measure.[65] These provisions, with revisions and compromises added along the legislative byways, remained substantially intact after congressional action. King visited the White House again on March 5 and argued the case to the president that a new bill needed to ban literacy tests and allow the appointment of federal registrars if black registration was at a low level in a given area. Johnson assured the black leader that legislation was on its way, but he did not reveal its content or the timing of his actions on the matter. King reported, "The President told me that Senator Dirksen had made a commitment to support a voting rights bill."[66]

Sunday, March 7, marked the turning point for the black voting rights struggle. Bloody Sunday, as it came to be called, riveted national attention on the excesses of Alabama law enforcement violence and the determination of southern blacks to obtain the vote. It brought the nation into active support for new, effective legislation. Despite a threat by Governor George Wallace to halt a proposed march from Selma to Montgomery, the state capital, to protest inequitable registration practices, six hundred marchers led by Hosea Williams of the SCLC and John Lewis of SNCC attempted to go forward with their plans.

They marched out of Selma and crossed onto the Edmund Pettus Bridge, where they halted before a phalanx of state troopers and sheriff's deputies on horseback. The marchers were told to go back. Hosea Williams asked, "May we have a word with the major?" Major John Cloud of the state police replied, "There is no word to be had." The exchange was repeated and followed by a moment of silence, and then "the troopers rushed forward . . . blurring into a flying wedge as they moved. The wedge moved with such force that it seemed almost to pass over the waiting column instead of through it." The *New York Times* report continued, "The first 10 or 20 Negroes were swept to the ground screaming, arms and legs flying. . . . The Negroes cried out as they crowded together for protection, and the whites [civilians] on the sidelines whooped and cheered." That evening the motion picture "Judgement at Nuremberg" was interrupted on national network programming by scenes of tear gas and nightsticks "flailing at the heads of marchers. The Negroes broke and ran. . . . Troopers and possemen, mounted and unmounted, went after them."[67] The violence and beatings by state troopers and local sheriff's deputies became a symbol of what was wrong in the South. Across the nation the anger of black and white citizens was palpable.

King quickly went to Selma for the next attempted march to Montgomery, and his pleas to white clergymen across the country to join him brought 450 clerical allies into the turmoil of the small Alabama enclave.[68] But he was caught in a political dilemma. Federal judge Frank M. Johnson ordered the march to be delayed until he could conduct a hearing and rule on the constitutionality of Governor Wallace's ban. In addition, President Johnson immediately issued a statement urging that the court order be obeyed. King had never violated a federal court order; but his followers, especially the more militant younger SNCC marchers, demanded that he confront the state police immediately. King understood that he could lose control of the Selma demonstrations if he did not take action, yet he needed the good will and the support of the president and the federal courts for the movement to keep these allies firmly on their side. Johnson provided his ally with a way out. He sent Governor Collins to Selma to get both sides to back down from the immediate confrontation. Collins quietly secured the agreement of King and the state police to allow the marchers to go up to the bridge for a symbolic confrontation and to turn around unmolested. At 5:00 A.M. on the day of the planned march, Katzenbach called King and urged him to obey the court order. King, despite misgivings, went along with Collins's proposal; and on March 9 the marchers went up to the bridge, prayed, and returned to Brown Chapel.[69] Judge Johnson did not approve plans for the march until March 17, and the march took place, with federal troops providing protection, on March 23.

But events beyond the control of the leaders moved matters before the march proceeded. On March 9 Reverend James J. Reeb, a Boston welfare worker who had come to Selma in response to King's plea, was assaulted while quietly walking with another civil rights supporter. He died on March 11. The president was in the middle of a discussion with sixty members of Congress in the East Room of the White House, a discussion in which he emphasized the need for voting legislation, when he was interrupted by a White House aide and told of Reeb's death. Johnson left the meeting and called the minister's wife and father.[70] Demonstrations and prayer vigils of support for the Selma demonstrators took place across the nation.

On March 12 Governor Wallace asked for an audience with the president, and on Saturday, March 13, he flew to Washington.[71] During this meeting, the president told the governor that if the state of Alabama could not or would not maintain law and order, he "would not hesitate one moment to send in federal troops."[72] Little was decided at this meeting; but when Johnson and Wallace went outside for a radio and television news conference in the Rose Garden, the president took charge. "Last Sunday," he noted, "a group of Negro Americans in Selma, Alabama, attempted peacefully to protest the denial of the most basic political right of all—the right to vote. They were attacked and brutally beaten." Johnson then launched a withering assault on Alabama law enforcement officials. The president closed by telling the nation that these events could not be repeated, and he promised that "this Monday, I will send to Congress a request for legislation."[73] A defeated Wallace had little to say.

On Sunday evening, March 14, Johnson met with the House and Senate leadership, and at the urging of Speaker John McCormack and Hubert Humphrey, he agreed to address a televised joint session of Congress to introduce the legislation.[74] Johnson's speech electrified the nation. He identified Selma with Lexington, Concord, and Appomattox and declared, "Our mission is at once the oldest and the most basic of this country: to right wrong, to do justice, to serve man." He orated, "In our time we have come to live with moments of great crisis. . . . But rarely in any time does an issue lay bare the secret heart of America itself . . . a challenge to the values, the purposes and the meaning of our nation. The issue of equal rights for American Negroes is such an issue."[75]

The president told the Congress and the nation, "The time for waiting is gone. Outside this chamber is the outraged conscience of a nation—the grave concerns of many nations—and the harsh judgement of history on our acts." In the next forty-eight hours he would send Congress legislation "striking down restrictions . . . which have been used to deny Negroes the right to vote. . . . establish a simple, uniform standard" for registration, "send federal officials empowered to Register Negroes wherever state officials refuse to register them . . . and ensure that properly registered individuals are not prohibited from voting." He closed his speech with a powerful cry: "Their cause must be our cause too. It is not just Negroes, but it is all of us, who must overcome the crippling legacy of bigotry and injustice. And we shall overcome." His last sentence came from the movement's anthem, repeatedly sung at gatherings and marches.

From the outset it was clear that the administration's voting rights bill would be enacted into law with little determined southern resistance in evidence.[76] The country had changed too much since the sit-ins and the freedom rides and the 1963 March on Washington. Black rights could no longer be pigeonholed in congressional committees or held hostage to the threat of a filibuster. The critical discussions on the White House bill were between Everett Dirksen and Mike Mansfield, and they reached agreement on its substance before it was sent to the Hill.[77] On March 17 the White House-Mansfield-Dirksen bill arrived in the Senate. Sixty-six senators cosponsored this voting rights proposal. The day after it arrived in the Senate, by a vote of sixty-seven to thirteen, the bill was sent to James Eastland's Judiciary Committee with instructions that it be reported back to the body by April 9.[78] On the day it was sent to the Judiciary Committee, Eastland told his Senate colleagues, "This bill would apply to only five states. It is sectional legislation. It is regional legislation."[79] He was quite right, but voting discrimination based on race was largely a sectional problem. The movement and its allies were now in control. The liberals squabbled among themselves about the best method to obtain southern black voting rights, but the legislation encountered no serious difficulties.

On May 21, after a desultory southern filibuster permitted by the Senate leadership out of deference to tradition more than anything else, the Senate voted cloture by a seventy to thirty vote; and on May 26 the upper chamber passed the bill by a seventy-seven to nineteen margin. Senators Albert Gore and Ross Bass of Tennessee and Ralph Yarborough of Texas joined the majority, while only southerners voted nay. Senator Richard Russell wrote an ally, "The self-styled 'liberals' are in such a majority now in the Senate that our small band of Southern constitutionalists can muster only about twenty votes. . . . I know of no action that I could take [for our cause] which would be helpful."[80] In the House on July 9, 221 Democrats and 112 Republicans cast their votes in favor of the voting rights proposal with minor amendments; 21 Republicans and 61 Democrats voted against passage. Thirty-six southerners, including three Republicans, voted for passage of the bill. By a vote of 328 to 74, on August 3 the House adopted the Conference

Committee compromise, which substantially ratified the administration bill. The next day the Senate accepted the conference compromise by a vote of 79 to 18, with Senator Smathers of Florida joining the other southern supporters of the measure.[81]

The day before Johnson signed the bill into law, Russell, wrote of his former protégé's current civil rights stance: "Our opinions are so completely at variance that we do not discuss what I regard as his extreme position on this issue."[82] On August 6 Lyndon Johnson conducted an elaborate ceremony as he signed the Voting Rights Act of 1965 in the Capitol Rotunda. At the signing ceremony, he called it "one of the most monumental laws in the entire history of American freedom."[83] This was one of the few times that the Texan's hyperbole was consistent with the event at hand.

Within days of the signing, federal voting registrars and observers were sent into the covered states. The results were astonishing. Johnson reported to the nation on August 25, "In the 19 days since I signed into law the Voting Rights Act of 1965 . . . a total of 27,385 Negroes in 13 counties in 3 Southern States have qualified to vote. And they represent nearly one-third of the potential applicants in all of those 13 counties."[84] Nearly a quarter of a million black voters were added to the voting roles of the covered states in the first five months of the act's existence.[85] Black voter registration in the covered states went from 26.8 percent of the age-eligible population immediately prior to passage of the act to 55.0 percent by the summer of 1966.[86] Of course, evasion and subterfuge were employed in various localities; but in sum, Martin Luther King, Jr., was right when he wrote to Lyndon Johnson during the summer of 1965: "I am convinced that you will go down in history as the president who issued the second and final Emancipation Proclamation."[87]

King and Johnson parted company over the next two years as the black leader increasingly attacked the president's Vietnam War policies. King also expanded his vision to include the social-economic deprivation of blacks and whites across the nation and the class biases of the nation. The liberal assumption, shared by almost all of the black leaders and their white allies, was that black economic equality and black social equality would quickly follow from black possession of the ballot. King recognized the deeper societal problems linked to race, class, and political power, and he undertook a new crusade on behalf of the underprivileged. He died in 1968 by an assassin's bullet while leading a march of sanitation workers who wanted fair wages and improved job conditions.

The black movement itself split apart as younger, more fervent, more antiwhite, and less institutionally oriented blacks demanded black power *now* while older, more establishment-oriented black leaders tried to assess where the movement should move next within the institutional establishment. The 1966 elections witnessed a Republican resurgence that included a net gain of forty-seven seats in the House, seven more seats than the Democrats won in 1964, and six seats in the Senate. Lurleen Wallace succeeded her husband as governor of Alabama, and California elected a new, right-wing Republican governor, Ronald Reagan. *Newsweek* entitled a preelection article "Politics: The White Backlash of 1966" and reported that for the first time since the early 1960s, whites now felt the administration was "pushing civil rights too fast." The white populace rapidly withdrew its support from the movement as violence and black riots swept across 128 cities over the next several years. Major areas of Detroit, St. Louis, Chicago, Los Angeles, Washington, and Miami were destroyed by fires and vandalism.[88]

The 1968 elections also bore witness to antiblack voting. After the 1968 presidential election was over, Kevin P. Phillips, a special assistant to Nixon campaign manager John N. Mitchell, wrote *The Emerging Republican Majority*, a book that set down the core Republican racial strategy for the decades to come. "Obviously," he maintained, "the GOP can build a winning [national] coalition without Negro votes. Indeed, Negro-Democratic mutual identification was a major source of Democratic loss [in 1968] . . . in many sections of the nation." White reaction to "Negro enfranchisement and integration . . . had to result in political realignment." The new Republican party would be built upon blue-collar and white-collar voters of growing towns and suburban centers in the South, the West, and the Midwest. This new majority would inevitably overwhelm the decaying central-city–based liberalism of the Northeast.[89] White resistance and resentment of black "preferences" engineered by the liberal Democrats were to be sources of new Republican voters in the years to come.

Despite the increasing white resistance to new civil rights measures, Johnson stayed the course with the more moderate elements of the civil rights movement and even succeeded in having a fair housing bill passed into law in 1968. When asked at one of his last presidential news conferences what he regarded as his "greatest accomplishment," Johnson answered succinctly, "the Voting Rights Act."[90] LBJ could not face reelection under the cloud wrought by his Vietnam War policies, but his civil rights policies remain a model of presidential achievement. Twenty years after Johnson left the presidency, his one-time foe Joseph Rauh wrote: "Without President Johnson's leadership and determination there would have been no Civil Rights Act of 1964, nor any Voting Rights Act of 1965, nor any Fair Housing Act of 1968. Lyndon Johnson was the greatest civil rights President in my lifetime."[91] Ambition for office and Democratic politics had moved Johnson where few believed he would go. He had evolved from an ordinary east-Texas politician into an extraordinary national leader.

Epilogue

Many forms of government have been tried, in this world
of sin and woe. No one pretends that democracy is perfect
or all-wise. Indeed, it has been said that democracy is the
worst form of government except all those other forms
that have been tried from time to time.

Winston Churchill

THE KENNEDY-JOHNSON YEARS mark the high point of
civil rights accomplishments in the post–World War II years.
At the movement's insistence the Second Reconstruction was
enacted into law, and civil rights battles since then have evolved
around the implementation and interpretation of these laws.[1]
John Kennedy provided presidential recognition of the moral
legitimacy of civil rights and moved, however reluctantly, to enact major civil rights legislation. Lyndon Johnson supported a
strengthened civil rights bill and boldly led the Congress and
the South to accept it. He used the convergence of his needs
and the movement's to produce the strongest voting rights law
ever enacted. This movement and these two presidents irrevocably altered the basis of the nation's political alignments. In
the process of changing the legal basis of the black civil rights,
the basis of domestic political alliances was also changed.

The 1964 presidential election was a critical turning point
for the GOP in the South.[2] In the face of repeated Democratic
presidential calls for federal intervention to undermine the
southern racial-caste system, Goldwater and the Republicans
who followed him spoke of states' rights and a limited federal
role. Passage of the Voting Rights Act reinforced southern
whites' departure from the party of their forebears.[3] Southern
whites have not cast a majority of their votes for a Democratic

presidential nominee since 1964. The GOP's lily-white southern base became a major component of the Republican surge
that has carried every presidential election since 1964, with the
exception of Jimmy Carter's post-Watergate victory of 1976.[4]
Not one southern state cast its electoral college votes for the
Democratic presidential nominee in 1968, 1972, 1984, or 1988.
In 1980, with native son Jimmy Carter on the ballot, Georgia
was the only southern state to go Democratic. Prior to 1960,
Republicans had not won a southern United States Senate seat
in the twentieth century. Since 1960 they have consistently won
Senate seats throughout Dixie. The GOP held 6 percent of the
South's congressional seats in 1960 and 32 percent in 1972.[5]
Goldwater went where the ducks were, and he brought home a
great catch for the GOP.

On the other side of the political upheaval, the enfranchisement of southern blacks gave rise to the election of black public
officials across the South. More blacks currently hold elective
state and local offices in Mississippi than in any other state in
the nation.[6] Since the 1970s, statewide black and white Democratic voting coalitions have become a powerful factor in southern politics.[7] In 1986, Mike Espy became the first black
congressman elected from Mississippi since the end of the First
Reconstruction, and John Lewis, the fiery SNCC youngster of
the 1960s, won the Atlanta congressional seat vacated by Andrew Young. William Jefferson (La.), Harold Ford (Tenn.) and
Craig Washington (Tex.) are also black Democrats currently
serving in the House. Virginia elected a black Democratic governor in 1988. In Georgia a black Democrat contested the runoff primary for governor in 1990, and in North Carolina a
black Democrat was nominated for a United States Senate seat
in the same year. Both were defeated. In North Carolina the
campaign took on an especially ugly tone; an explicit appeal to
white reaction and racism carried the day for the Republican
victor, Jesse Helms. The political alliances of the New Deal
were transformed by the civil rights events of the 1960s, which
in turn created the political alliances that followed.

Neither Kennedy nor Johnson came to the presidency as
a civil rights radical or transformer of the political system.
Quite the opposite could be inferred from their prepresidential

records. Kennedy was a moderate tied to a highly pragmatic, rational view of politics and public policy. Johnson was a moderate tied to majority building and compromises in Senate caucus politics. Each man, however, was moved by the dynamics of election, the occurrence of crises, and a shifting political landscape brought on by the civil rights movement.

John Kennedy and Lyndon Johnson were political schemers. They maneuvered, made promises, and again maneuvered as political necessity dictated. That is what politicians do in democracies where political ambition and political power are tied to office and office is tied to votes. The civil rights events to which Kennedy and Johnson reacted often resulted from risks taken and plans carried out by political idealists; it was the idealists who moved public opinion and political leaders.[8] Thus did the politics of democracy prevail. In their drive for power the politicians moved to where the votes were, and they moved where the idealists led them.

NOTES

Transcripts of interviews conducted by the author are in his possession.

ABBREVIATIONS USED IN NOTES

ADA	Files of the Americans for Democratic Action
AUL	Atlanta University Library
BUL	Boston University Library
DDEL	Dwight D. Eisenhower Library
DSG	Files of the Democratic Study Group
JFK	Papers of John F. Kennedy
JFKL	John F. Kennedy Library
LBJ	Papers of Lyndon B. Johnson
LBJL	Lyndon B. Johnson Library
LC	Library of Congress
MCA	Microfilm Corporation of America
MHS	Minnesota Historical Society
MLK	Papers of Martin Luther King, Jr.
MLKC	Martin Luther King, Jr., Center for Social Change
MSL	Moorland-Spingarn Research Center, Howard University Library
NUL	National Urban League
PPP:DDE	Public Papers of the Presidents: Dwight D. Eisenhower
PPP:JFK	Public Papers of the Presidents: John F. Kennedy
PPP:LBJ	Public Papers of the Presidents: Lyndon B. Johnson
PUL	Princeton University Library
RBRL	Richard B. Russell Library
TCS	Theodore C. Sorenson Papers
WHCF	White House Central File

PROLOGUE

1. Downs, *Economic Theory of Democracy*, 28, 34–35.

2. Jack Walker, "A Critique of the Elitist Theory of Democracy," *American Political Science Review* 60 (1966): 292; Kingdon, *Agendas*, 3–4.

3. Kingdon, *Agendas*, 207; Polsby, *Political Innovation in America*, 165–174.

4. Schattschneider, *Semi-Sovereign People*, 71.

5. The Second Reconstruction is the term employed in Woodward, *Strange Career of Jim Crow*, 8.

6. Myrdal, *American Dilemma*.

7. Key, *Southern Politics*.

8. McAdam, *Political Process*, 77–82.

9. Friedel, *FDR and the South*; Sitkoff, *New Deal for Blacks;* Blum, *Progressive Presidents*, 132–136; Weiss, *Farewell to the Party of Lincoln*.

10. Clark Clifford, interview with author, 7 March 1989. See also Sitkoff, "Harry Truman," 597–616; Bernstein, "Ambiguous Legacy."

11. W. C. Berman, *Politics of Civil Rights*, 79–135, esp. 112; Robert Bendiner, "The Route of the Bourbons," *Nation* 167 (24 July 1948): 91–93.

12. Morris, *Origins of the Civil Rights Movement*.

I PURSUING THE PRESIDENCY

1. John F. Kennedy to Roy Wilkins, 6 May 1958, NAACP 3, B-204, LC.

2. Roy Wilkins to John F. Kennedy, 29 May 1958, NAACP 3, B-204, LC.

3. John F. Kennedy to Roy Wilkins, 6 June 1958, NAACP 3, B-204, LC.

4. See, for example, the following exchange of letters: M. R. Goldman to John F. Kennedy, 30 June 1959; John F. Kennedy to M.R. Goldman, 14 July 1959, NAACP 3, B-204, LC.

5. John F. Kennedy to Roy Wilkins, 18 July 1958, NAACP 3, B-204, LC.

6. See Kearns Goodwin, *The Fitzgeralds and the Kennedys*; and R. J. Whalen, *Founding Father*.

7. Sorenson, *Kennedy*, 15–16.

8. Richard Cushing, oral history interview by Carl Solberg, 11 March 1969, Solberg Papers, Box 16, 30.E.12.4F, MHS.

9. On Joseph Kennedy's involvement in John Kennedy's Senate elections see Collier and Horowitz, *The Kennedys*, 148 ff.

10. Quoted in Burns, *John Kennedy*, 155.

11. Quoted in Leuchtenburg, *Shadow of FDR*, 76. See also Irwin Ross, *New York Post*, 30, 31 July, 1 August 1956.

12. Quoted in Leuchtenburg, *Shadow of FDR*, 77.

13. Burns, *John Kennedy*, 53; Roosevelt, *On My Own*, 163–164; Steinberg, *Mrs. R.*, 343.

14. Sorenson, *Kennedy*, 51–55; Schlesinger, *Thousand Days*, 20–21; Schlesinger, *Robert Kennedy*, 106–115.

15. Irwin Ross, *New York Post*, 30 July 1956; Hamby, *Liberalism and Its Challengers*, 192–193; Martin and Plant, *Front Runner, Dark Horse*, 202.

16. D. C. Lord, *John F. Kennedy*, 44–46; Sorenson, *Kennedy*, 48–78; Burner and West, *The Torch Is Passed*, 76–77; Hamby, *Liberalism and Its Challengers*, 189.

17. W. O. Douglas, *Court Years*, 302.

18. David S. Broder, *Washington Post*, 10 April 1960.

19. Sorenson, *Kennedy*, 529.

20. Key, *Southern Politics;* Schattschneider, *Semi-Sovereign People.*.

21. Kennedy, *Profiles in Courage*, 152–153.

22. Quoted in Woffard, *Kennedys and Kings*, 31.

23. O'Neill and Novak, *Man of the House*, 82, 90.

24. Wofford, *Kennedys and Kings*, 21; Brauer, *Second Reconstruction*, 19.

25. "Mississippi," 11 October 1957, JFK, Pre-Presidential Papers, Box 26, JFKL; John F. Kennedy to Joseph P. Kennedy, 29 June 1956, TCS, Box 9, JFKL.

26. Lee White, oral history interview by Joe B. Frantz, 28 September 1970, LBJL, 1–2. The Johnson quotation is from Goodwin, *Remembering America*, 790.

27. Quoted in O'Donnell, Powers, and McCarthy, *Johnny We Hardly Knew Ye*, 146.

28. Adlai Stevenson to John F. Kennedy, 26 August 1956, JFK, Selected Pre-Election Name Files, Box 434, JFKL.

29. Marvin Griffin to John F. Kennedy, 18 October 1956, JFK, Presidential Office Files, Special Events, Box 1, JFKL.

30. Brauer, *Second Reconstruction*, 20.

31. "Speeches, 1956," TCS, Box 16, JFKL.

32. Land, "Kennedy's Southern Strategy," 41–63.

33. There are many accounts of the legislative battle over the 1957 Civil Rights Act. The most insightful may be found in J. W. Anderson, *Eisenhower, Brownell, and the Congress;* Evans and Novak, *Exercise of Power*, 119–140; and Lawson, *Black Ballots*, 140–202.

34. Herbert Tucker to John F. Kennedy, 21 June 1957; Ruth Batson to John F. Kennedy, 24 June 1957; John F. Kennedy to Herbert Tucker, 24 June 1957; John F. Kennedy to Ruth Batson, 29 June 1957, JFK, Pre-Presidential Papers, Box 458, JFKL.

35. John F. Kennedy to Ruth Batson, 1 August 1957; John F. Kennedy to J. P. Coleman, 1 August 1957; John F. Kennedy to Luther Hodges, 1 August 1957; John F. Kennedy to Marvin Griffin, 1 August 1957, JFK, Pre-Presidential Papers, Box 458, JFKL.

36. "The South's Choice after Johnson," n.d., TCS, Box 22, JFKL.

37. Burns, *John Kennedy*, 250. See also Wicker, *JFK and LBJ*, 18–19.

38. Roy Wilkins to Peter Arlos, 16 May 1958, NAACP 3, B-204, LC.

39. Roy Wilkins to John F. Kennedy, 29 May 1958, NAACP 3, B-204, LC.

40. John F. Kennedy to Roy Wilkins, 6 June 1958, NAACP 3, B-204, LC.

41. M. R. Goldman to John F. Kennedy, 30 June 1959; John F. Kennedy to M. R. Goldman, 14 July 1959, NAACP 3, B-204, LC.

42. Joseph L. Rauh, Jr., interview with author, 30 August 1988; John F. Kennedy to Roy Wilkins, 18 July 1958, NAACP 3, B-204, LC.

43. Ambrose, *Nixon*, 434–436, Martin Luther King, Jr., to Richard M. Nixon, 30 August 1957, quoted in Ambrose, *Nixon*, 434.

44. Martin Luther King, Jr., to Earl Mazo, 2 September 1958, MLK, Box 28, BUL.

45. Phillip Snowden to John F. Kennedy, 21 July 1958, JFK, Pre- Presidential Papers, Box 47, JFKL; John F. Kennedy to Philip David Fine, 14 August 1958, TCS, Box 9, JFKL; John F. Kennedy to Lewis Weinstein, 14 August 1958, TCS, Box 9, JFKL; memorandum, n.d., attached to letter from W. Montague Cobb to John F. Kennedy, 14 September 1958, TCS, Box 13, JFKL.

46. Herbert Tucker to Roy Wilkins, 2 October 1958; Roy Wilkins to Herbert Tucker, 16 October 1958, NAACP 3, B-204, LC.

47. Wilkins and Mathews, *Standing Fast*, 274.

48. Roy Wilkins to John F. Kennedy, 9 December 1958, TCS, Box 9, JFKL.

49. Harry Ashmore to John A. Blatnik, 31 December 1958, Stevenson Papers, Box 761, PUL.

50. Ed E. Reid to Theodore Sorenson, 22 November 1958, TCS, Box 21, JFKL.

51. Theodore Sorenson, "Agenda for Discussion with Senators," 8 September 1959, TCS, Box 21, JFKL; "Prospects for 1960," n.d., TCS, Box 22, JFKL.

52. Brauer, *Second Reconstruction*, 27.

53. Harris Wofford, oral history interview by Larry Hackman, 29 November 1965, JFKL, 7.

54. Wofford, *Kennedys and Kings*, 37–38.

55. Harris Wofford, oral history interview by Larry Hackman, 29 November 1965, Box 7, JFKL, 7–8.

56. Wofford, *Kennedys and Kings*, 47.

57. Harris Wofford to Martin Luther King, Jr., 13 May 1960, MLK, Box 30, BUL.

58. On the legislative struggle over the 1960 Civil Rights Act, see: D. M. Berman, *A Bill Becomes a Law*.

59. T. H. White, *Making of the President, 1960*.

60. Arthur Schlesinger, Jr., to Adlai Stevenson, 8 June 1960, Stevenson Papers, Box 398, PUL. On Stevenson's refusal to enter the presidential contest, see *New York Times*, 14 June 1959. On the liberal rejection of Johnson see, for example, Violet M. Gunther, "To Record," 6 April 1960, ADA, ser. 6, no. 96, MCA.

61. *New York Times*, 6 May, 4 June 1959.

62. Solberg, *Humphrey: A Biography;* Sundquist, *Dynamics of the Party System,* 250–52.

63. Transcript of "Interview between Drew Pearson, Jack Anderson, and Hubert Humphrey," 12 April 1960, Box 64, 42.C.5.10F, Humphrey Papers, MHS. See also Solberg, *Humphrey: A Biography,* 213.

64. John Kennedy quoted in Joseph L. Rauh, Jr., oral history interview by Paige Mulhollan, 30 July 1969, 2:2, LBJL; Rauh quoted in Rauh, interview with author, 20 February 1988, 1. See also Rauh, oral history interview by Carl Solberg, 12 November 1980, Box 16, 30.11.10E, Solberg Papers, MHS, 5.

65. Arthur Schlesinger, Jr., to Adlai Stevenson, 16 June 1960, Stevenson Papers, Box 798, PUL.

66. James M. Burns, Henry Steele Commanger, Jr., Kenneth Galbraith, Hon. Edith Green, Arthur S. Goldberg, Gilbert A. Harrison, Hon. Phileo Nash, Allen Nevins, William T. Patrick, Jr., Joseph L. Rauh, Jr., John L. Saltonstall, Jr., Massachusetts State Senator Roger Tuby, and Hon. John D. Voelker, "An Important Message of Interest to All Liberals," 17 June 1960, ADA, ser. 6, no. 94, MCA.

67. Garrow, *Bearing the Cross,* 138–139.

68. John F. Kennedy to Martin Luther King, Jr., 10 November 1959, MLK, Box 90, BUL.

69. Martin Luther King, Jr., to Chester Bowles, 24 June 1960, MLK, Box 3, BUL.

70. Harris Wofford, oral history interview by Larry Hackman, 29 November 1965, JFKL, 1–33.

71. *New York Times,* 24, 25 June 1960.

72. T. H. White, *Making of the President, 1960,* 397. See also Schlesinger, *Thousand Days,* 847.

73. Paul Butler quoted in Wilkins and Mathews, *Standing Fast,* 275–276.

74. Wofford, *Kennedys and Kings,* 51–52. Joseph Rauh, oral history interview by Paige Mulhollan, 30 July 1969, 2–16, LBJL; Rauh, interview by author, 30 August 1988, 2.

75. D. B. Johnson, *National Party Platforms,* 599.

76. Leuchtenburg, *Shadow of FDR,* 88–89. The roll-call vote, by state, may be found in: Runyon, Verdini, and Runyon, *Source Book,* 81–83.

77. Joseph L. Rauh, oral history interview by Paige Mulhollan, 30 July 1969, 2:18, LBJL.

78. Kenneth P. O'Donnell, oral history interview by Larry H. Hackman, 23 July 1969, 1:11, JFKL.

79. Theodore Sorenson to John F. Kennedy, 29 June 1960, TCS, Box 21, JFKL. See also Sorenson, "Values of John F. Kennedy," 8.

80. Bowles, *Promises to Keep,* 297, J. Lindsey Almond, oral history interview by Larry H. Hackman, 7 February 1968, JFKL, 2–3.

81. T. H. White, *Making of the President, 1960,* 199.

82. Schlesinger, *Thousand Days,* 47–48; Sorenson, *Kennedy,* 184–187.

83. George E. Reedy, interview with author, 27 October 1990, 3.

84. The conversation between O'Neill and Rayburn is from O'Neill and Novak, *Man of the House*, 93–95; the conversation between O'Neill and Boggs is from Hardeman and Bacon, *Rayburn: A Biography*, 78.

85. Schlesinger, *Thousand Days*, 50–61; T. H. White, *Making of the President, 1960*, 199–204, O'Donnell, Powers, and McCarthy, *Johnny We Hardly Knew Ye*, 222–227, Kenneth P. O'Donnell, oral history interview by Larry H. Hackman, 23 July 1969, 2:10, JFKL; Ernest F. Hollings, interview with author, 8 March 1989, 1; O'Brien, interview by author, 19 July 1989, 7.

86. Clarence Mitchell, oral history interview by Thomas H. Baker, 30 April 1969, 1:20, LBJL.

87. James Farmer, oral history interview by Thomas H. Baker, 30 October 1969, LBJL, 2.

88. Wilkins and Mathews, *Standing Fast*, 276.

89. Woodcock quoted in Miller, *Lyndon, An Oral Biography*, 258.

90. O'Donnell, Powers and McCarthy, *Johnny We Hardly Knew Ye*, 227.

91. T. H. White, *Making of the President, 1960*, 205–207; Nixon, *Six Crises*, 313–318; D. B. Johnson, *National Party Platforms*, 618–620.

92. *New York Times*, 28 July 1960.

93. NAACP, "Statement on Congressional Civil Rights Record of Presidential and Vice-Presidential Candidates," August 1960, LBJ, United States Senate, 1949–1961, Box 6, LBJL.

94. ADA, ser. 6, no. 48, MCA.

95. Roy Wilkins to Carter Wilson, 8 September 1960, NAACP 3, B-399, LC.

96. Wofford, *Kennedys and Kings*, 58.

97. Press release, "Statement of John F. Kennedy," 26 August 1960, NAACP 3, B-399, LC.

98. Arthur M. Schlesinger, Jr., to John F. Kennedy, 26, 30 August 1960, Stevenson Papers, Box 798, PUL.

99. Senate Committee on Commerce, *Report: Speeches, Remarks, Press Conferences and Statements of Senator John F. Kennedy* 87th Cong., 1st sess., 1961, 69. See also press release, "From the Offices of Senator Joseph F. Clark (D. Pa.) and Representative Emanuel Celler (D. N.Y.)," 16 September 1960, Celler Papers, Box 272, LC.

100. Garrow, *Bearing the Cross*, 142; Harris Wofford, oral history interview by Larry Hackman, 29 November 1965, JFKL, 14; Wofford, interview with author, 20 February 1988, 1.

101. Martin Luther King, Jr., oral history interview by Berl Bernhard, 9 March 1964, JFKL, 4–5.

102. Wofford, *Kennedys and Kings*, 11; Martin Luther King, Jr., oral history interview by Berl Bernhard, 9 March 1964, JFKL, 10.

103. The Shriver-Kennedy interchange and the Shriver-Wofford discussion are from Wofford, *Kennedys and Kings*, 18; and Harris Wofford, interview with author, 20 February 1988, 1–2. Shriver is also quoted on this episode in Parmet, *Presidency of John Fitzgerald Kennedy*, 55.

104. C. King, *My Life With Martin Luther King, Jr.*, 196.

105. L. Martin, "Organizing Civil Rights," 94.

106. Differing accounts of this episode appear in, Wofford, *Kennedys and Kings*, 14–22. Harris Wofford, oral history interview by Larry Hackman, 29 November 1965, JFKL, 16; Robert F. Kennedy and Burke Marshall, joint oral history interview by Anthony Lewis, 4 December 1964, JFKL, 513. Hereafter, Robert Kennedy and Burke Marshall are noted separately in references made to this oral history. An edited text of this oral history may be found in E.O. Guthman and J. Shulman, eds., *Robert Kennedy: In His Own Words* (New York: Bantam, 1988), 66–230.

107. Siegenthaler, "Civil Rights in the Trenches," 105; Harris Wofford, interview with author, 20 February 1988, 2.

108. Robert Kennedy, oral history interview by Anthony Lewis, 4 December 1964, JFKL, 413–414. Louis Martin, oral history interview by Robert Wright, 25 March 1970, MSL; Siegenthaler, "Civil Rights in the Trenches," 105.

109. T. H. White, *Making of the President, 1960*, 323.

110. Lodge quoted in Nixon, *Six Crises*, 377. See also Matusow, *Unravelling of America*, 24.

111. *New York Times*, 27 October 1960; Nixon, *Six Crises*, 390–391; E. Frederick Morrow, oral history interview by Thomas E. Soapes, 23 February 1977, DDEL, 8. The statement proposed on behalf of Nixon may be found in "Suggested Statement Dictated by Judge Lawrence E. Walsh," 31 October 1960, Official File, 142-A-4, DDEL. See also Nixon, *Six Crises*, 362–363.

112. Martin Luther King, Jr., news release, 1 November 1960, MLK, 4, Box 33, Folder 29, BUL.

113. The Robert Kennedy quote is from Robert Kennedy, oral history interview by Anthony Lewis, 4 December 1964, JFKL, 517. All other quoted material in this section is from Harris Wofford, interview with author, 20 February 1988, 2. On this incident see also Wofford, *Kennedys and Kings*, 24. The press, as well as most everybody else, originally underestimated the impact of the Kennedy telephone calls. Anthony Lewis points out that the Washington bureau of the *New York Times* originally filed "a substantial" story on the Kennedy call to Dr. King, but this was cut to three paragraphs when published (*Portrait of a Decade*, 31).

114. Eleanor Roosevelt is quoted in Arthur Schlesinger, Jr., to John F. Kennedy, 14 November 1960, JFK, President's Office Files, Box 165, JFKL.

115. Martin Luther King, Jr., oral history interview by Berl Bernhard, 9 March 1964, JFKL, 12–13.

116. Cosman, "Presidential Republicanism in the South," 303–322.

117. *New York Times*, 27 November 1960; *Crisis* 68 (1961): 5–14; Sigel, "Race and Religion," 446; Ladd and Hadley, *Transformation*, 112.

118. Converse, "Major Political Realignment in the South," 234, 240; Carmines and Stimson, "Structure and Sequence of Issue Evolution," 901–920.

2 AN INTIMIDATED PRESIDENT

1. James MacGregor Burns, oral history interview by William H. Brubeck, 14 May 1965, JFKL, 71.

2. Harris Wofford, oral history interview by Larry Hackman, 29 November 1965, JFKL, 32.

3. PPP:JFK, 1961, 157.

4. O'Brien, *No Final Victories*, 112.

5. Bolling, *House Out of Order*, 210–220.

6. Wilkins and Mathews, *Standing Fast*, 296.

7. Discussion of this struggle may be found in Hardeman and Bacon, *Rayburn: A Biography*, 447–465; and O'Neill and Novak, *Man of the House*, 165–167.

8. Hardeman and Bacon, *Rayburn: A Biography*, 449–450.

9. Quoted in Hardeman and Bacon, *Rayburn: A Biography*, 451.

10. The 4 February 1961 Rayburn conversation with Hardeman is found in Hardeman and Bacon, *Rayburn: A Biography*, 452.

11. John Kennedy quoted in Sorenson, *Kennedy*, 382. See also Robert F. Kennedy, oral history interview by John Bartlow Martin, 29 February 1964, JFKL, 44. In the Martin interview, Robert Kennedy states: "The President always pointed to that [Rules Committee fight] later on. When people were wondering why he had to go slow . . . to deal with Congress—it was said here we had Sam Rayburn, therefore the Texas delegation. We had the maximum strength—the Democrats—and yet you [*sic*] only won it by a couple of votes." Another indication of southern power in the Congress is that, when JFK became president, southerners chaired ten of the twenty standing House committees and nine of the sixteen standing Senate committees. Sixty-two of the ninety-eight southern House members voted against the administration on the vote to expand the Rules Committee. See also Herbert Edelsberg and David A. Brody, "Civil Rights in the 87th Congress, First Session," mimeo, Washington, D.C., Anti-Defamation League of B'nai B'rith, n.d., ADA, Legislative File, ser. 5, no. 47, MCA; O'Brien, *No Final Victories*, 105–106; Wicker, *JFK and LBJ*, 73.

12. Roy Wilkins, oral history interview by Berl Bernhard, 13 August 1964, JFKL, 34.

13. Harris Wofford, "Memo to President-Elect John Kennedy on Civil Rights-1961," 30 December 1960, Robert Kennedy Papers, Box 21, JFKL; Fleming, "Federal Executive and Civil Rights," 923; Berl Bernhard, oral history interview by John Stewart, 17 June 1968, JFKL, 2.

14. Anonymous Kennedy White House staff members quoted in Light, *The President's Agenda*, 105.

15. P. H. Douglas, *In the Fullness of Time*, 195.

16. Lawrence F. O'Brien, interview with author, 19 July 1989.

17. PPP: JFK, 1961, 22.

18. Joseph L. Rauh, Jr., interview with author, 30 August 1988, 4.

19. M. L. King, "Equality Now," 93.

20. Arnold Aaronson and Roy Wilkins to Theodore Sorenson, 6 February 1961, TCS, Civil Rights File, JFKL; Roy Wilkins, oral history interview by Berl Bernhard, 13 August 1964, JFKL, 5. See also Matusow, *Unravelling of America*, 63.

21. Unsigned memo to Mike Feldman, 16 February 1961, JFK, President's Office Files, Staff Memoranda, Box 2, JFKL.

22. PPP: JFK, 1961, 157.

23. Schlesinger, *Thousand Days*, 651; Sorenson, *Kennedy*, 534; Burke Marshall, oral history interview by Anthony Lewis, 13 June 1964, JFKL, 61.

24. Schlesinger, *Thousand Days*, 849–850.

25. *Congressional Record*, 79th Cong., 1st sess., 4 May 1961, vol. 107:7340.

26. *New York Times*, 10 May 1961.

27. Herbert Edelsberg and David A. Brody, "Civil Rights in the 88th Congress, First Session," mimeo, Washington, D.C., Anti-Defamation League of B'nai B'rith, n.d., ADA, Legislative File, ser. 5, no. 47, MCA, 6.

28. *New York Times*, 11 May 1961; Roy Wilkins, "Statement on White House Attitude Towards Civil Rights Legislation," 10 May 1961, NAACP, Transfile 2, "Government—National, Bills, 1957–1959," LC.

29. Roy Wilkins, "[To] All Participating Organizations [of the Leadership Conference on Civil Rights]," memorandum, 12 May 1961, ADA, Legislative File, ser. 5, no. 48, MCA.

30. Wicker, *JFK and LBJ*, 88.

31. Ripley, *Kennedy and Congress*, 22.

32. M. L. King, *Stride toward Freedom*, 131–132.

33. L. Martin, "Organizing Civil Rights," 94.

34. See, e.g., Sorenson, *Kennedy*, 532. The five black federal judges included the future Supreme Court Justice Thurgood Marshall and the first black female jurist, Marjorie Lawson. At least one critic of the Kennedy position has pointed out that the administration could have rotated judges from other districts to fill vacancies in the South if nonsegregationist judges could not be confirmed for the region (see Miroff, *Pragmatic Liberalism*, 241). An excellent analysis of the Kennedy southern judicial appointments may be found in Hamilton, *Bench and the Ballot*.

35. Burke Marshall, oral history interview by Louis Oberdorfer, 29 May 1964, JFKL, 16; Robert F. Kennedy, oral history interview by John Bartlow Martin, 29 February 1964, JFKL, 1:10. The Kennedy-Douglas discussion concerning the Wright appointment is from W. O. Douglas, *Court Years*, 127.

36. A good description of Cox's appointment is in: Jack Bass and Walter DeVries, *The Transformation of Southern Politics: Social Changes and Political Consequences Since 1945* (New York: Basic Books, 1976), 164-68. On the appointment of southern judges from the Kennedy perspective see Schlesinger, *Robert Kennedy*, 330–334.

37. Robert F. Kennedy, oral history interview by Anthony Lewis, 4 December 1964, JFKL, 3:38, 4:7.

38. Roy Wilkins, telegram to Robert F. Kennedy, 22 June 1961, NAACP Transfile 2, "Government—National, Kennedy, John F., General, 1961–1963," LC.

39. *New York Times*, 9 March 1964.

40. Quoted in Schlesinger, *Robert Kennedy*, 332.

41. Quoted in J. Bass and DeVries, *Transformation of Southern Politics*, 171.

42. Quoted in Wofford, *Kennedys and Kings*, 163–164. See also Burke Marshall, oral history interview by Larry Hackman, 19–20 January 1970, JFKL, 962; and Dulles, *Civil Rights Commission*, 179–180.

43. Robert F. Kennedy to John A. Hannah, 15 December 1962, NAACP, Transfile 2, "Government-National, Civil Rights Commission, 1961–1964," LC.

44. Robert F. Kennedy to Dr. John A. Hannah, 26 March 1963; Dr. John A. Hannah to Mr. Attorney General, 2 January 1963, NUL, pt. 2, 1a, Box 52, LC.

45. Reverend Theodore M. Hesburgh, oral history interview by Joseph E. O'Connor, 27 March 1966, LBJL, 11, 13. See also "Chronology of Events—U.S. Commission On Civil Rights," n.d., NUL, pt.2, 1a, Box 52, LC.

46. Quoted in Wofford, *Kennedys and Kings*, 161.

47. Roy Wilkins to "NAACP Members in New Jersey," 30 August 1961, NAACP Transfile 2, "Government—National, Civil Rights Commission, 1961–1964," LC.

48. *Afro-American* (Baltimore), 11 March 1961.

49. See, e.g., Robert E. Gilbert, "John F. Kennedy and Civil Rights for Black Americans," *Presidential Studies Quarterly* 12 (1982): 387–388; Fleming, "Federal Executive," 932–935; Matusow, *Unravelling of America*, 20–96; Brauer, *Second Reconstruction*, 61–88; A. Lewis, *Portrait of a Decade*, 117–119; Schlesinger, *Thousand Days*, 851–852; Sorenson, *Kennedy*, 532.

50. "Statistical Summary"; Muse, *Ten Years of Prelude*; Sarratt, *Ordeal of Desegregation*.

51. Roy Wilkins to John F. Kennedy, 28 December 1961, NAACP, Transfile 2, "Government—National, Kennedy, John F., General, 1961-1963," LC.

52. Nicholas deB Katzenbach to Byron White, 10 October 1961, TCS, Box 30, JFKL.

53. Sorenson, *Kennedy*, 504.

54. Lee White, oral history interview by Joe B. Frantz, 28 September 1970, LBJL, 83–85. An analysis of this episode that is sympathetic to JFK may be found in Brauer, *Second Reconstruction*, 205–209.

55. Lee White to John F. Kennedy, 13 November 1961, TCS, Box 30, JFKL.

56. Lee White to John F. Kennedy, 13 November 1961, TCS, Box 30, JFKL.

57. PPP:JFK, 1962, 832. On the delays and the issuance of the order see Harris Wofford, oral history interview by Larry Hackman, 3 February 1969, LBJL, 154–156.

58. *Pittsburgh Courier*, 1 December 1962.

59. L. Martin, "Organizing Civil Rights," 89.

60. Brauer, *Second Reconstruction*, 68.

61. See Ambrose, *Eisenhower*," 620.

62. Roy Wilkins to Harris Wofford, 5 April 1961, NAACP, Transfile 2, "Government—National, General, 1956–1965," LC. See also Wilkins and Mathews, *Standing Fast*, 282.

63. Wilkins and Mathews, *Standing Fast*, 284–285. See also Roy Wilkins, oral history interview by Robert Wright, 29 April, 5 May 1970, MSL; Clarence Mitchell, oral history interview by Thomas H. Baker, 30 April 1969, LBJL, 11–12.

64. Burke Marshall, "Congress, Communication, and Civil Rights," 66. Marshall states, "The Department of Justice was intended to be and became the focal point of civil rights matters in the Kennedy administration." From the beginning, John Kennedy understood the sensitive role of the department. The president-elect first offered the position of attorney general to Abraham Ribicoff, a Kennedy intimate and governor of Connecticut. Ribicoff turned him down because he believed that a Jewish attorney general would only intensify the antagonisms that were bound to occur in the coming years. Ribicoff later became John Kennedy's secretary of Health, Education and Welfare.

65. Robert F. Kennedy, oral history interview, by John Bartlow Martin, 29 February 1964, JFKL, 54.

66. Harris Wofford, oral history interview by Larry Hackman, 3 February 1969, LBJL, 128.

67. Martin Luther King, Jr., oral history interview by Berl Bernhard, 9 March 1964, JFKL, 14.

68. Roy Wilkins, oral history interview by Berl Bernhard, 13 August 1964, JFKL, 14.

69. Navasky, *Kennedy Justice*, 445–446.

70. Robert F. Kennedy, oral history interview by John Bartlow Martin, 29 February 1964, JFKL, 54, by Anthony Lewis, 4 December 1964, JFKL, 529–530.

71. Wofford, *Kennedys and Kings*, 95.

72. Sorenson, *Kennedy*, 537–538. See also Robert F. Kennedy, oral history interview by Anthony Lewis, 4 December 1964, JFKL, 588–596.

73. Robert F. Kennedy, oral history interview by Anthony Lewis, 4 December 1964, JFKL, 396, 586–587.

74. Lichtman, "Federal Assault," 346–367.

75. Garrow, *Protest at Selma*, 13.

76. "A Review of Activities of the Department of Justice in Civil Rights in 1964," with cover letter by Nicholas Katzenbach, 6 January 1965, Marshall Papers, Box 16, JFKL.

77. William L. Taylor, oral history interview by Steven F. Lawson, October 1972, Columbia University Oral History Collection, Columbia University, 11.

78. U.S. Commission on Civil Rights, *Report* (1959), 98–106.

79. U.S. Commission on Civil Rights, *Political Participation* (1968), 12–13; idem, *Report: Voting* (1961), 100; idem, *Report* (1959), 141. Wofford, "Notre Dame Conference," 328–367, esp. 336.

80. Katzenbach, "Origin of Kennedy's Civil Rights," 51.

81. Morris, *Origins of the Civil Rights Movement*, 174–228.

82. Virginia Durr to Burke Marshall, 27 April 1961, Marshall Papers, Box 4, JFKL.

83. Wofford, *Kennedys and Kings*, 151–152.

84. Farmer, *Lay Bare the Heart*, 1–32, 195–207; Meier and Rudwick, *CORE*, 135–158; Carson, *In Struggle*, 31–44.

85. On the argument that the civil rights movement was engendering an irreversible momentum see McAdam, *Political Process*, 117–145. Morris, *Origins of the Civil Rights Movement*.

86. Ibid., 125; Robert F. Kennedy, oral history interview by Anthony Lewis, 6 December 1964, JFKL, 2:7.

87. Martin Luther King, Jr., oral history interview by Berl Bernhard, 9 March 1964, JFKL, 22, 24; Wofford, *Kennedys and Kings*, 156.

88. *New York Times*, 25 May 1961.

89. Farmer, *Lay Bare the Heart*, 205–206.

90. Siegenthaler, "Civil Rights in the Trenches," 111. Richard Gid Powers argues: "President Kennedy did not have the political strength that would let him make that total commitment [to civil rights], and so in asking the FBI to take the lead in the Southern civil rights struggle, the administration was asking it to help overthrow a caste system, to fight a civil war. For Hoover to risk that, he needed far more political backing than Kennedy could give him. The administration was simply not strong enough politically for Hoover to take any risks on its behalf, even if he had wanted to." (*Secrecy and Power*, 369). Of course, there is considerable doubt that Hoover ever wanted to commit his forces in support of civil rights. He believed the movement was riddled with communists and communist sympathizers, and he was not about to get involved in a struggle in which the rewards were questionable and the political costs could be extremely high. As a consequence, the FBI leader stood by as his agents watched the violence. Furthermore, the FBI conducted its own campaign of innuendo and intimidation against the black-rights movement and its leadership (see Garrow, *FBI and Martin Luther King*).

91. Robert F. Kennedy, oral history interview by Anthony Lewis, 6 December 1964, JFKL, 2:575.

92. Burke Marshall, oral history interview by Louis Oberdorfer, 29 May 1964, JFKL, 25–36; Robert F. Kennedy, oral history interview by Anthony Lewis, 4 December 1964, JFKL, 559.

93. Fred Shuttlesworth, oral history interview by James Mosby, September 1968, MSL, 10.

94. Martin Luther King, Jr., "Report on Meeting," 26 May 1961, MLK, Box 58, 7, BUL.

95. Robert F. Kennedy, oral history interview by Anthony Lewis, 4 December 1964, JFKL, 573.

96. Burke Marshall, oral history interview by Larry Hackman, 19–20 January 1970, JFKL, 41.

97. The conversation and aftermath is reported in Wofford, *Kennedys and Kings*, 155–156.

98. Harris Wofford to Kenneth O'Donnell, 2 June 1961, WHCF, Box 804, JFKL.

99. Wofford, *Kennedys and Kings*, 190.

100. PPP:JFK, 1961, 517.

101. Quoted in Dulles, *Civil Rights Commission*, 104.

102. On the freedom ride and the ICC order see Meier and Rudwick, *CORE*, 135–144.

103. James Farmer, oral history interview by John Britton, 28 September 1968, MSL, 18–19.

104. Roy Wilkins, oral history interview by Berl Bernhard, 13 August 1964, JFKL, 10.

105. Thurgood Marshall, oral history interview by Berl Bernhard, 7 April 1964, JFKL, 8.

3   A RELUCTANT PARTICIPANT

1. John Lewis, oral history interview by Steven F. Lawson, 1970, Columbia University Oral History Collection, Columbia University, 4.

2. Quoted in Brauer, *Second Reconstruction*, 85.

3. Schlesinger, *Thousand Days*, 850; Carson, *In Struggle*, 37.

4. Schlesinger, *Thousand Days*, 850, 853.

5. Harold C. Fleming, interview with author; 4 April 1985; Mary Jane Eddy, interview with author, 1 May 1986; Harold C. Fleming, interview with David J. Garrow, 10 January 1983, transcript in possession of Garrow; Leslie W. Dunbar to William Hinson, Jr., 19 April 1976, Voter Education Project, T-111, Robert Woodruff Library, Special Collections, Emory University. On the Voter Education Project see Lomax, "Kennedys Move in on Dixie," 27–33; and Watters and Cleghorn, *Climbing Jacob's Ladder*.

6. Robert F. Kennedy to Harold C. Fleming, 28 February 1961; 8 March 1961, Files of the Southern Regional Council, 75-1-71-26, AUL; John F. Kennedy to Harold C. Fleming, 30 September 1960, 3 October 1960, Files of the Southern Regional Council, 75-1-71-20, AUL.

7. Harold C. Fleming, interview with author, 4 April 1985, 2. Fleming is also quoted on this matter in Navasky, *Kennedy Justice*, 118–119.

8. Southern Regional Council, "Minutes of the Executive Committee," 27 July 1961, Files of the Southern Regional Council, 75-1-8-6, AUL. Leslie Dunbar to Stephen R. Currier, 5 September 1961, Files of the Southern Regional Council, 75-5-34-3, AUL; Burke Marshall, "To Voter Registration File," memorandum, 31 July 1961, Marshall Papers, Box 34, JFKL. On the

different perceptions of the protection promised by the federal government see Sitkoff, *Struggle for Black Equality,* 114 ff.

9. This discussion relies extensively on Meier and Rudwick, *CORE,* 173–174. Navasky, *Kennedy Justice,* 117–118; Watters and Cleghorn, *Climbing Jacob's Ladder,* 46–48; Harold C. Fleming, interview with author, 4 April 1985.

10. Wiley Branton, oral history interview by James Mosby, 11, 16 January 1969, MSL, 30–31.

11. Harold Fleming, interview with author, 4 April 1985.

12. Robert Kennedy, oral history interview by Anthony Lewis, 6 December 1964, 3, JFKL, 3:27.

13. Martin Luther King, Jr., oral history interview by Berl Bernhard, 9 March 1964, JFKL, 22.

14. Quoted in Meier and Rudwick, *CORE,* 175.

15. Carson, *In Struggle* 139–142; Zinn, *SNCC,* 59; Charles F. McDew, oral history interview by Katherine M. Shannon, 24 August 1967, MSL, 71–72.

16. Wiley Branton to John Doar, 19 June 1963, Wiley Branton to Burke Marshall, 19 June 1963, Files of the Southern Regional Council, 75-5-34-3, AUL; Wiley Branton to Burke Marshall, 28 July 1964, and Wiley Branton to Robert F. Kennedy, 18 July 1964, Files of the Southern Regional Council, 75-6-34-4, AUL.

17. Burke Marshall to Leslie W. Dunbar, 30 March 1962, Files of the Southern Regional Council, 75-1-71-2, AUL.

18. "Minutes of the Annual Meeting," 21 November 1964, Files of the Southern Regional Council, 75-1-6-32, AUL.

19. This represents an increase of 629,942 southern black voters. See Watters and Cleghorn, *Climbing Jacob's Ladder,* 376–377.

20. Carson, *In Struggle,* 41.

21. Charles F. McDew, interview with author, 24 July 1985.

22. Carson, *In Struggle,* 97; Watters and Cleghorn, *Climbing Jacob's Ladder,* 64–65; Charles F. McDew, interview with author, 24 July 1985.

23. Lawson, *Black Ballots,* 250–287. Marshall gave the most thorough articulation of his position in a series of lectures presented at Columbia University. These lectures were published as a book, *Federalism and Civil Rights.* See also his "Federal Protection of Negro Voting Rights," 455–467.

24. Charles F. McDew, interview with author, 24 July 1985, 9–10.

25. Quoted in Carson, *In Struggle,* 49.

26. Timothy Jenkins interview is in Raines, *My Soul Is Rested,* 231.

27. Leslie Dunbar to William Hinson, Jr., 19 April 1976, Voter Education Project, T-111, Robert Woodruff Library, Special Collections, Emory University.

28. Quoted in Navasky, *Kennedy Justice,* 118.

29. Leslie Dunbar, oral history interview by Robert E. Martin, 5 September 1968, MSL, 2. See also Zinn, "Kennedy the Reluctant Emancipator," 373–376. Matusow, *Unravelling of America,* 71.

30. Harold C. Fleming, interview with author, 4 April 1985. See also: Southern Regional Council, *Federal Executive* 26–27.

31. The Meredith admission to the University of Mississippi has received much scholarly attention. See, for example, W. Lord, *Past That Would Not Die*; Silver, *Mississippi*; Dorman, *We Shall Overcome*, 11–143; Schlesinger, *Thousand Days*, 858–867; Brauer, *Second Reconstruction*, 180–204; A. Lewis, *Portrait of a Decade*, 214–224.

32. For a chronology of the events in late September see *New York Times*, 1 October 1961.

33. W. Lord, *Past That Would Not Die*, 190–191.

34. Quoted in Brauer, *Second Reconstruction*, 192–193.

35. PPP:JFK, 1962, 726–728.

36. Quoted in Peter Maas, *Look*, 28 March 1961.

37. Katzenbach, "Origin of Kennedy's Civil Rights," 52.

38. Thurgood Marshall, oral history interview by Berl Bernhard, 7 April 1964, JFKL, 5.

39. See M. L. King, "Who Is Their God?" 209–211.

40. Lawson, *Black Ballots*, 290–297; Sundquist, *Politics and Policy*, 254–257.

41. *New York Times*, 3 January 1962.

42. PPP:JFK, 1962, 8.

43. Burke Marshall to the president, "Constitutionality of Poll Tax Legislation," n.d., Lee White Files, Box 1, JFKL.

44. Sorenson, *Kennedy*, 535.

45. Senate Committee on the Judiciary, *Hearings on Literacy Tests*, 87th Cong., 2d sess. 1962, 261 ff, 454; J. Francis Polhaus to Clarence Mitchell, memo, 12 March 1963, NAACP, Transfile 2, "Government—National, Bills, 1963," LC.

46. Stewart, "Independence and Control," 187–188.

47. Joseph Rauh, "Statement Telephoned March 28, 1963, to AP, UPI, *Post, Star*," ADA, Legislative File, ser. 5, no. 47, MCA; Joint Release, Glenn Beall, Clifford Case, Hiram Fong, Jacob Javits, Kenneth Keating, Thomas Kuchel, Hugh Scott, "Republicans Introduce Civil Rights Bills," ADA, Legislative File, ser. 5, no. 47, MCA; Press Release, "Republicans Introduce Civil Rights Bills," 28 March 1963, NAACP, Transfile 2, "Government-National, Bills, 1963," LC; *Congressional Quarterly Weekly Report* 21 (5 April 1963): 527.

48. *Congressional Quarterly Weekly Report* 21 (5 April 1963): 527.

49. Wilkins and Mathews, *Standing Fast*, 285.

50. Senate Committee on the Juridiary, *Hearings on Literacy Tests*, 87th Cong., 2d sess., 1962, 227.

51. Herman Edelsberg and David A. Brody, "Civil Rights in the 87th Congress, Second Session," mimeo, Washington, D.C., Anti-Defamation League of B'nai B'rith, 1 January 1963, ADA, Legislative File, ser. 5, no. 47, MCA.

52. PPP:JFK, 1962, 382–383.

53. *New York Times*, 10, 11, 13, 15, 16, 17, May 1962. See also Brauer, *Second Reconstruction*, 132–137; Lawson, *Black Ballots*, 290–293.

54. *Time* 79 (18 May 1962): 16.

55. Sorenson, *Kennedy*, 534.

56. Roy Wilkins to William Miller, 14 June 1962, NAACP, Transfile 2, "Government—National, Elections, Republican Party," LC.

57. Raines, *My Soul Is Rested*, 361–366.

58. Watters, *Down to Now*, 206.

59. Reverend Samuel Wells quoted in Garrow, *Bearing the Cross*, 218.

60. Martin Luther King, Jr., to A. Philip Randolph, 5 October 1962, Southern Christian Leadership Conference Papers, 19:54, MLKC. On the Albany, Georgia, struggle as a critical turning point in the movement see Garrow, *Protest at Selma*, 221, and *Bearing the Cross*, 173–230.

61. M.L. King, "Fumbling on the New Frontier," 193.

62. Gar Alperovitz and Kim Willerson, "The Leaderless Liberals," *Nation* 195 (8 September 1962): 103–105.

63. M. L. King, *Why We Can't Wait*, 143.

64. Hazel Gaudet Erskine, "The Polls: Kennedy as President," *Public Opinion Quarterly* 28 (1964): 336.

65. Lou Harris to the president, 19 November 1962, JFK, President's Office File, Special Correspondence, JFKL. See also *New York Times*, 8 November 1962.

4 A RELUCTANT COMMITMENT

1. PPP:JFK, 1963, 11–14.

2. Martin Luther King, Jr., oral history interview by Berl Bernhard, 9 March 1964, JFKL, 17; Fred Shuttlesworth, oral history interview by James Mosby, September 1968, MSL, 62.

3. Robert Kennedy, "A Report on the Progress of Civil Rights by the Attorney General Robert Kennedy to the President," 24 January 1963, Marshall Papers, Box 16, JFKL.

4. Cernoria D. Johnson memorandum to Whitney M. Young, Alexander J. Allen, and Nelson C. Jackson, 23 January 1963, NUL, pt. 2, 1a, Box 24, LC.

5. Juanita Mitchell, interview with author, 22 October 1987.

6. *Congressional Quarterly Weekly Report* 21 (16 February 1963): 191.

7. Berl I. Bernhard and William L. Taylor to Lee White, 21 February 1963, TCS, Box 30, JFKL.

8. Burke Marshall, oral history interview by Louis Oberdorfer, 29 May 1964, JFKL, 1:46

9. Joseph L. Rauh, Jr., oral history interview by Katherine Shannon, 28 August 1967, MSL, 66.

10. M. L. King, "Bold Design," 260.

11. Herman Edelsberg and David A. Brody, "Civil Rights in the 88th Congress, First Session," mimeo, 1963, ADA, Legislative File, ser. 5, no. 47, MCA.

12. Robert F. Kennedy, oral history interview by John Bartlow Martin, 1 March 1964, JFKL, 134.

13. M. L. King, *Why We Can't Wait*, 54; *Congressional Quarterly Weekly Report* 21 (15 March 1963): 336. The most thorough examination of King's role in the Birmingham demonstrations is in Garrow, *Bearing the Cross*, 231–296. See also Fairclough, *To Redeem the Soul*, 111–140.

14. M. L. King, *Why We Can't Wait*, 23, 157.

15. M. L. King, "Bold Design," 260.

16. Schlesinger, *Thousand Days*, 874.

17. *New York Times*, 13 April 1963.

18. Wyatt T. Walker, oral history interview by John H. Britton, 11 October 1967, MSL, 62–63. See also *New York Times*, 3–8 May 1963.

19. Carter, "Role of the Civil Rights Commission," 10–17.

20. John A. Hannah, letter to the president, 16 April 1963, with attached "Interim Report of the United States Commission on Civil Rights," White House Staff Files, Lee C. White File, Box 23, JFKL.

21. Schlesinger, *Thousand Days*, 953; Sorenson, *Kennedy*, 488.

22. Quoted in Carter, "Role of the Civil Rights Commission," 12.

23. PPP:JFK, 1963, 494.

24. Schlesinger, *Thousand Days*, 959.

25. PPP:JFK, 1963, 372.

26. Burke Marshall, oral history interview by Anthony Lewis, 14 June 1964, JFKL, 97–98.

27. Viorst, *Fire in the Streets*, 219; Gentile, *March on Washington*, 21; Joseph L. Rauh, Jr., interview with author, 30 August 1988, 5.

28. *New York Times*, 12, 13 June 1963.

29. Louis Martin to the attorney general, 13 May 1963, White House Staff File, Box 365a, JFKL.

30. Burke Marshall, "Demonstrations—Chronology, June, 1963–Sept., 1963," Marshall Files, Box 32, JFKL.

31. "Statement by the AFL-CIO Executive Council on Civil Rights, St. Louis, Missouri," 14 May 1963, Files of the Leadership Conference on Civil Rights, Subject File, ser. E, Box 5, LC.

32. PPP:JFK, 1963, 408.

33. John F. Kennedy telegram to George C. Wallace, White House Staff Files, Lee C. White File, Box 19, JFKL.

34. Sorenson, *Kennedy*, 494.

35. Burke Marshall, oral history interview by Anthony Lewis, 14 June 1964, JFKL, 101, 103–105; Norbert A. Schlei, oral history interview by John Stewart, 20–21 February 1964, JFKL, 44.

36. PPP:JFK, 1963, 423.

37. Brauer, *Second Reconstruction*, 243; Schlesinger, *Robert Kennedy*, 355–361.

38. Schlesinger, *Robert Kennedy*, 358–359.

39. Ibid., 359.

40. PPP:JFK, 1963, 423.

41. Lyndon Baines Johnson, "Edison Dictaphone Recording, LBJ—[Theodore C.] Sorenson," LBJ, 3 June 1963, LBJL. The Johnson quotes in the next three paragraphs are also from this source. A thorough analysis of Johnson's advice to President Kennedy at this point in time may be found in Riccards, "Rare Counsel," 395–398. On Johnson as vice-president see Evans and Novak, *Exercise of Power*, 305–334.

42. Walter Lippman, *Washington Post*, 28 May 1963.

43. *Congressional Record*, vol. 109, 6 June 1963, 10262.

44. Stewart, "Independence and Control," 171ff.

45. John P. Roche to Mr. President, 6 June 1963, ADA, ser. 5, no. 47, MCA.

46. Harris, "How Whites Feel about Negroes," 44–57; *Washington Post*, 9 December 1963.

47. Sundquist, *Politics and Policy*, 488.

48. *New York Times*, 10 June 1963.

49. Robert F. Kennedy, oral history interview by Anthony Lewis, 4 December 1964, JFKL, 777.

50. John F. Kennedy to Dwight D. Eisenhower, 10 June 1963, TCS, Box 30, JFKL. Eisenhower quoted in *New York Times*, 13 June 1963, Sorenson, *Kennedy*, 561.

51. *New York Times*, 11, 12, 13 June 1963.

52. Quoted by Jack Anderson, *Washington Post*, 11 June 1963. See also *New York Times*, 11 June 1963.

53. Lyndon B. Johnson to Theodore C. Sorenson, 10 June 1963, TCS, Box 30, JFKL.

54. *New York Times*, 12 June 1963.

55. Schlesinger, *Thousand Days*, 881.

56. PPP:JFK, 1963, 468–471; *New York Times*, 12 June 1963.

57. Roy Wilkins to John F. Kennedy, 12 June 1963, NAACP, Transfile 2, "Government—National, Kennedy, John F., General, 1961–1963," LC.

58. Martin Luther King, Jr., to President John F. Kennedy, 12 June 1963, WHCF, Box 1478, JFKL.

59. Lawrence F. O'Brien, interview with author, 19 July 1989.

60. Aaron Henry, oral history interview by Thomas H. Baker, 12 September 1970, MSL, 17.

61. *New York Times*, 13 June 1963.

62. *Washington Post*, 2 July 1963.

63. PPP:JFK, 1963, 523.

64. Audiotape log 101.4, 29 July 1963, White House Staff Files, JFKL.

65. Mike Mansfield to the president, 13 June 1963, TCS, Box 30, JFKL. See also C. Whalen and B. Whalen, *Longest Debate*, 153.

66. *New York Times*, 18 June 1963.

67. Sorenson, *Kennedy*, 561–562; Katzenbach, "Origin of Kennedy's Civil Rights," 53.

68. Harris Wofford to Martin Luther King, Jr., 18 June 1963, Southern Christian Leadership Conference Papers, 27:24, MLKC.

69. Herman Edelsberg and David A. Brady, "Civil Rights in the 88th Congress, First Session," mimeo, Anti-Defamation League of B'nai-B'rith, Spring 1963, Legislative File, ADA, ser. 5, no. 47, MCA.

70. Viorst, *Fire in the Streets*, 221–222.

71. Schlesinger, *Thousand Days*, 883.

72. PPP:JFK, 1963, 272.

73. Sundquist, *Politics and Policy*, 263.

74. Leslie Dunbar, "Annual Report of the Executive Director of the Southern Regional Council, A Review of Program Activities During 1963, February 1964," Files of the Southern Regional Council, 75-1-7-5, AUL.

75. Robert F. Kennedy, oral history interview by Anthony Lewis, 6 December 1964, vol. 5, JFKL, 3.

76. Schlesinger, *Thousand Days*, 883.

77. William Connell to Hubert H, Humphrey, 26 June 1963, Humphrey Papers, Box 593, MHS.

78. Quoted in Navasky, *Kennedy Justice*, 99.

79. Robert Kennedy, oral history interview by Anthony Lewis, 4 December 1964, JFKL, 776.

80. Ibid., 6 December 1964, JFKL, 783; Lee White, "Record of Presidential Meetings with Leadership Groups," n.d., White House Staff Files, Lee C. White Files, Box 19, JFKL; Burke Marshall, oral history interview by Anthony Lewis, 14 June 1964, JFKL, 110–111.

81. Frederick Kappel, letter to members of the business council, 17 July 1963, attached to Lee White memorandum, 17 July 1963, White House Staff Files, Lee C. White Files, Box 19, JFKL.

82. Garfinkel, *When Negroes March*, 38; A. Philip Randolph, oral history interview by John Martin, 14 January 1969, MSL, 57–58; Gentile, *March on Washington*, 14; Jervis Anderson, *A. Philip Randolph*, 323–325; D. L. Lewis, *King: A Biography*, 214; Garrow, *Bearing the Cross*, 271–273.

83. A. Philip Randolph to Whitney M. Young, Jr., 26 March 1963, NUL, pt. 2, 1a, Box 25, LC.

84. Muse, *American Negro Revolution*, 7–10; Meier and Rudwick, *CORE*, 224.

85. Whitney M. Young, Jr., to A. Philip Randolph, 13 April 1963, NUL, pt. 2, 1a, Box 25, LC.

86. Richard Russell to William Knowland, 24 June 1963, Russell Papers, Box 1 J.10, RBRL.

87. Charles C. Diggs, Jr., to Martin Luther King, Jr., 27 June 1963, Southern Christian Leadership Conference Papers, 24:26, MLKC.

88. Martin Luther King, Jr., to Charles C. Diggs, Jr., 17 July 1963, Southern Christian Leadership Conference Papers, 24:26, MLKC.

89. Schlesinger, *Thousand Days*, 884–886; Wilkins and Mathews, *Standing Fast*, 290–291.

90. The conversation in this and the next three paragraphs, except where noted otherwise, is drawn from Schlesinger, *Thousand Days*, 884–885.

91. Wilkins and Mathews, *Standing Fast*, 291.

92. Joseph L. Rauh, Jr., interview with author, 30 August 1988, 6.

93. Schlesinger, *Thousand Days*, 384. On the alleged communist infiltration of the SCLC see Schlesinger, *Thousand Days*, 382–385; Garrow, *FBI and Martin Luther King*, 21–77; Garrow, *Bearing the Cross*, 272–273; Powers, *Secrecy and Power*, 372–377; Raines, *My Soul Is Rested*, 430–431.

94. King quoted in Raines, *My Soul Is Rested*, 431.

95. Schlesinger, *Thousand Days*, 384.

96. Robert F. Kennedy, oral history interview by Anthony Lewis, 6 December 1964, JFKL, 919.

97. Garrow, *FBI and Martin Luther King, Jr.*, 41.

98. William Sullivan Report to Herbert Hoover, 23 August 1963, quoted in Powers, *Secrecy and Power*, 375.

99. Martin Luther King, Jr., to Jack O'Dell, 3 July 1963, Southern Christian Leadership Conference Papers, 18:39, MLKC. Sorenson, in *Kennedy*, notes: "One civil rights leader was privately persuaded to reject some communists who had infiltrated his movement" (565). This is an obvious reference to the King-O'Dell-Levison affair and is, unfortunately, a distortion of the matter.

100. PPP:JFK, 1963, 531.

101. Schlesinger, *Robert Kennedy*, 387.

102. Lee White, oral history interview by Joe B. Frantz, 28 September 1970, LBJL, 157–158; *Newsweek* (29 July 1963): 63.

103. Lee White, oral history interview by Joe B. Frantz, 28 September 1970, LBJL, 163–164; Lee White to the president, 22 August 1963, JFK, President's Office Files, Subjects, JFKL.

104. Roy Wilkins, press release, "Wilkins Sees J.F.K.'s Proposals as not Meeting Today's Needs," 22 June 1962, NAACP, Transfile 2, "Government—National, Kennedy, John F., General, 1961–1963," LC.

105. *New York Times*, 26 June 1965.

106. Schlesinger, *Thousand Days*, 886–887; Gentile, *March on Washington*, 65.

107. Sorenson, *Kennedy*, 566.

108. Press release, "Civil Rights Legislation Not Enough Say Big Five," 27 July 1963, NAACP, Transfile 2, "Civil Rights, General, 1963–1964," LC.

109. Arnold Aaronson to Cooperating Organizations, 25 July 1963, Leadership Conference on Civil Rights, Organizations File, Box 4, LC.

110. Roy Wilkins and Arnold Aaronson to all Cooperating Organizations, "Memorandum on the Principal Activities of the Leadership Conference on Civil Rights from 1963 to July, 1966," n.d., Leadership Conference on Civil Rights, Subject File, ser. E, Box 6, LC.

111. Edward D. Hollander to Chairman and National Board Members, 12 July 1963, ADA, ser. 5, no. 47, MCA.

112. House Committee on the Judiciary, *Hearings on Voting Rights*, 88th Cong. 1st sess., 1963. The legislative history of the 1964 Civil Rights Act may be found in Whalen and Whalen, *Longest Debate*. The Kennedy-Lindsay ex-

change that follows may be found on pages 6–7 in the latter study, as are Wirtz's comments.

113. C. Whalen and B. Whalen, *Longest Debate*, 22–23.

114. News release, "News From the AFL-CIO, For Release, A.M. Papers, Thursday, August 22, 1963"; James Roosevelt letter to Jack [John H.] Biedler, 16 August 1963, Leadership Conference on Civil Rights, Subject File, ser. E, Box 5, LC.

115. Schlesinger, *Robert Kennedy*, 376.

116. Burke Marshall, oral history interview by Anthony Lewis, 22 December 1964, JFKL, 917–918.

117. Gentile, *March on Washington*, 62–63; Schlesinger, *Robert Kennedy*, 376–377.

118. Carson, *In Struggle*, 92; Mary Jane Eddy, interview with author, 1 May 1986.

119. Lester, *Look Out, Whitey!*, 12–13.

120. D. L. Lewis, *King: A Biography*, 219.

121. Thomas J. Hanlon, memorandum to Whitney M. Young, Jr., 13 August 1963, NUL, pt. 2, 1a, Box 25, LC.

122. PPP:JFK, 1963, 529.

123. *New York Times*, 30 August 1987.

124. Sorenson, *Kennedy*, 566.

125. *New York Times*, 29 August 1963.

126. Meier, "Who Are the 'True Believers'? 480–481.

127. Sorenson, *Kennedy*, 504.

128. PPP:JFK, 1963, 645.

129. Transcript of "March on Washington . . . Report by the Leaders," 28 August 1963, White House Subject Files, Box 365, JFKL; audiotape log 108.2, 28 August 1963, White House Subject Files, Box 505, JFKL.

130. Roy Wilkins, oral history interview by Robert Wright, 1 April 1969, MSL, 10.

131. Sorenson writes in *Kennedy*: "He doubted that any vote in Congress had been changed. He doubted segregationists had been converted. But he felt that the march had helped to unite the adherents of civil rights more closely; and merely the absence of violence in such a large and restless throng had awakened new interest and won new adherents in white America" (567).

132. Audiotape log 108.2, White House Subject Files, Box 505, JFKL.

133. *Washington Post*, 16 October 1963.

134. Audiotape log 108.2, 28 August 1963, White House Subject Files, JFKL. The quote in the next paragraph is also from this source.

135. Arnold Aaronson, to All Cooperating Organizations, 30 August 1963, Leadership Conference on Civil Rights, Organizations File, Box 4, LC.

136. Quoted in *Congressional Quarterly Weekly Report* (20 September 1963): 1632.

137. David Cohen to Beryl Radin, 31 October 1963, ADA, Legislative File, ser. 5, no. 88, MCA; Kastenmeier, transcript, "CBS Reports: Filibuster—

Birth Struggle of a Law," broadcast 18 March 1964, 9; Robert W. Kastenmeier, oral history interview by Ronald Grele, 25 October 1965, JFKL, 14–15.

138. C. Whalen and B. Whalen, *Longest Debate*, 35–38.

139. Arnold Aaronson, to Cooperating Organizations, 27 September 1963, ADA, ser. 5, no. 47, MCA.

140. Roy Wilkins, to All NAACP Branches and Youth Council Officials, 2 October 1963, NAACP, Transfile 2, "Government—National, Bills, 1963," LC.

141. C. Whalen and B. Whalen, *Longest Debate*, 40.

142. Robert Kastenmeier, oral history interview by Ronald Grele, 25 October 1965, JFKL, 14–15.

143. Quoted in C. Whalen and B. Whalen, *Longest Debate*, 38.

144. John F. Kennedy meeting with Eugene Carson Blake, audiotape log 113.2, 30 September 1963, White House Subject Files, JFKL.

145. Quoted in C. Whalen and B. Whalen, *Longest Debate*, 46.

146. Roy Wilkins, news release, "Kennedys Opposed on Softer Civil Rights Bill," 26 October 1963, NAACP, Transfile 2, "Government—National, Civil Rights Act of 1964, Miscellany, 1963," LC. See also David Cohen to Beryl Radin, 30 October 1963, ADA, Legislative File, ser. 5, no. 47, MCA.

147. Joseph L. Rauh, Jr., oral history interview by Katherine Shannon, 28 August 1967, MSL, 62–63.

148. Quoted in *Congressional Quarterly Weekly Report* (18 October 1963): 1814.

149. Clarence Mitchell to Emanuel Cellar, 18 October 1963, Cellar Papers, Box 463, LC.

150. Quoted in C. Whalen and B. Whalen, *Longest Debate*, 54. See also *New York Times*, 24 October 1963, 1E.

151. C. Whalen and B. Whalen, *Longest Debate*, 58–59; Scheele, *Charlie Halleck*, 225–227.

152. C. Whalen and B. Whalen, *Longest Debate*, 66; *New York Times*, 30 October 1963. Provisions of the bill and the specific committee votes may be found in *Congressional Quarterly Almanac* (Washington, D.C.: Congressional Quarterly, 1963), 349–351.

153. Lee White to Lawrence O'Brien, 30 October 1963, Lee White Files, Box 22, JFKL.

154. Nicholas deB Katzenbach, oral history interview by Larry Hackman, 8 October 1969, JFKL, 75–76.

155. Theodore Sorenson and Lawrence O'Brien to the president, 10, 17, 22 September, 22 October 1963, TCS, Box 59, JFKL.

156. PPP:JFK, 1963, 584.

157. *New York Times*, 2 November 1963; Scheele, *Charlie Halleck*, 225–227; Sorenson, *Kennedy*, 562.

158. John A. Blatnik to Democratic Study Group Members, 13 November 1963, DSG, Box 72, LC.

159. Bayard Rustin to Martin Luther King, Jr., 5 November 1963, Southern Christian Leadership Conference Papers, 20:39, MLKC.

160. Sorenson, *Kennedy*, 568.

161. Harris, "How Whites Feel about Negroes," 44–57.

162. *Washington Post*, 21 July 1963.

163. Gallup, *Gallup Poll*, 3:1828–1851.

164. Bradlee, *Conversations with Kennedy*, 190; O'Donnell, Powers, and Mc-Carthy, *Johnny We Hardly Knew Ye*, 445; Sorenson, *Kennedy*, 849.

165. Schlesinger, *Thousand Days*, 895; O'Neill and Novak, *Man of the House*, 176.

166. Lawrence F. O'Brien, interview with author, 19 July 1989, 6.

167. Evans and Novak, *Exercise of Power*, 466.

5   FROM TEXAN TO NATIONAL POLITICIAN

1. Lyndon Baines Johnson, speeches in Austin, Texas, 22 May 1948, and in Texarkana, Texas, 22 May 1948; additional speeches along these lines were made by Johnson on 18, 20 July, 13, 19 August 1948, LBJ, Statements of Lyndon B. Johnson, vol. 1, Box 1, LBJL.

2. James H. Rowe to Lyndon B. Johnson, 23 February 1949, LBJ, Civil Rights, United States Senate, 1949–1961, Box 1, LBJL.

3. Elliott, "Union Sentiment in Texas," 463.

4. L. B. Johnson, *Vantage Point*, 155.

5. R. B. Johnson, *Family Album*, 69–71; Kearns, *Johnson and the American Dream*, 30; W. S. White, *Professional LBJ*, 93.

6. Dyer, "LBJ and the Politics of Civil Rights."

7. Kearns, *Johnson and the American Dream*, 55.

8. Lyndon B. Johnson, interview in *Pittsburgh Courier*, 9 July 1960.

9. Lee C. White, interview with author, 6 March 1989, 3.

10. Kearns, *Johnson and the American Dream*, 230; Billington, "Johnson and Blacks," 26–42. Caro, *Path to Power*, 166–172.

11. On Johnson's appointment to Kleberg's staff see Miller, *Lyndon: An Oral Biography*, 36–37.

12. Kearns, *Johnson and the American Dream*, 84; Frank Horne quoted in Miller, *Lyndon: An Oral Biography*, 56.

13. Billington, "Johnson and Blacks," 31.

14. National Youth Administration Files, LBJ, Box 11, LBJL.

15. Friedel, *FDR and the South*, 65; Blum, *Progressive Presidents*, 132–136. Longaker, *Presidency and Individual Liberties*, 42, 91. The two most comprehensive, and contrasting, studies of FDR and blacks are Sitkoff, *New Deal For Blacks*, and Weiss, *Farewell to the Party of Lincoln*.

16. Leuchtenburg, *Shadow of FDR*, 121.

17. Quoted in Dugger, *Politician*, 138.

18. On the Texas challenge see Blumenthal, "Getting It All Wrong," 29–36. The Texas Regulars did slate an anti-Roosevelt set of electors in 1944, and

oil money supported a full-blown general election campaign for the slate. They were, however, unsuccessful: FDR won 822,000 votes, Dewey 191,000, and the regulars 135,000 (see Blumenthal, "Getting It All Wrong," 34).

19. Mary McLeod Bethune to Lyndon B. Johnson, 3 May 1937, LBJ, Pre-Presidential Papers, Box 2, LBJL.

20. Frantz, "Opening a Curtain," 3–26.

21. Keyserling quoted in Miller, *Lyndon: An Oral Biography*, 72.

22. Hubert H. Humphrey, oral history interview by Michael L. Gillette, 20 June 1977, 2:5, LBJL. Hamby points out, however, that from 1943 through 1948 LBJ always voted against prounion legislation (*Liberalism and Its Challengers*, 13).

23. L. B. Johnson, *Vantage Point*, 155.

24. W. S. White, *Professional LBJ*, 139–140. George Reedy recalls that FDR asked Vinson to help place LBJ on the Naval Affairs Committee (Reedy letter to author, April 11, 1991).

25. Billington, "Johnson and Blacks," 32–33.

26. Johnson, speeches in Austin, Texas, 22 May 1948, in Texarkana, Texas, 22 May 1948. Johnson also made speeches with racist overtones in Sherman, Texas, 18 July 1948; Waco, Texas, 20 July 1948; San Antonio Texas, 13 August 1948; and Fort Worth, Texas, 19 August 1948 (LBJ, Statements of Lyndon B. Johnson, vol. 1, Box 1, LBJL).

27. Billington, "Johnson and Blacks," 34–36. A highly critical but thorough review of LBJ's maneuvering in this election is in Caro, *Means of Ascent*; a useful counter to Caro is in Robert Dallek, *Lone Star Rising: Lyndon Johnson and His Times* (New York: Oxford University Press, 1991).

28. Dyer, "LBJ and the Politics of Civil Rights," 70.

29. Dugger, *Politician*, 344–345.

30. Lyndon B. Johnson to James H. Rowe, 15 March 1949, LBJ, Civil Rights, United States Senate, 1949–1961, Box 1, LBJL. In subsequent correspondence Rowe refers to LBJ's arguments as "medieval," and Johnson terminates this interchange with the comment: "We are both dogmatic, both sure we are right" (see Rowe to Johnson, 18 April 1949, and Johnson to Rowe, 22 April 1949).

31. Lyndon B. Johnson, *Congressional Record*, 81st Cong., 1st sess., 2041–2049.

32. Richard Russell to J. Strom Thurmond, 17 February 1948, Russell Papers, Civil Rights Series, 10:45, RBRL.

33. Lyndon Johnson to A. E. Holland, 2 March 1949, LBJ, Pre-Presidential Papers, Box 1, LBJL.

34. "Resolution on Civil Rights," San Antonio Branch, NAACP, 6 January 1950; Lyndon Johnson to Harry V. Burns, 18 January 1950, LBJ, Pre-Presidential Papers, Box 2, LBJL.

35. Carter Wesley, *Houston Informer*, 6 February 1954.

36. Joseph L. Rauh, Jr., oral history interview by Paige Mulhollan, 30 July 1969, 2:5, LBJL. V. O. Key argued in *Southern Politics* that Texas was "more western than southern" (254), but Senator Johnson was hearing and responding to the call of the South.

37. Fite, *Richard B. Russell, Jr.*, 268; Johnson quoted in Dugger, *Politician*, 343.

38. Claudia T. (Lady Bird) Johnson, oral history interview by Hugh Cates, 28 June 1977, LBJL, 3, 8. See also Kearns, *Johnson and the American Dream*, 110. George E. Reedy notes that Sam Rayburn also viewed Johnson in this light (*LBJ: A Memoir*, 43).

39. George E. Reedy, interview with author, 4–5 March 1991, 1; W. S. White, *Professional LBJ*, 169.

40. Leslie Carpenter, "Whip from Texas," *Colliers* (17 February 1951).

41. Dugger, *Politician*, 373–77; Evans and Novak, *Exercise of Power*, 226–227.

42. Mooney, *Irreverent Chronicle*, 10–13, 16.

43. *New York Times*, March 12, 1950; Richard B. Russell to H. Broughton, 14 November 1950, Russell Papers, Political Series, 6:31, RBRL; Ralph Huitt quoted in Miller, *Lyndon: An Oral Biography*, 154.

44. Lyndon Johnson to Richard Russell, 2 January 1953, LBJ, Johnson Senate File, Master File Index, Box 162, LBJL.

45. Richard M. Nixon, oral history interview by Hugh Cates and Robert G. Stephens, Jr., 13 April 1978, RBRL, 16. See also Robert Troutman, Jr., oral history interview by Hugh Cates, 4 March 1971, RBRL, 22.

46. James Rowe, Jr., to Carl McGowan, 29 January 1953, Stevenson Papers, Box 378, PUL.

47. Reedy, *LBJ: A Memoir*, xiii; Evans and Novak, *Exercise of Power*, 63–64; Stewart, "Two Strategies of Leadership," 61; Huitt, "Democratic Party Leadership," 338; Sundquist, *Politics and Policy*, 400.

48. Joseph L. Rauh, oral history interview by Paige Mulhollan, 30 July 1969, 2:14, LBJL, 19.

49. Reedy, *LBJ: A Memoir*, 206.

50. TRB, *New Republic* 131 (6 December 1954): 2; Branyan and Hon Lee, "Art of the Possible," 213–233.

51. Harry McPherson, interview with author, 6 March 1989, 3; W. S. White, *Professional LBJ*, 199.

52. Wilkins and Mathews, *Standing Fast*, 296.

53. Press release of Richard Russell, 17 May 1954, reprinted in *Congressional Record*, 83d Cong., 2d sess., 18 May 1954, 6750.

54. Quoted in *New York Times*, 28 May 1954.

55. Speech Senate Floor, 18 May 1954, LBJ, Statements of Lyndon B. Johnson, 1948–2 August 1957, vol. 2, Box 2, LBJL.

56. "The Declaration of Constitutional Principles" and Senate commentary on the statement may be found in *Congressional Record*, 84th Cong., 2d sess., 12 March 1956, 4459–4460. On the authorship of the manifesto, see Richard Russell to M. Hayes Mizell, 13 April 1962, Russell Papers, Dictation Series, 10:299, RBRL. Russell's text of the manifesto may be found in Speech/Media Series, Russell Papers, 3:33, RBRL.

57. *New York Times*, 13 March 1956. Stennis quoted in Miller, *Lyndon: An Oral Biography*, 188.

58. Richard Russell to W. H. Bridges, 27 March 1956, Russell Papers, Early Office Series, 4:199, RBRL. See also, Fite, *Richard B. Russell, Jr.*, 336.

59. *New York Times*, 30 July 1956.

60. Lyndon Johnson to Charles L. Hatcher, 18 May 1956, LBJ, Civil Rights, United States Senate, 1949–1961, Box 7, LBJL.

61. *Washington Post*, 3 July 1955; Patrick McMahon, *Time* 61 (22 June 1953): 23; "Knowland and Johnson in 1956?" *American Mercury* 79 (October 1954): 40; Philip Graham quoted in David Halberstam, *The Powers That Be* (New York: Knopf, 1979), 307; Ashmore, *Hearts and Minds*, 308.

62. George E. Reedy, letter to author, 11 April 1991.

63. McPherson, *Political Education*, 142; George Reedy to Lyndon Johnson, 3 December 1956, LBJ, Civil Rights, United States Senate, 1949–1961, Box 7, LBJL; Steinberg, *Sam Johnson's Boy*, 467. See also McPherson, "Johnson and Civil Rights," 57; and Harry McPherson, oral history interview by Thomas Baker, 5 December 1968, LBJL, 13.

64. Lyndon Johnson to Allen Duckworth, 9 March 1957, LBJ, Civil Rights, United States Senate, 1949–1961, Box 2, LBJL; Kearns, *Johnson and the American Dream*, 147. One study of LBJ's role in the 1957 Civil Rights Act legislative fight is in Evans and Novak, *Exercise of Power*, 119–163.

65. Richard Russell, *Congressional Record*, 85th Cong., 1st sess., 2 July 1957, 1077.

66. Johnson quoted in Miller, *Lyndon: An Oral Biography*, 371; first Reedy quote from Miller, *Lyndon: An Oral Biography*, 206; second Reedy quote from George Reedy, interview with author, 27 October 1990, 2.

67. George E. Reedy, interview with author, 4–5 March 1991, 4. This matter is also discussed in two extensive letters Reedy wrote to me on 7 and 11 April 1991. Mr. Reedy insightfully argues that LBJ did get *a* civil rights bill into law and that this broke the civil rights logjam. Given the composition of the Senate, the bill would not have become law had the strong liberal position been maintained. In this sense, Reedy notes, LBJ forever changed the Senate's civil rights legislative agenda.

68. *Congressional Quarterly Weekly Report* (30 March 1956): 1393; Richard H. Rovere, "Letter from Washington," *New Yorker* (31 August 1957): 72; staff memorandum, n.d., LBJ, Civil Rights, United States Senate, 1949–1961, Box 3, LBJL.

69. The remarks by Brownell are from Herbert Brownell, interview with author, 27 October 1990, 2–3. The first Eisenhower quote is from Lyon, *Eisenhower*, 74; Russell's Senate comments may be found in *Congressional Record*, 85th Cong., 1st sess., 2 July 1957, 10771–10774; 10 July 1957, 11291–11294; 22 July 1957, 12287–12292, and in *New York Times*, 11 July 1957; Eisenhower's second statement is from PPP:DDE, 1957, 52.

70. *New York Times*, 18 July 1957; Everett M. Dirksen, oral history interview by Joe B. Frantz, 30 July 1969, 2:3, LBJL, 1.

71. Quoted in Kearns, *Johnson and the American Dream*, 150.

72. George E. Reedy, interview with author, 4–5 March 1991, 4.

73. *Congressional Record*, 85th Cong., 1st sess., 1 August 1957, 13355–13356; Harry F. Byrd to Lyndon Johnson, 2 August 1957, LBJ, Senate Papers, Congressional Correspondence, Box 4, LBJL; Richard Russell to Roy V.

Harris, 9 August 1957, Russell Papers, Civil Rights Series, 10:84, RBRL; Transcript, "Senator Russell's conversation with Carter Pittman," 2 September 1957, Russell Papers, Dictation Series, IF2, RBRL. Evans and Novak provide the story of this maneuvering in *Exercise of Power*. Lawson also provides an excellent study of the 1957 civil rights battle, *Black Ballots*, 140–202.

74. *Congressional Record*, 85th Cong., 1st sess., 16112, 16477–16478, 16784. PPP:DDE, 1957, 587; Lawson, *Black Ballots*, 196–199.

75. The Church quotes here and in the next paragraph are from Miller, *Lyndon: An Oral Biography*, 209–210.

76. Johnson quoted in ibid., 212; Russell quoted by Strom Thurmond in *Congressional Quarterly Guide to American Government, Spring, 1988* (Washington, D.C.: Congressional Quarterly, 1988), 43.

77. Lyndon Johnson to George B. Fleming, 29 July 1957, LBJ, Civil Rights, United States Senate, 1949–1961, Box 3, LBJL. Much of this correspondence may be found in box 2 of the Johnson Senate Civil Rights collection.

78. Newspaper clippings on this subject, from across Texas, may be found in News Clippings, Civil Rights, LBJ, United States Senate, 1949–1961, Box 15, LBJL.

79. Emanuel Celler, oral history interview by Thomas H. Baker, 19 March 1969, LBJL, 3.

80. *New York Times*, 1 September 1957.

81. C. Vann Woodward to Lyndon Johnson, 6 November 1957, LBJ, Civil Rights, United States Senate, 1949–1961, Box 2, LBJL.

82. Richard Russell to James W. Talbert, 29 August 1957, Russell Papers, Civil Rights Series, IF2, RBRL. See also Richard Russell to Mr. and Mrs. G. M. Jackson, 23 September 1957, Russell Papers, Civil Rights Series, 10:83, RBRL.

83. Richard Russell to President Dwight D. Eisenhower, 26 September 1957; Richard Russell to Secretary of Defense Charles E. Wilson, 26 September 1957, Russell Papers, Dictation Series, IF2, RBRL.

84. Richard Russell, press release, 24 September 1957, Russell Papers, Civil Rights Series, 10:52, RBRL; Richard Russell, book telegram, 27 September 1957, Russell Papers, Civil Rights Series, 10:83, RBRL.

85. Lyndon Johnson, Speech on Senate Floor, 24 September 1957, LBJ, Statements of Lyndon B. Johnson, 5 August 1957 to 27 October 1959, Box 3, LBJL.

86. The first quotation is from Lyndon Johnson to J. P. Kidd, 24 September 1957, LBJ, Civil Rights, United States Senate, 1949–1961, Box 3, LBJL; the second quotation is from Johnson to J. R. Black, 8 October 1957, LBJ, Civil Rights, United States Senate, 1949–1961, Box 5, LBJL. Box 5 of this series contains much of Johnson's correspondence on this matter.

87. Harry S. Ashmore to John A. Blatnik, 31 December 1958, Stevenson Papers, Box 761, PUL.

88. *New York Times*, 10 January 1959.

89. *Congressional Record*, 86th Cong., 1st sess., 6.

90. *New York Times*, 9–13, January 1959.

91. Quoted in *New York Times*, 13 January 1959. See also *Congressional Record*, 86th Cong., 1st sess., 207–208, 298, 446, 492–494.

92. *New York Times*, 10 January 1959.

93. See Richard B. Russell, press release, 13 January 1959, Russell Papers, Civil Rights Series, 10:117, RBRL.

94. *New York Times*, 10, 13 January 1959.

95. Dean Acheson to Lyndon Johnson, 18 December 1958, LBJ, Civil Rights, United States Senate, 1949–1961, Box 4, LBJL.

96. The most in-depth study of the legislative struggle over the 1960 Civil Rights Act is D. M. Berman, *A Bill Becomes a Law*. See also Sundquist, *Politics and Policy*, 239–250, and Lawson, *Black Ballots*, 220–249.

97. See comments by Paul Douglas, Hubert Humphrey, and others in *New York Times*, 21, 22 January 1959.

98. *Congressional Record*, 86th Cong., 1st sess., 20 January 1959, 875–877.

99. Lyndon Johnson to "Dear Friend," 27 January 1959, LBJ, Civil Rights, United States Senate, 1949–1961, Box 10, LBJL.

100. PPP:DDE, 1959, 164–167.

101. *Congressional Record*, 86th Cong., 1st sess., 14 September 1959, 19567.

102. *Congressional Record*, 86th Cong., 2d sess., 15 February 1960, 2470; *New York Times*, 14–16 February 1960.

103. *New York Times*, 16 February 1960.

104. Johnson and Russell quoted in Miller, *Lyndon: An Oral Biography*, 226–227.

105. Harry McPherson, interview with author, 24 July 1989, 5.

106. Gerry W. Siegel, "Analysis of H.R. 8601, Civil Rights Bill," 25 March 1960, LBJ, Civil Rights, United States Senate, 1949–1961, Box 13, LBJL.

107. *Congressional Record*, 86th Cong., 2d sess., 24 March 1960, 6452–6455.

108. *Congressional Record*, 86th Cong., 2d sess., 4 April 1960, 7166, 8 April 1960, 7218, 7225.

109. *New York Times*, 4 April 1960; *Congressional Record*, 86th Cong., 2d sess., 7225.

110. Clark and Johnson quoted in Miller, *Lyndon: An Oral Biography*, 229; Paul H. Douglas, "The 1960 Civil Rights Bill: The Struggle, the Final Results, and the Reasons," *Journal of Intergroup Relations* 1 (Summer 1960): 82. See also Longaker, *Presidency and Individual Liberties*, 52. Longaker reaches the conclusion that the "sense of the minimum degree of moderation which Congress would accept, dominated the proceedings."

111. Lyndon Johnson, Radio Speech in Texas, 11 April 1960, LBJ, Statements of Lyndon B. Johnson, Box 4, LBJL.

112. Hawk and Kirby, "Federal Protection of Negro Voting Rights," 1053–1213. Marshall quoted in *New York Times*, 22 April 1960.

113. See, for example, Longaker, *Presidency and Individual Liberties*, 52.

114. T. H. White, *Making of the President, 1960*, 156.

115. Quote in Richard Russell to Price Daniel, 18 November 1959, Russell

Papers, Dictation Series, IC2, RBRL. See also Hardeman and Bacon, *Rayburn: A Biography*, 432.

116. Reedy, *LBJ: A Memoir*, 43.

117. George Reedy to Lyndon Johnson, 10 July 1960, LBJ, Statements of Lyndon B. Johnson, Box 4, LBJL. See also Miller, *Lyndon: An Oral Biography*, 242. Reedy notes that Johnson "had no consistent strategy" in 1960 and blew hot and cold over whether to pursue the nomination. "Ambiguity . . . killed his candidacy" (Reedy letter to author, April 11, 1991).

118. T. H. White, *Making of the President, 1960*, 397.

119. Wofford, *Kennedys and Kings*, 51–52. Joseph L. Rauh, Jr., oral history interview by Paige Mulhollan, 30 July 1969, 2:16, LBJL.

120. O'Neill and Novak, *Man of the House*, 93–95.

121. The first Johnson quote is in Miller, *Lyndon: An Oral Biography*, 256; the second is in Evans and Novak, *Exercise of Power*, 280. See also Kearns, *Johnson and the American Dream*, 168.

122. Joseph Rauh, Jr., oral history interview by Paige Mulhollan, 30 July 1969, 2:2, LBJL, 18; Clarence Mitchell, oral history interview by Thomas H. Baker, 30 April 1969, LBJL, 1:20; James Farmer, oral history interview by Thomas H. Baker, 30 October 1969, LBJL, 2; Woodcock quoted in Miller, *Lyndon: An Oral Biography*, 258; Joseph Rauh, Jr., interview with author, 20 February 1988, 1.

123. Richard Russell to Hon. John J. Jones, 18 July 1960; Richard Russell to Dr. Robert P. Coggins, 26 July 1960, Russell Papers, Dictation Series, IC2, RBRL.

124. Richard Russell to Charles A. Rowland, 17 December 1960, Russell Papers, Dictation Series, IC2, RBRL.

125. Quoted in Miller, *Lyndon: An Oral Biography*, 273; and Reedy, *LBJ: A Memoir*, 121.

126. Quoted in Ashmore, *Hearts and Minds*, 370. On the JFK-LBJ-RFK relationship see also Burke Marshall, oral history interview by Anthony Lewis, 14 June 1964, JFKL, 111–112; and Reedy, *LBJ: A Memoir*, 133.

127. Wilkins and Mathews, *Standing Fast*, 297; Whitney Young, Jr., oral history interview by Thomas H. Baker, 18 June 1969, LBJL.

128. James Farmer, oral history interview by Thomas H. Baker, 30 October 1969, LBJL, 6–7; Louis Martin, oral history interview by David G. McComb, 14 May 1969, LBJL, 14–15.

129. Robert F. Kennedy, oral history interview by Anthony Lewis, 4 December 1964, 4:23, JFKL, 27; Schlesinger, *Robert Kennedy*, 335–337.

130. Quoted in Schlesinger, *Robert Kennedy*, 361.

131. Lyndon Baines Johnson, "Edison Dictaphone Recording, LBJ—[Theodore C.] Sorenson," LBJ, 3 June 1963, LBJL, 14.

132. See Schlesinger, *Robert Kennedy*, 361–362; Robert F. Kennedy, oral history interview by Anthony Lewis, 4 December 1964, 6:7, JFKL.

133. Lyndon Johnson, Speech at Wayne State University, 6 January 1963, LBJ, Statements of Lyndon B. Johnson, Box 8, LBJL.

134. *Washington Post*, 30 May 1963. *New York Times*, 1 June 1963.

135. Lyndon Baines Johnson, "Edison Dictaphone Recording, LBJ—[Theodore C.] Sorenson," LBJ, 3 June 1963, LBJL. Quotes here and to the end of the chapter are from this source.

136. L. Baker, *Johnson Eclipse*, 253; Lawrence O'Brien, interview with author, 19 July 1989, 4.

6   CREATING A LIBERAL PRESIDENCY

1. Jack Valenti, interview with author, 5 October 1990, 1; C. Whalen and B. Whalen, *Longest Debate*, 63.

2. PPP:LBJ, 1963–1964, 9.

3. *New York Times*, 29 November 1963.

4. Quoted in C. Whalen and B. Whalen, *Longest Debate*, 76.

5. Kearns, *Johnson and the American Dream*, 199.

6. Lawrence F. O'Brien, interview with author, 19 July 1989, 3.

7. Ibid.

8. L. B. Johnson, *Vantage Point*, 95. Johnson personalized this feeling of northern antipathy. After leaving the presidency he told Doris Kearns, "All the historians are Harvard people. It just isn't fair. Poor old Hoover from West Branch, Iowa had no chance with that crowd. Nor did Andrew Johnson from Tennessee. Nor does Lyndon Johnson from Stonewall, Texas." He added: "They'll get me no matter how hard I try. . . . The reviews are in the hands of my enemies in the *New York Times* and the Eastern magazines—so I don't have a chance" (Kearns, *Johnson and the American Dream*, 372–373). See also Miller, *Lyndon: An Oral Biography*, 390.

9. PPP:LBJ, 1965, 284.

10. L. B. Johnson, *Vantage Point*, 38. Johnson's remarks along these lines are also recalled by Jack Valenti (Jack Valenti, interview with author, 5 October 1990, 1).

11. Harry McPherson, interview with author, 24 July 1989, 2.

12. L. B. Johnson, *Vantage Point*, 157–158.

13. Quoted in *New York Times*, 2 July 1989. Valenti confirmed the *Times*'s account of this conversation, Jack Valenti, interview with author, 5 October 1990, 2.

14. Richard Russell to Charles R. Bloch, 27 November 1963, Russell Papers, Dictation Series, IF2, RBRL.

15. Kearns, *Johnson and the American Dream*, 161, 154.

16. Lyndon Johnson to Allen Duckworth, 9 March 1957, LBJ, Civil Rights, United States Senate, 1949–1961, Box 2, LBJL; Kearns, *Johnson and the American Dream*, 57.

17. L. B. Johnson, *Vantage Point*, 155.

18. Evans and Novak, *Exercise of Power*, 350.

19. McPherson, "Johnson and Civil Rights," 49–50.

20. Wilkins and Mathews, *Standing Fast*, 295–296.

21. President's Appointment File (Diary Backup), 2 December 1963, with memorandum from Lee White attached, Box 2, LBJL; President's Appointment File (Diary Backup), 3 December 1963, Box 2, LBJL; *New York Times*, 4 December 1963.

22. Farmer, *Lay Bare the Heart*, 293–296.

23. President's Appointment File (Diary Backup), 5 December 1963, with attached memoranda from Lee C. White and Willard Wirtz, Box 2, LBJL.

24. On the effort of Johnson to reign in black demonstrations see Miroff, "Presidential Leverage," 2–23.

25. "The Democratic Vice-Presidential Campaign," 4 December 1963, ser. 6, no. 102, ADA.

26. Joseph L. Rauh, Jr., letter to Ms. Joyce Tucker, 29 May 1988, copy in possession of the author.

27. Ibid.; Joseph L. Rauh, Jr., to Lyndon B. Johnson, 9 December 1963, Rauh Papers, Box 24, LC.

28. Henry Hall Wilson to Lawrence F. O'Brien, 2 December 1963, White House Aides Files, Wilson Files, Civil Rights Folder, Box 2, LBJL.

29. Mike Manatos to Lawrence F. O'Brien, 4 November 1963, White House Aides Files, Manatos Files, 1963–1965 folder, Box 6, LBJL.

30. Minutes of Leadership Meeting, President's Appointment File (Diary Backup), 3 December 1963, Box 2, LBJL; *New York Times*, 4 December 1964.

31. *New York Times*, 5 December 1963, 26.

32. *New York Times*, 6 December 1963.

33. PPP:LBJ, 1963–1964, 1:22.

34. *New York Times*, 6 December 1963.

35. *Congressional Quarterly Weekly Report* 22 (10 January 1964): 48.

36. *Afro-American* (national edition), 11 January 1964.

37. C. Whalen and B. Whalen, *Longest Debate*, 36–67.

38. *Washington Post*, 16 January 1964, A-2.

39. *New York Times*, 18 January 1964.

40. Joseph L. Rauh, Jr., "Notes on Meeting: President Johnson, Clarence Mitchell, and Joe Rauh," 21 January 1964, Rauh Papers, Box 26, LC; Joseph L. Rauh, Jr., oral history interview by Paige Mulhollan, 8 August 1969, LBJL. See also Wilkins, *Standing Fast*, 299–300.

41. Joseph L. Rauh, Jr., interview with author, 28 March 1990.

42. Lyndon Baines Johnson to Mark A. Hannah, 21 January 1964, LBJ, Ex FG 629-1, Box 375, WHCF, LBJL.

43. PPP:LBJ, 1964, 28, 35.

44. Arnold Aronson to Cooperating Organizations, 27 January 1964, ADA, Legislative File, ser. 5, reel 48, no. 47, MCA.

45. Lawrence F. O'Brien to the president, "Summary of Agency Reports on Legislation," 27 January 1964, White House Aides Files, Wilson Files, Wilson: Legislative Reports, Box 3, LBJL.

46. *Congressional Quarterly Weekly Report* (21 February 1964): 365; Whitten quoted in *Congressional Quarterly Weekly Report* (14 February 1964): 296.

47. Raymond Wolfinger, comment, see "Roundtable of Participants."

48. *Congressional Quarterly Weekly Report* (14 February 1964): 293, 294. See also Deputy Attorney General Nicholas deB Katzenbach's comments on McCulloch's role in Katzenbach, oral history interview by Paige R. Mulhollan, 23 November 1968, LBJL, 17.

49. Clarence Mitchell, oral history interview by Thomas H. Baker, 30 April 1969, LBJL, 27–28.

50. Joseph L. Rauh, Jr., interview with author, 28 March 1990.

51. Quoted in Miller, *Lyndon: An Oral Biography*, 367–368.

52. President's Appointment File (Diary Backup), 11 February 1964, Box 4, LBJL.

53. "Notes on the First Congressional Leadership Breakfast Held by the President on 3 December 1963," President's Appointment File (Diary Backup), Box 2, LBJL.

54. Nicholas deB Katzenbach, "Lyndon Johnson and the Civil Rights Revolution: A Panel Discussion," in *Lyndon Baines Johnson and the Uses of Power*, ed. Bernard Firestone and Robert C. Vogt (New York: Greenwood, 1988), 179.

55. Stewart, "Independence and Control," 173.

56. C. Whalen and B. Whalen, *Longest Debate*, 155.

57. Nicholas deB Katzenbach to Lawrence F. O'Brien, "Re: Civil Rights Legislation," n.d., White House Aides Files, Mike Manatos Files, Box 6, LBJL.

58. Jack Valenti, oral history interview by Joe B. Frantz, 12 July 1972, LBJL, 5:11–12; Bornet, *Presidency of Lyndon Johnson*, 122–123.

59. Stewart, "Independence and Control," 93–94.

60. Ibid., 181–182.

61. Hubert H. Humphrey, oral history interview by Michael L. Gillette, 20 June 1977, tape 2, 3:9, LBJL.

62. Clarence Mitchell and John G. Stewart, oral history interview by W. Connel, 15 March 1979, MHS, 6.

63. Quoted in Miller, *Lyndon: An Oral Biography*, 368–370. The daily newsletter may be found in Papers of the Leadership Conference on Civil Rights, Legislative File, Box 9, LC.

64. *Congressional Quarterly Weekly Report* (13 March 1964): 491.

65. Clarence Mitchell and John G. Stewart, oral history interview by W. Connel, 15 March 1979, MHS, 5.

66. *New York Times*, 22 March 1964.

67. The LCCR commanders repeatedly pushed for grassroots mail to be sent to the Hill and reminded the congressmen that they would be remembered for their actions when election time arrived (see, e.g., Clarence Mitchell to Roy Wilkins, 20 March 1964, NAACP, Transfile 2, "Government—National, Civil Rights Act of 1964, General Correspondence, 1963–1964," LC). Mitchell implored Wilkins to "give us a snow storm of mail to senators" to counter anti-rights mail coming in (Roy Wilkins to Hon. John V. Lindsay, 2 April 1964, ibid.). Wilkins let Lindsay know that he was aware of his support

for the civil rights bill and told him "[you] deserve the support of voters at the polls next November" (Clarence Mitchell to Mildred Bond, 27 March 1964, ibid.). "We get reports from Senate offices that you have been busy on behalf of the bill. Please keep up the good work and get others to help. Republicans now show that pro–civil rights mail is now increasing. Please continue the good work that you are doing by getting the letters to Washington" (Roy Wilkins to John A. Morsell, 17 April 1964, ibid.).

68. Hubert H. Humphrey, memorandum, n.d., Humphrey Papers, Personal, Civil Rights Bill—1964, 24.G.5.85, MHS.

69. *New York Times*, 29 April 1964.

70. Murray Kempton, "The Senate: Mr. Humphrey's Conquering Hosts," *New Republic* (4 April 1964): 8.

71. Leadership Conference on Civil Rights, memorandum 2, 5 August 1963, ser. D, Box 4, LC.

72. Sundquist, *Politics and Policy*, 268.

73. Joseph L. Rauh, Jr., oral history interview by Katherine Shannon, 28 August 1967, MSL.

74. Mathew Ahmann to Catholic Interracial Councils and Other Contacts in twenty Midwestern and Southwestern States, "Re: Proceedings of the Catholic Convocation for Civil Rights held in Omaha, May 5," 8 May 1964, ADA, Legislative File, ser. 5, reel 88, no. 47, MCA.

75. Richard Russell, *Congressional Record*, 88th Cong., 2d sess., vol. 110, 10 June 1964, 13309.

76. PPP:LBJ, 1964–1965, 421.

77. *Washington Post*, 4 March 1964.

78. PPP:LBJ, 1963–1964, 342.

79. *Washington Post*, 8 March 1964.

80. PPP:LBJ, 1963–1964, 410.

81. *New York Times*, 10 March 1964; PPP:LBJ, 1963–1964, 374.

82. *New York Times*, 2 March 1964.

83. See, e.g., *New York Times*, 5, 17, 18 April, 7, 13 May; Lee C. White to Lyndon B. Johnson, "Civil Rights Activities During the First 100 Days," 15 April 1964, LBJ, Ex HU 2, Box 1, WHCF, LBJL.

84. See, e.g., his 9 April 1964 remarks to business leaders and his 27 April 1964 remarks to members of the United States Chamber of Commerce, PPP:LBJ, 1963–1964, 449, 562; his 17 April 1964 comments to editors attending the American Society of Newspaper Editors, ibid., 482; his 29 April 1964 talk to religious leaders who participated in the National Interreligious Convocation on Civil Rights, ibid., 588–589.

85. PPP:LBJ, 1963–1964, 182–184.

86. Stewart, "Independence and Control," 198.

87. *New York Times*, 8 April, 6, 7, 21 May 1964; *Congressional Quarterly Weekly Report* (22 May 1964): 1000–1001.

88. Frady, *Wallace*, 45.

89. *New York Times*, 8 April 1964.

90. *Congressional Quarterly Weekly Report* (15 May 1964): 948.

91. Richard Goodwin to the President, 4 May 1964, Ex HU 2, Box 2, WHCF, LBJL; Eric Goldman to Lyndon Johnson, 4, 12 May 1964, LBJ, Ex LE HU 2, Box 65, WHCF, LBJL.

92. Loevy, "Books of Law," 117.

93. Clarence Mitchell to Roy Wilkins, 22 May 1964, NAACP, Transfile 2, "Government—National, Civil Rights Act of 1964, General Correspondence, 1964," LC.

94. *New York Times*, 16 April 1964; PPP:LBJ, 1963–1964, 429–430, 457, 521–522, 653.

95. L. B. Johnson, *Vantage Point*, 29.

96. PPP:LBJ, 1963–1964, 482.

97. Stephen Horn, Senatorial Log, 1964, folder no. 2, 29 April 1964 meeting, MHS, 130; C. Whalen and B. Whalen, *Longest Debate*, 164.

98. *New York Times*, 6 May 1964.

99. Stewart, "Independence and Control," 247; *New York Times*, 7 May 1964; PPP:LBJ, 1963–1964, 618.

100. Stephen Horn and Raymond Wolfinger, comments, see "Roundtable of Participants," 1 September 1989.

101. C. Whalen and B. Whalen, *Longest Debate*, 184; Stewart, "Independence and Control," 249–254; *Washington Post*, 14 May 1964; *New York Times*, 14, 15 May 1964.

102. *New York Times*, 20 May 1964.

103. *New York Times*, 14 May 1964.

104. Clarence Mitchell to Roy Wilkins, 22 May 1964, NAACP, Transfile 2, "Government—National, Civil Rights Act of 1964, General Correspondence, 1964," LC; Clarence Mitchell and John G. Stewart, oral history interview by W. Connel, 15 March 1979, MHS.

105. MacNeil, *Dirksen*, 235.

106. Mike Manatos, internal file memorandum, 25 May 1964, White House Aides File, Mike Manatos Files, Box 6, LBJL.

107. *New York Times*, 25 May 1964.

108. Stewart, "Independence and Control," 263–265; Drew, "Politics of Cloture," 19–23.

109. Stewart, "Independence and Control," 272.

110. Mike Manatos, memorandum for the files, 8 June 1964, White House Aides Files, Mike Manatos Files, Box 6, LBJL.

111. *Congressional Record*, 88th Cong., 2d sess., 10 January 1964, 12866.

112. Mark A. Arnold, "The Drama of a Senate Cloture Vote and How Civil Rights Forces Won It," *National Observer* (15 June 1964): 1.

113. Stephen Horn, comments, see "Roundtable of Participants," 1 September 1989; *New York Times*, 22 May 196.

114. Solberg, *Humphrey: A Biography*, 225.

115. Hubert H. Humphrey, memorandum, n.d., Humphrey Papers, 24.G.5.65, MHS, 18–20.

116. Mike Manatos to Hobart Taylor, 11 June 1964, White House Aides Files, Mike Manatos Files, Box 8, LBJL.

117. *Congressional Record*, 88th Cong., 2d sess., 18 June 1964, 13825 and 14012.

118. Richard B. Russell to John F. Echols, 1 July 1964, Russell Papers, Civil Rights Series, 10:47, RBRL.

119. Stewart, "Independence and Control," 288; *Congressional Record*, CX, 88th Cong., 2d sess., 14982.

120. *New York Times*, 3 July 1964; PPP:LBJ, 1963–1964, 842–844.

121. M. L. King, Jr., *Why We Can't Wait*, 146.

122. Quoted in Firestone and Vogt, *Uses of Power*.

123. See, e.g., Califano, *Presidential Nation*, 215; C. Whalen and B. Whalen, *Longest Debate*, 174, 187–188, 203; Stewart L. Udall to Lyndon B. Johnson, 17 May 1964, LBJ, Ex LE/HU 2, Box 65, WHCF, LBJL.

124. Nicholas deB Katzenbach, oral history interview by Paige R. Mulhollan, 12 November 1968, LBJL, 22.

125. L. B. Johnson, *Vantage Point*, 257.

126. Evans and Novak, *Exercise of Power*, 378; James Reston, *New York Times*, 19 June 1964; Theodore Hesburgh, oral history interview by Paige R. Mulhollan, 17 February 1971, LBJL, 11.

127. "Text of Radio Address Recorded by Senator Allen J. Ellender of Louisiana, For Presentation over Radio Station WWL, New Orleans, Louisiana, at 7:15 P.M. CST, Saturday, July 4, 1964," and "Bill Fulbright Reports from the United States Senate, The Civil Rights Law," in Leadership Conference on Civil Rights, Subject File, ser. E, Box 7, LC.

128. Quoted in *Congressional Quarterly Weekly Report* (3 July 1964): 1331.

129. Russell quoted in *New York Times*, 16 July 1964; Ramsey Clark, oral history interview by James Mosby, 17 December 1968, MSL, 11. See also "Voluntary Compliance Widespread," *Afro-American*, 11 July 1964.

130. M. L. King, *Why We Can't Wait*, 146.

131. TRB, *New Republic* (2 May 1964): 4.

7 FORGING THE ELECTION COALITION

1. PPP:LBJ, 1963–1964, 1:705.

2. McAdam, *Political Process*, 160.

3. COFO's constituent groups included the Congress of Racial Equality, the Student Nonviolent Coordinating Committee, the Southern Christian Leadership Conference, and the state of Mississippi NAACP chapter. SNCC and CORE came to dominate the COFO operation. Among the best studies of the MFDP are McLemore, "Mississippi Freedom"; Walton, *Black Political Parties*; and Colby, "Protest and Party." On the 26 April 1964 founding meeting of the MFDP, see McLemore, "Mississippi Freedom," 107. A study of the MFDP 1964 Democratic National Convention challenge, which makes extensive use of the DNC records at the Johnson Library, is Bass, "Presidential Party Leadership," 85–101.

4. Quoted in Raines, *My Soul Is Rested*, 287, 274.

5. The most extended defense of the Kennedy administration's argument of its limited ability to enter into these cases may be found in Marshall, *Federalism and Civil Rights*. A profile of the white Freedom Summer volunteers may be found in Rothschild, *Case of Black and White*, 31–47.

6. Forman, *Making of Black Revolutionaries*, 372–373.

7. Carson, *In Struggle*, 111.

8. Belfrage, *Freedom Summer*, 22.

9. Nicholas deB Katzenbach to Lee White, "Memorandum for the President," 21 May 1964, White House Aides Files, Lee White Files, Box 6, LBJL.

10. Robert Kennedy to Lyndon Johnson, 5 June 1964, LBJ, Ex FG 135, Box 1, WHCF, LBJL.

11. Lee White to Burke Marshall, 17 June 1964, White House Aides Files, Lee White Files, Box 6, LBJL; Lee White to Lyndon Johnson, 17 June 1964, LBJ, Ex HU 2-7, Box 55, WHCF, LBJL.

12. *New York Times*, 22 June 1963.

13. PPP:LBJ, 1963–1964, 808.

14. Allen W. Dulles, "Mississippi Trip, Tuesday Evening, June 23, 1964," Dulles Papers, Box 125, PUL. The quotation is from presidential press secretary George Reedy, "News Conference #306," 24 June 1964, Dulles Papers, Box 126, PUL.

15. Allen W. Dulles, "Chronology of Trip to Mississippi," 26 June 1964, Dulles Papers, Box 125, PUL; "Notes for My Guidance in Reporting to the President," n.d., Dulles Papers, Box 125, PUL, 4.

16. Stephen A. Gill, telegram to the president, 26 June 1964, Ex HU 2/ST 24, Box 27, WHCF, LBJL.

17. Nicholas deB Katzenbach to Lyndon Johnson, 1 July 1964, Ex HU 2/ST 24, Box 26, WHCF, LBJL.

18. "The Harris Survey," *Washington Post*, 6 July 1964.

19. PPP:LBJ, 1963–1964, 854.

20. Quoted in Powers, *Secrecy and Power*, 408–409.

21. Watters, *Down to Now*, 301.

22. *New York Times*, 4, 9 August 1964. In 1967 seven white men were convicted in federal court of violating the civil rights of the three activists and sentenced to prison terms. The deputy sheriff of Meridian, Cecil Price, was one of the individuals convicted. The state of Mississippi never filed murder charges, a state offense, against the men.

23. John Lewis to Lyndon Johnson, 19 August 1964, Ex HU 2/ST 24, Box 27, WHCF, LBJL.

24. Hoffman, *Mississippi Notebook*, 28.

25. Watters and Cleghorn, *Climbing Jacob's Ladder*, appendix 2; U.S. Commission on Civil Rights, *Political Participation*, 12–13. By 1964, despite the brave and bloodied effort of the civil rights forces, the black registration figure was raised to only 6.7 percent. By contrast, 62.7 percent of the age-eligible white Mississippi population was registered to vote in 1964.

26. McLemore, "Mississippi Freedom," 112–117.

27. T. H. White, *Making of the President, 1964* (New York: Atheneum, 1965), 93.

28. F. C. White, *Suite 3505*, 20–98; Rusher, *Rise of the Right*, 87–127.

29. T. H. White, *Making of the President, 1964*, 132.

30. Goldwater, *Conscience of a Conservative*, 35; and Goldwater, *Why Not Victory?*

31. *New York Times*, 2 April 1964.

32. Quoted in Stewart Alsop, "Can Goldwater Win?" *Saturday Evening Post*, 24 August 1963, 14.

33. MacNeil, *Dirksen*, 238; *New York Times*, 18 June 1964; *Congressional Record*, 88th Cong., 2d sess., vol. 110, 18 June 1964, 14319.

34. T. H. White, *Making of the President, 1964*, 192, 205.

35. Runyon, Verdini, and Runyon, *Source Book*, 91–93.

36. *New York Times*, 17 July 1964.

37. T. H. White, *Making of the President, 1964*, 217.

38. Goldwater and Casserly, *Goldwater*, 199.

39. Kessel, *Goldwater Coalition*.

40. *New York Times*, 20 July 1964.

41. Ibid., 19 July 1964.

42. Martin Luther King, Jr., news release, 16 July 1964, MLK, 20:15, MLKC.

43. T. H. White, *Making of the President, 1964*, 221–231.

44. Henry H. Wilson, Jr., to Lawrence F. O'Brien, 8 July 1964, White House Aides Files, Wilson Files, Campaign 1964 File, LBJL.

45. PPP:LBJ, 1963–1964, 890–891.

46. Hobart Taylor, Jr., to Lyndon Johnson, 17 July 1964, Ex HU 2, Box 2, WHCF, LBJL.

47. Roy Wilkins to Martin Luther King, Jr., James Farmer, Whitney M. Young, Jr., A. Philip Randolph, and John Lewis, 22 July 1964, NAACP, Transfile 2, "Government—National, Elections, Miscellany, 1964," LC.

48. Dwight D. Eisenhower to Milton Eisenhower, 17 July 1964, Eisenhower Papers, Post-Presidential Appointment Book, Box 2, DDEL.

49. Lee White, memorandum for the White House Files, 6 July 1964, Ex HU 2, Box 2, WHCF, LBJL.

50. Wilkins and Mathews, *Standing Fast*, 303. Johnson consistently called for the public to understand that the riots were linked to legitimate, underlying grievances. See, for example, *New York Times*, 12, 18 July 1964; Lee White to Lyndon Johnson, "Notes for Meeting with Negro Leaders," 18 August 1964, Ex HU 2, Box 3, WHCF, LBJL.

51. Lyndon Johnson, telephone call to Roy Wilkins, 27, 28 July 1964, LBJ, Daily Diary, LBJL. For a view of these events that sees the president as more directly manipulating this meeting see Miroff, "Presidential Leverage," 12–13.

52. Farmer, *Lay Bare the Heart*, 298–299; James Farmer, oral history interview by Thomas H. Baker, 30 April 1969, LBJL, 2.

53. "Statement of Civil Rights Organization Leaders," 29 July 1964, NAACP, Transfile 2, "Civil Rights, General, 1963–1964," LC; *New York Times*, 30 July 1964.

54. *New York Times*, 2 August 1964.

55. Gallup, *Gallup Poll*, 3:1881, 1894, 1896, 1902. In July Goldwater was favored over Johnson in the South by 51 percent to 40 percent. By August the Goldwater-Johnson figures were 47 percent to 46 percent. See also *New York Times*, 24 August 1964. The Johnson lead was never seriously threatened by Goldwater (*New York Times*, 6 October, 3 November 1964).

56. John Stewart, oral history interview by Carl Solberg, 21 June 1970, MHS, 6.

57. Marion Barry, oral history interview by Katherine Shannon, 30 October 1967, MSL, 42.

58. McLemore, "Mississippi Freedom," 128–129.

59. Joseph L. Rauh, Jr., oral history interview by Katherine Shannon, 16 June 1967, MSL, 310. Unless otherwise noted, the chronology of various pressures brought on Rauh to stop the challenge is from this source.

60. Garrow, *Bearing the Cross*, 347; U.S. Congress, Senate Select Committee, *Intelligence Activities and the Rights of Americans*, 94th Cong. 2d sess., 26 April 1976, 2:117–118. Approximately thirty FBI agents were involved in this surveillance, which included hidden room microphones and telephone taps on Martin Luther King, Jr.

61. Joseph L. Rauh, Jr., oral history interview by Katherine Shannon, 16 June 1967, MSL, 313.

62. Jack T. Conway, interview with author, 21 June 1990, 1–2. The material in this paragraph and the next paragraph is drawn from this interview and from Joseph L. Rauh, Jr., interview with author, June 29, 1990, 2.

63. Joseph L. Rauh, Jr., "Remarks in Rebuttal of Joseph L. Rauh, Jr., of the Mississippi Freedom Democratic party, before the Credentials Committee of the Democratic National Convention," 22 August 1964, Rauh Papers, appendix, Box 86, LC.

64. Carson, *In Struggle*, 124.

65. *New York Times*, 19 August 1964.

66. Evans and Novak, *Exercise of Power*, 435–448. On Humphrey as the popular choice of the convention delegates for the vice-presidential nomination see *New York Times*, 31 July 1964. On Johnson's lecture, see Bayard Rustin, telephone conversation with Ralph Helstein, 19 July 1964, FBI King File, MLKC.

67. On the black leadership position, see Arnold Aronson, "Memo to Co-operating Organizations," 13 August 1964, NUL, pt. 2, 1a, Box 2, LC; Roy Wilkins to NAACP Branch and Youth Group Presidents, "Re: Support for Mississippi Freedom Party Delegation at Democratic National Convention in Atlantic City, New Jersey," 12 August 1964, NAACP 3, B-375, LC; news release, "Seat Freedom Delegates, NAACP Urges Democrats," 21 August 1964, NAACP, Transfile 2, "Government—National, Elections, Democratic Party, 1964," LC.

68. Evans and Novak, *Exercise of Power*, 452; George Reedy, news conference transcript, 19 August 1964, National Security Files, vol. 1, LBJL.

69. Solberg, *Humphrey: A Biography*, 174–175; Joseph L. Rauh, Jr., oral history interview by Paige R. Mulhollan, 30 July 1969, LBJL, 2:16–18; Hubert H. Humphrey, oral history interview by Joe B. Frantz, 17 August 1971, tape 1, LBJL, 37–38.

70. Harry McPherson, oral history interview by Thomas H. Baker, 24 March 1969, tape 2, LBJL, 10.

71. John Stewart, oral history interview by Carl Solberg, 21 June 1970, MHS, 6.

72. Humphrey, *Education of a Public Man*, 299.

73. Joseph L. Rauh, Jr., "Remarks in Rebuttal of Joseph L. Rauh, Jr., Mississippi Freedom Democratic party, before the Credentials Committee of the Democratic National Convention," 22 August 1964, Rauh Papers, appendix, Box 86, LC.

74. Holt, *Summer That Didn't End*, 168–169; T. H. White, *Making of the President, 1964*, 291–292. See also the oral history transcript in Watters and Cleghorn, *Climbing Jacob's Ladder*, 362–375.

75. Joseph L. Rauh, Jr., interview with author, 29 June 1990, 2.

76. Jack T. Conway, interview with author, 21 June 1990, 2–3.

77. Joseph L. Rauh, Jr., interview with author, 29 June 1990, 2; Jack T. Conway, interview with author, 21 June 1990, 4.

78. Jack T. Conway, interview with author, 21 June 1990, 5–6. The material on the Johnson-Reuther relationship is largely drawn from this interview.

79. Ibid., 5.

80. Joseph L. Rauh, Jr., oral history interview by Katherine Shannon, 16 June 1967, MSL, 338.

81. Joseph L. Rauh, Jr., to Leslie McLemore, 16 June 1965, Rauh Papers, Box 86, LC.

82. Walter F. Mondale, interview with author, 23 July 1990, 1.

83. Ibid., 1–2.

84. Jack T. Conway, interview with author, 21 June 1990, 4–5.

85. Joseph L. Rauh, Jr., interview with author, 29 June 1990, 2.

86. Ibid., 3.

87. Joseph L. Rauh, Jr., oral history interview by Katherine Shannon, 16 June 1967, MSL, 341–345.

88. *New York Times*, 26 July 1964.

89. Aaron Henry, interview with author, 23 July 1990.

90. Viorst, *Fire in the Streets*, 265; Joseph L. Rauh, Jr., interview with author, 29 June 1990, 3.

91. Joseph L. Rauh, Jr., interview with author, 29 June 1990, 2.

92. Wilkins and Mathews, *Standing Fast*, 305–306.

93. Joseph L. Rauh, Jr., oral history interview by Katherine Shannon, 16 June 1967, MSL, 353.

94. Forman, *Making of Black Revolutionaries*, 302. McLemore, "Mississippi Freedom," 153.

95. Forman, *Making of Black Revolutionaries*, 393; John Lewis, oral history interview by Steven F. Lawson, 1970, Columbia University Oral History Collection, 8.

96. Aaron Henry and Ed King to John W. McCormack, Chairman, Democratic National Convention, 26 August 1964, Rauh Papers, Box 86, LC.

97. Aaron E. Henry, "Position Paper," 29 August 1964, Rauh Papers, Box 86, LC. ᷄

98. Quoted in Garrow, *Bearing the Cross*, 349.

99. Matusow, *Unravelling of America*, 142.

100. Joseph L. Rauh, Jr., oral history interview by Paige R. Mulhollan, 30 July 1969, LBJL, 3:7–8.

101. Charles Diggs to Elizabeth Hirshfield, 27 August 1964, Mississippi Freedom Democratic Party Files, Box 4, MLKC.

102. D. B. Johnson, *National Party Platforms* , 641. On LBJ's role in putting the platform together see Evans and Novak, *Exercise of Power*, 86–87.

8 THE SECOND GREAT EMANCIPATOR

1. Goodwin, *Remembering America*, 302.

2. Evans and Novak, *Exercise of Power*, 481.

3. Election results from *New York Times*, 4, 5 November 1964; Rovere, "Letter From Washington," 126.

4. O'Brien, *No Final Victories*, 178.

5. Grantham, *Life and Death of the Solid South*, 159–161.

6. Cosman, *Five States for Goldwater*; Wildavsky, "Goldwater Phenomenon," 386–413; Sundquist, *Dynamics of the Party System*, 352–375.

7. Thomas P. O'Neil, Jr., to Martin Luther King, Jr., 5 January 1965, MLK, 24:28, MLKC.

8. Larry O'Brien, memorandum to the president, 23 October 1964, WHCF, Wilson Files, Box 3, LBJL.

9. Evans and Novak, *Exercise of Power*, 467. See also Sundquist, *Politics and Policy*, 467.

10. Bill Moyers, letter to author, 27 August 1985, copy in possession of the author.

11. Lawrence F. O'Brien, interview with author, 19 July 1989, 11.

12. See, e.g., Evans and Novak, *Exercise of Power*, 467.

13. Southern Regional Council, "What Happened in the South?" 15 November 1964, news release, Files of the Southern Regional Council, 75-17-3-38, AUL.

14. Louis Martin to John M. Bailey, "Operation Dixie, 1964–1965," 17 November 1964, LBJ, Legislative Background, Voting Rights Act of 1965, Box 1, LBJL.

15. Lee White to the president, "Voting Rights," 18 November 1964, LBJ, Ex HU 2, Box 3, WHCF, LBJL.

16. Task Force Issue Paper, "Civil Rights," 17 June 1964, WHCF, Lee White Files, Box 3, LBJL.

17. Hobart Taylor, Jr., to the president, 27 November 1964, Ex HU, Box 3, WHCF, LBJL.

18. Matthew Reese, Jr., "Voting Participation and Registration," Confidential Report, December 1964, WHCF, Fred Panzer Files, Box 500, LBJL.

19. Clarence Mitchell, oral history interview by Thomas H. Baker, 30 April 1969, tape 2, LBJL, 3.

20. Lawson, *Black Ballots*, 299.

21. U.S. Commission on Civil Rights, *Voting Rights Act: The First Months*, (1965), 9.

22. New York Times, 5 November 1964.

23. White House Diary and Diary Backup, LBJ, 18 December 1964, LBJL; Lee White to President Johnson, "Possible Items for Discussion with Dr. Martin Luther King," 3 December 1964, name file, Martin Luther King, Jr., LBJL.

24. W. Baker, *Selma, 1965*, 5–6.

25. Quoted in Garrow, *Bearing the Cross*, 368. The best analysis of the Selma episode is in Garrow, *Protest at Selma*.

26. Kearns, *Johnson and the American Dream*, 228; Goldman, *Tragedy of Lyndon Johnson*, 318; L. B. Johnson, *Vantage Point*, 161–162.

27. Lawrence F. O'Brien, interview with author, 19 July 1989, 10.

28. Katzenbach quoted in Firestone and Vogt, *Uses of Power*, 180.

29. Jack Valenti, oral history interview with Joe B. Frantz, 18 October 1969, LBJL, 2:36.

30. Nicholas deB Katzenbach to Lyndon B. Johnson, 28 December 1964, Justice Department Administrative History, vol. 7, pt. Xa, LBJL.

31. Lee White to Bill Moyers, "Legislation to Facilitate Registration for Federal Elections," 30 December 1964, WHCF, Lee White Files, Box 3, LBJL.

32. A thorough analysis of the Voting Rights Act of 1965 may be found in Garrow, *Protest at Selma*.

33. House Committee on the Judiciary, *Hearings on Voting Rights*, H.R. 6400, 89th Cong., 1st sess., 1965, S. Rept. 1564. See especially the testimony of Theodore Hesburgh, 258 ff.; Nicholas deB Katzenbach, 9 ff.; and Burke Marshall, 305 ff.

34. Nicholas deB Katzenbach to the president, "A Review of the Activities of the Department of Justice in Civil Rights in 1964," 6 January 1965, Marshall Files, Box 16, JFKL.

35. Garrow, *Protest at Selma*, 2.

36. "Lou Harris Poll," *Washington Post*, 9 January 1965.

37. *New York Times*, 3 January 1965, 4 January 1965, 19–21 January 1965.

38. PPP:LBJ, 1965, 1:5.

39. News conference, "Background Basis from W.H. Officials," with George Reedy, McGeorge Bundy, and William Moyers, 4 January 1964, LBJ, Legislative Background, Voting Rights Act of 1965, Box 1, LBJL.

40. Arnold Aronson to Cooperating Organizations, 9 January 1965, Leadership Conference on Civil Rights, Organizations File, Box 4, LC.

41. King, "Equality Now," 92; Wofford, *Kennedys and Kings*, 38.

42. "Justice Department Weekly Legislative Report to Lawrence O'Brien," 11 January 1965, Reports on Pending Legislation, Box 8, LBJL. See also Larry O'Brien to the president, 12 January 1965, WHCF, Files of Mike Manatos, Box 2, LBJL.

43. *New York Times*, 1, 4 February 1965.

44. See, e.g., George Meany (president, AFL-CIO) to President Lyndon B. Johnson, 3 February 1965; A. Philip Randolph to President Lyndon B. Johnson, 1 February 1965; Michael J. Quill (president, Transport Workers Union) to President Lyndon B. Johnson, 5 February 1965; James Forman (Student Violent Coordinating Committee) to President Lyndon B. Johnson, 4 February 1965; Harry Van Arsdale (New York City Central Labor Council) to Lyndon B. Johnson, 4 February 1965; David Siegal (president, National Restaurant and Bartenders Employees International Union) to President Lyndon B. Johnson, 5 February 1965, Ex HU 2/ST 1, Box 27, WHCF, LBJL.

45. Martin Luther King, Jr., to Andrew Young, Selma Jail Notes, 1–5 February 1965, MLK, MLKC, 22–26.

46. Lee C. White to Lyndon B. Johnson, 3 February 1965, Ex HU 2/ST 1, Box 24, WHCF, LBJL.

47. PPP:LBJ, 1965, 130–131.

48. *New York Times*, 7 February 1965.

49. Statement of Martin Luther King, Jr., 7 February 1965, MLK, 21:11, MLKC.

50. Martin Luther King, Jr., "Selma Notes on Strategy and Statements," February 1965, MLK, 22:6, MLKC; Lee C. White to the president, 8 February 1965, name file, Martin L. King, Jr., Ex HU 2, Box 3, LBJL; Jack Valenti to Mr. President, 9 February 1965, name file, Martin L. King, Jr., Ex HU 2, Box 3, LBJL.

51. *New York Times*, 10 February 1965. See also Lee C. White, memorandum for the president, 8 February 1965, WHCF, Ex HU 2, Box 3, WHCF, LBJL.

52. Frank Thompson, Jr., to Executive Committee, Steering Committee, "Buddy System Whips, Voting Rights Strategy Meeting, Tuesday, February 6th—4:00 P.M," 1 February 1965, DSG, Box 74, LC.

53. *New York Times*, 4, 10 February 1965.

54. Charles C. Diggs, Jr., to President Lyndon B. Johnson, 10 February 1965, LBJ, Legislative Background, Voting Rights Act of 1965, Box 1, LBJL.

55. Quoted in Raines, *My Soul Is Rested*, 337.

56. Nicholas deB Katzenbach, "Weekly Report—Major Legislation," 15 February 1965, "Reports on Legislation," 8 February–16 March 1965, LBJ, LBJL; Lawson, *Black Ballots*, 309.

57. Nicholas deB Katzenbach, oral history interview by Paige R. Mulhollan, 23 November 1968, LBJL, 25. On the failure of the First Reconstruction voting legislation see Kousser, "Undermining of the First Reconstruction," 27–46.

58. U.S. Commission on Civil Rights, *Hearings in Jackson, Mississippi* , 16–20 February 1965. See also *New York Times*, 21 May 1965.

59. *New York Times*, 24 February 1965.

60. Lawrence O'Brien to the president, 1 March 1965, White House Aides Files, Mike Manatos Files, Box 2, LBJL.

61. Ramsey Clark, "Comment," in Firestone and Vogt, *The Uses of Power*, 174.

62. Senate Committee on the Judiciary, *Hearings on Voting Rights, 1965*, 89th Cong., 1st sess., 1965, S. Rept. 1564, 163.

63. Harold Barefoot Sanders, oral history interview by Joe B. Frantz, 3 November 1969, tape 3, LBJL, 3.

64. "An Act," 5 March 1965, Justice Department Administrative History, vol. 7, pt. Xa, LBJL. The basis for the selection of this particular automatic formula is discussed in *New York Times*, 11, 12 April 1965, E5.

65. Bickel, *Politics and the Warren Court*, 121. The state of Alaska was also covered under the formula, but this occurred because of the large number of servicemen stationed there. Subsequently, the act was not enforced in Alaska.

66. *New York Times*, 6 March 1965; Garrow, *Protest at Selma*, 69.

67. *New York Times*, 8 March 1965.

68. *New York Times*, 8, 9 March 1965; Dean Peerman and Martin E. Marty, "Selma: Sustaining the Momentum," *Christian Century* (24 March 1965): 358–359.

69. *New York Times*, 10 February 1965; Wagy, "Governor LeRoy Collins," 403–420.

70. *New York Times*, 12 March 1965.

71. George C. Wallace telegram to Mr. President, 12 March 1965, LBJ, Ex HU 2/ST 1, Box 24, WHCF, LBJL. Lyndon B. Johnson to George Wallace, 12 March 1965, LBJ, Ex HU 2/ST 1, Box 24, WHCF, LBJL.

72. L. B. Johnson, *Vantage Point*, 163.

73. PPP:LBJ, 1965, 274–281.

74. White House Daily Diary and Appointment File, 14 March 1965, Box 4, LBJL; L. B. Johnson, *Vantage Point*, 164.

75. PPP:LBJ, 1965, 187–191.

76. Congressional Quarterly, *Congress and the Nation* (Washington, D.C.: Congressional Quarterly, Inc., 1969), 2:357.

77. Ramsey Clark to Bill Moyers, 13 March 1865, White House Aides Files, Bill Moyers Files, Box 6, LBJL; Larry O'Brien to the president, 10 March 1965, LBJ, Ex HU 2–7, Box 55, WHCF, LBJL; Sundquist, *Politics and Policy*, 273.

78. *Congressional Quarterly Weekly Report* (19 March 1965): 434–435.

79. James Eastland, *Congressional Record*, 89th Congress, 1st sess., 18 March 1965, 5228.

80. Richard B. Russell to Bruce Myrick, 28 July 1965, Russell Papers, Civil Rights Series, 10:47, RBRL.

81. See *Congressional Quarterly Weekly Report*, (28 May 1965):1007, (16 July 1965):1402–1403, and (13 August 1965):1595–1597. The complete text of the Voting Rights Act of 1965 may be found in U.S. Commission on Civil Rights, *Voting Rights Act of 1965*.

82. Richard B. Russell to Zac Crittenden, 5 August 1965, Russell Papers, Political Series, 6:23, RBRL. On Johnson's devotion to Russell see Harry McPherson, oral history interview by Thomas H. Baker, 5 December 1968, tape 1, LBJL, 20.

83. PPP:LBJ, 1965, 2:842.

84. Ibid., 361–362.

85. Congressional Quarterly, *Congress and the Nation*, 2:357.

86. U.S. Commission on Civil Rights, *Political Participation*, (1968), 12–13.

87. Martin Luther King, Jr., to Lyndon B. Johnson, MLK, 13:7, MLKC.

88. Muse, *American Negro Revolution*. See also *Report of the National Advisory Commission on Civil Disorders*; *Newsweek*, 10 October 1966, 27–28. See also *New York Times*, 22 October, 9 November 1966.

89. Phillips, *Emerging Republican Majority*, 467–468, 473. On the importance of Phillips's arguments to Republican political strategy see Rusher, *Rise of the Right*, 226. An excellent analysis of the impact in Texas of this Republican strategy is provided in Davidson, *Race and Class in Texas Politics*.

90. PPP:LBJ, 1968, 1354.

91. Joseph L. Rauh, Jr., letter to Ms. Joyce Tucker, 29 May 1988, copy in possession of the author.

EPILOGUE

1. Chafe, "The End of One Struggle, the Beginning of Another," 188; Davidson, *Minority Vote Dilution*; Thernstrom, *Whose Votes Count?*; Parker, *Black Votes Count*; Graham, *The Civil Rights Era*; Detlefsen, "Triumph of the Race-Conscious State."

2. Pomper, "From Confusion to Clarity," 415–428; Carmines and Stimson, *Issue Evolution*, 188; Bass and DeVries, *Transformation of Southern Politics*, 79; Wildavsky, "Goldwater Phenomenon," 386–413.

3. Bensel, *Sectionalism and American Political Development*, 253.

4. Phillips, *Emerging Republican Majority*, 187; Axelrod, "Where the Votes Come From," 11–20; Axelrod, "Presidential Election Coalitions in 1984," 281–284.

5. On the changed political South see Grantham, *Life and Death of the Solid South*; Lamis, *Two-Party South*; Black and Black, *Politics and Society in the South*.

6. Joint Center for Political Studies, *Black Elected Officials: A National Roster* (Washington, D.C.: Joint Center for Political Studies, 1989); Cavanagh and Stockton, *Black Elected Officials and Their Constituencies*; Sonenshein, "Can Black Candidates Win Statewide Elections?" 219–242.

7. Lamis, *Two-Party South*, 20–43.

8. Burstein, "Public Opinion," 170.

BIBLIOGRAPHY

ARCHIVAL MATERIALS

Americans for Democratic Action. Papers. Microfilm Corporation of America.

Celler, Emanuel. Papers. Library of Congress.

Democratic Study Group. Files. Library of Congress.

Dulles, Allen W. Papers. Seeley G. Mudd Manuscript Library, Princeton University.

Eisenhower, Dwight D. Papers. Dwight D. Eisenhower Library, Abilene, Kansas.

Horn, Stephen. Senatorial Log, 1964. Minnesota Historical Society, Minneapolis.

Humphrey, Hubert H. Papers. Minnesota Historical Society, Minneapolis.

Johnson, Lyndon Baines. Papers. Lyndon Baines Johnson Library, Austin.

Justice Department Administrative History. Lyndon Baines Johnson Library, Austin.

Kennedy, John F. Papers. John F. Kennedy Library, Boston.

Kennedy, Robert F. Papers. John F. Kennedy Library, Boston.

King, Martin Luther, Jr. Papers (including the FBI's King file). Martin Luther King, Jr., Center for Social Change, Atlanta.

————. Papers. Mugar Library, Boston University.

Leadership Conference on Civil Rights. Files. Library of Congress.

Manatos, Mike. Files. Lyndon Baines Johnson Library, Austin.

Marshall, Burke. Papers. John F. Kennedy Library, Boston.

Mississippi Freedom Democratic Party. Papers. Martin Luther King, Jr., Center for Social Change, Atlanta.

National Association for the Advancement of Colored People. Papers. Library of Congress.

National Urban League. Papers. Library of Congress.

Panzer, Fred. Files. Lyndon Baines Johnson Library, Austin.

Rauh, Joseph L., Jr. Papers. Library of Congress.

Russell, Richard B. Papers. Richard B. Russell Library, University of Georgia, Athens.

Solberg, Carl. Papers. Minnesota Historical Society, Minneapolis.

Sorenson, Theodore C. Papers. John F. Kennedy Library, Boston.

Southern Christian Leadership Conference. Papers. Martin Luther King, Jr., Center for Social Change, Atlanta.

Southern Regional Council. Files. Robert Woodruff Library, Special Collections, Atlanta University Library.

Stevenson, Adlai. Papers. Seeley G. Mudd Manuscript Library, Princeton University Library.

Voter Education Project. Files. Robert Woodruff Library, Special Collections, Emory University, Atlanta.

White, Lee. Files. John F. Kennedy Library, Boston.

Wilson, Henry Hall. Files. Lyndon Baines Johnson Library, Austin.

INTERVIEWS CONDUCTED
BY THE AUTHOR

Brownell, Herbert. Austin, Texas. 27 October 1990.

Clifford, Clark. Washington, D.C. 7 March 1989.

Conway, Jack T. Sarasota, Florida. 21 June 1990.

Eddy, Mary Jane. New York, New York. 1 May 1986.

Fleming, Harold C. Washington, D.C. 4 April 1985.

Henry, Aaron. Clarksdale, Mississippi. 23 July 1990.

Hollings, Ernest F. Washington, D.C. 8 March 1989.

McDew, Charles F. Kent, Ohio. 24 July 1985.

McPherson, Harry. Washington, D. C. 6 March 1989 and 24 July 1989.

Mitchell, Juanita. Baltimore, Maryland. 22 October 1987.

Mondale, Walter F. Minneapolis, Minnesota. 23 July 1990.

O'Brien, Lawrence F. New York, New York. 19 July 1989.

Rauh, Joseph L., Jr. Washington, D.C. 20 February 1988, 30 August 1988, and 28 March 1990. Orlando, Florida. 6 June 1990 and 29 June 1990.

Reedy, George E. Austin, Texas. 27 October 1990. Orlando, Florida. 4–5 March 1991.

Valenti, Jack. Orlando, Florida. 5 October 1990.

White, C. Lee. Washington, D.C. 6 March 1989.

Wofford, Harris. Hempstead, New York. 20 February 1988.

ORAL HISTORIES AND
OTHER INTERVIEWS

Almond, J. Lindsey. 7 February 1968. John F. Kennedy Library.

Barry, Marion. 30 October 1967. Ralph J. Bunche Oral History Collection, Moorland-Spingarn Research Center, Howard University.

Bernhard, Berl. 17 June 1968. John F. Kennedy Library.

Branton, Wiley. 11, 16 January 1969. Ralph J. Bunche Oral History Collection, Moorland-Spingarn Research Center, Howard University.

Burns, James MacGregor. 14 May 1965. John F. Kennedy Library.

Celler, Emanuel. 19 March 1969. Lyndon Baines Johnson Library.

Clark, Ramsey. 17 December 1968. Ralph J. Bunche Oral History Collection, Moorland-Spingarn Research Center, Howard University.

Cushing, Richard. 11 March 1969. Minnesota Historical Society.

Dirksen, Everett M. 30 July 1969. Lyndon Baines Johnson Library.

Dunbar, Leslie. 5 September 1968. Ralph J. Bunche Oral History Collection, Moorland-Spingarn Research Center, Howard University.

Elman, Philip. 1984. Columbia University Oral History Project, Columbia University.

Farmer, James. 30 October 1969. Lyndon Baines Johnson Library.

————. 28 September 1968. Ralph J. Bunche Oral History Collection, Moorland-Spingarn Research Center, Howard University.

Fleming, Harold C. Interview by David J. Garrow, 10 January 1983, Washington, D.C.

Henry, Aaron. 12 September 1970. Ralph J. Bunche Oral History Collection, Moorland-Spingarn Research Center, Howard University.

Hesburgh, Theodore. 27 March 1966 and 17 February 1971. Lyndon Baines Johnson Library.

Humphrey, Hubert H. 17 August 1971 and 20–21 June 1977. Lyndon Baines Johnson Library.

Johnson, Claudia T. 28 June 1977. Lyndon Baines Johnson Library.

Kastenmeier, Robert W. 25 October 1965. John F. Kennedy Library.

Katzenbach, Nicholas. 8 October 1969. John F. Kennedy Library.

————. 12 and 23 November 1968. Lyndon Baines Johnson Library.

Kennedy, Robert F. 29 February 1964. John F. Kennedy Library.

Kennedy, Robert F., and Burke Marshall. Joint Oral History. 4, 6, and 22 December 1964. John F. Kennedy Library.

King, Martin Luther, Jr. 9 March 1964. John F. Kennedy Library.

Lewis, John. 1970. Columbia University Oral History Project, Columbia University.

McDew, Charles F. 24 August 1967. Ralph J. Bunche Oral History Collection, Moorland-Spingarn Research Center, Howard University.

McPherson, Harry. 5 December 1968 and 24 March 1969. Lyndon Baines Johnson Library.

Marshall, Burke. 29 May 1964, 13–14 June 1964, 4 and 22 December 1964, and 19–20 January 1970. John F. Kennedy Library.

Marshall, Thurgood. 7 April 1964. John F. Kennedy Library.

Martin, Louis. 14 May 1969. Lyndon Baines Johnson Library.

————. 25 March 1970. Ralph J. Bunche Oral History Collection, Moorland-Springarn Research Center, Howard University.

Mitchell, Clarence. 30 April 1969. Lyndon Baines Johnson Library.

Mitchell, Clarence and John Stewart. 15 March 1979. Joint Oral History, Minnesota Historical Society.

Morrow, E. Frederick. 23 February 1977. Dwight D. Eisenhower Library.

Nixon, Richard M. 13 April 1978. Richard Russell Library.

O'Donnell, Kenneth P. 23 July 1969. John F. Kennedy Library.

Randolph, A. Philip. 14 January 1969. Ralph J. Bunche Oral History Collection, Moorland-Spingarn Research Center, Howard University.

Rauh, Joseph L., Jr. 30 July and 8 August 1969. Lyndon Baines Johnson Library.

————. 12 November 1980. Minnesota Historical Society.

————. 16 June and 28 August 1967. Ralph J. Bunche Oral History Collection, Moorland-Spingarn Research Center, Howard University.

Sanders, Harold Barefoot. 3 November 1969. Lyndon Baines Johnson Library.

Schlei, Norbert A. 20–21 February 1964. John F. Kennedy Library.

Shuttlesworth, Fred. September 1968. Ralph J. Bunche Oral History Collection, Moorland-Spingarn Research Center, Howard University.

Sorenson, Theodore. 26 March 1964, 15 April 1964, 3 May 1964, 24 March 1969, and 23 July 1970. John F. Kennedy Library.

Stewart, John. 21 June 1970. Minnesota Historical Society.

Taylor, William L. October 1972. Columbia University Oral History Project, Columbia University.

Troutman, Robert, Jr. 4 March 1971. Richard Russell Library.

Valenti, Jack. 18 October 1969, 3 March 1971, and 12 July 1972. Lyndon Baines Johnson Library.

Walker, Wyatt T. 11 October 1967. Ralph J. Bunche Oral History Collection, Moorland-Spingarn Research Center, Howard University.

White, C. Lee. 28 September 1970. Lyndon Baines Johnson Library.

Wilkins, Roy. 13 August 1964. John F. Kennedy Library.

————. 1 April 1969, 29 April 1970, and 5 May 1970. Ralph J. Bunche Oral History Collection, Moorland-Spingarn Research Center, Howard University.

Wofford, Harris. 29 November 1965. John F. Kennedy Library.

————. 3 February 1969. Lyndon Baines Johnson Library.

Young, Whitney, Jr. 18 June 1969. Lyndon Baines Johnson Library.

PUBLIC DOCUMENTS

The following were printed at the Government Printing Office in Washington, D.C.

Congressional Record, 1942–1965.

Public Papers of the Presidents of the United States: Dwight D. Eisenhower, 1958–1962. 8 vols. 1959–1963.

Public Papers of the Presidents of the United States: John F. Kennedy, 1962–1964. 3 vols. 1963–1965.

Public Papers of the Presidents of the United States: Lyndon B. Johnson, 1964–1965. 3 vols. 1965–1966.

U.S. Commission on Civil Rights. *Hearings in Jackson, Mississippi*, February 16–20, 1965.

———. *Political Participation*, 1968.

———. *Report*, 1959.

———. *Report: Voting I*, 1961.

———. *The Voting Rights Act: The First Months*, 1965.

———. *The Voting Rights Act of 1965*, 1965.

U.S. Congress. House. Committee on the Judiciary. *Hearings on Voting Rights.* 88th Cong., 1st sess., 1963.

———. Committee on the Judiciary. *Hearings on Voting Rights: H. R. 6400.* 89th Cong., 1st sess., 1965.

———. Senate. Committee on Commerce. *Report: Speeches, Remarks, Press Conferences, and Statements of Senator John F. Kennedy.* 87th Cong., 1st sess., 1961.

———. Committee on the Judiciary. *Hearings on Literacy Tests and Voter Requirements in State and Federal Elections.* 87th Cong., 2d sess., 1962.

———. Committee on the Judiciary. *Hearings on Voting Rights: S. 1564.* 89th Cong., 1st sess., 1965.

———. Select Committee to Study Governmental Operations with Respect to Intelligence Activities. *Intelligence Activities and the Rights of Americans.* 94th Cong., 2d sess., 1976.

SELECTED BOOKS, ARTICLES, AND UNPUBLISHED MATERIALS

Ambrose, Stephen E. *Eisenhower.* Vol. 2, *The President.* New York: Simon and Schuster, 1984.

———. *Nixon: The Education of a Politician, 1913–1962.* New York: Simon and Schuster, 1987.

Anderson, Jervis. *A. Philip Randolph: A Political Portrait.* New York: Harcourt Brace Jovanovich, 1972.

Anderson, J. W. *Eisenhower, Brownell, and the Congress: The Tangled Origins of the Civil Rights Bill of 1956–1957.* Tuscaloosa: University of Alabama Press, 1964.

Ashmore, Harry S. *Hearts and Minds: The Anatomy of Racism from Roosevelt to Reagan.* New York: McGraw-Hill, 1982.

Axelrod, Robert. "Presidential Election Coalitions in 1984." *American Political Science Review* 80 (1986): 281–284.

———. "Where the Votes Come From: An Analysis of Electoral Coalitions, 1952–1968." *American Political Science Review* 66 (1972): 11–20.

Baker, Leonard. *The Johnson Eclipse.* New York: Macmillan, 1966.

Baker, Wilson. *Selma, 1965.* New York: Scribner, 1974.

Bass, Harold F., Jr. "Presidential Party Leadership and Party Reform:

Lyndon B. Johnson and the MFDP Controversy." *Presidential Studies Quarterly* 21 (1991): 85–101.

Bass, Jack, and Walter DeVries. *The Transformation of Southern Politics: Social Changes and Political Consequences Since 1945.* New York: Basic, 1976.

Belfrage, Sally. *Freedom Summer.* New York: Viking, 1965.

Bensel, Richard F. *Sectionalism and American Political Development.* Madison: University of Wisconsin Press, 1984.

Berman, Daniel M. *A Bill Becomes a Law: Congress Enacts Civil Rights Legislation.* New York: Macmillan, 1966.

Berman, William C. *The Politics of Civil Rights in the Truman Administration.* Columbus: Ohio State University Press, 1970.

Bernstein, Barton J. "The Ambiguous Legacy: The Truman Administration and Civil Rights." In *Politics and Policies of the Truman Administration,* ed. Barton J. Berstein. Chicago: Quadrangle Books, 1970.

Bickel, Alexander M. *Politics and the Warren Court.* New York: Harper and Row, 1965.

Billington, Monroe. "Lyndon B. Johnson and Blacks: The Early Years." *Journal of Negro History* 62 (1977): 26–42.

Black, Earl, and Merle Black. *Politics and Society in the South.* Cambridge, Mass.: Harvard University Press, 1987.

Blum, John Morton. *The Progressive Presidents: Theodore Roosevelt, Woodrow Wilson, Franklin D. Roosevelt, Lyndon Johnson.* New York: Norton, 1980.

Blumenthal, Sidney. "Getting It All Wrong: The Years of Robert Caro." *New Republic,* 4 June 1990, 29–36.

Bolling, Richard. *House Out of Order.* New York: Dutton, 1965.

Bornet, Vaugn. *The Presidency of Lyndon Johnson.* Lawrence: University Press of Kansas, 1983.

Bowles, Chester. *Promises to Keep: My Years in Public Life, 1949–1969.* New York: Harper and Row, 1971.

Bradlee, Benjamin. *Conversations with Kennedy.* New York: Norton, 1975.

Branch, Taylor. *Parting the Waters: America in the King Years, 1954–63.* New York: Simon & Schuster, 1988.

Branyan, Robert L., and R. A. Hon Lee. "Lyndon B. Johnson and the Art of the Possible." *Southwestern Social Science Quarterly* 45 (1964): 213–233.

Brauer, Carl M. *John F. Kennedy and the Second Reconstruction.* New York: Columbia University Press, 1977.

Burner, David, and Thomas R. West. *The Torch Is Passed: The Kennedy Brothers and American Liberalism.* New York: Atheneum, 1984.

Burns, James M. *John Kennedy: A Political Profile.* New York: Harcourt, Brace and World, 1961.

Burstein, Paul. "Public Opinion, Demonstrations, and the Passage of Antidiscrimination Legislation." *Public Opinion Quarterly* 43 (1979): 157–172.

Califano, Joseph. *A Presidential Nation.* New York: Norton, 1975.

Carmines, Edward G., and James A. Stimson. *Issue Evolution, Race, and the*

Transformation of American Politics. Princeton: Princeton University Press, 1989.

———. "On the Structure and Sequence of Issue Evolution." *American Political Science Review* 80 (1986): 901–920.

Caro, Robert A. *The Years of Lyndon Johnson*. Vol. 1, *The Path to Power*. New York: Vintage Books, 1983. Vol. 2, *Means of Ascent*. New York: Knopf, 1990.

Carson, Clayborne. *In Struggle: SNCC and the Black Awakening of the 1960s*. Cambridge, Mass.: Harvard University Press, 1981.

Carter, Barbara. "The Role of the Civil Rights Commission." *Reporter* 29 (4 July 1963): 10–17.

Cavanagh, Thomas E., and Denise Stockton. *Black Elected Officials and Their Constituencies*. Washington, D.C.: Joint Center for Political Studies, 1983.

Chafe, William H. "The End of One Struggle, the Beginning of Another." In *The Civil Rights Movement in America*, ed. Charles W. Eagles, 127. Jackson: University Press of Mississippi, 1986.

Colby, David C. "Protest and Party: A Revisionist Study of the Mississippi Freedom Democratic Party." Paper read at the annual meeting of the Southern Political Science Association, Nashville, Tennessee, November 1985.

Collier, Peter, and David Horowitz. *The Kennedys: An American Drama*. New York: Summit Books, 1984.

Converse, Philip E. "On the Possibility of Major Political Realignment in the South." In *Elections and the Political Order*, ed. Agnus Campbell, Philip E. Converse, Warren E. Miller, and Donald E. Stokes. New York: Wiley, 1966.

Cosman, Bernard. *Five States for Goldwater: Continuity and Change in Southern Voting Patterns*. Tuscaloosa: University of Alabama Press, 1965.

———. "Presidential Republicanism in the South." *Journal of Politics* 24 (1962): 303–322.

Davidson, Chandler. *Race and Class in Texas Politics*. Princeton: Princeton University Press, 1990.

———, ed. *Minority Vote Dilution*. Washington, D.C.: Howard University Press, 1984.

Detlefsen, Robert R. "Triumph of the Race-Conscious State: The Politics of Human Rights, 1980–1986." Ph. D. diss., University of California, Berkeley, 1988.

Dorman, Michael. *We Shall Overcome*. New York: Carlson, 1965.

Douglas, Paul H. *In the Fullness of Time*. New York: Harcourt Brace Jovanovich, 1971.

Douglas, William O. *The Court Years, 1939–1977: The Autobiography of William O. Douglas*. New York: Random House, 1980.

Downs, Anthony. *An Economic Theory of Democracy*. New York: Harper and Row, 1956.

Drew, Elizabeth B. "The Politics of Cloture." *Reporter* 31 (16 July 1964): 19–23.

Dugger, Ronnie. *The Politician: The Life and Times of Lyndon Johnson, The Drive for Power—from the Frontier to Master of the Senate.* New York: Norton, 1982.

Dulles, Foster Rhea. *The Civil Rights Commission: 1957–1965.* East Lansing: Michigan State University Press, 1968.

Dyer, Stanford Phillips. "Lyndon B. Johnson and the Politics of Civil Rights, 1935–1960: The Art of 'Moderate Leadership.'" Ph. D. diss., Texas A & M University, 1978.

Elliott, Claude. "Union Sentiment in Texas, 1861–1865." *Southwestern Historical Quarterly* 50 (1947): 449–477.

Evans, Rowland, and Robert Novak. *Lyndon Baines Johnson: The Exercise of Power.* New York: American Library, 1966.

Fairclough, Adam. *To Redeem the Soul of America: The Southern Leadership Conference and Martin Luther King, Jr.* Athens: University of Georgia Press, 1987.

Farmer, James. *Lay Bare the Heart: An Autobiography of the Civil Rights Movement.* New York: Arbor House, 1985.

Firestone, Bernard J., and Robert C. Vogt, eds. *Lyndon Baines Johnson and the Uses of Power.* New York: Greenwood, 1988.

Fite, Gilbert C. *Richard B. Russell, Jr., Senator from Georgia.* Chapel Hill, N.C.: University of North Carolina Press, 1991.

Fleming, Harold C. "The Federal Executive and Civil Rights: 1961–1965." *Daedalus* 94 (1965): 921–948.

Forman, James. *The Making of Black Revolutionaries.* New York: Macmillan, 1972.

Frady, Marshall. *Wallace.* New York: World, 1970.

Frantz, Joe B. "Opening a Curtain: The Metamorphosis of Lyndon B. Johnson." *Journal of Southern History* 45 (1979): 3–26.

Friedel, Frank. *FDR and the South.* Baton Rouge: Louisiana State University Press, 1965.

Gallup, George H. *The Gallup Poll: Public Opinion, 1935–1971.* 3 vols. New York: Random House, 1972.

Garfinkel, Herbert. *When Negroes March: The March on Washington Movement in the Organizational Politics for FEPC.* New York: Atheneum, 1973.

Garrow, David J. *Bearing the Cross: Martin Luther King, Jr., and the Southern Christian Leadership Conference.* New York: Morrow, 1986.

———. *The FBI and Martin Luther King, Jr.: From "Solo" to Memphis.* New York: Norton, 1981.

———. *Protest at Selma: Martin Luther King, Jr., and the Voting Rights Act of 1965.* New Haven: Yale University Press, 1978.

Gentile, Thomas. *March on Washington, August 28, 1963.* Washington, D.C.: New Day, 1983.

Gilbert, Robert E. "John F. Kennedy and Civil Rights for Black Americans." *Presidential Studies Quarterly* 12 (1982): 386–399.

Goldman, Eric F. *The Tragedy of Lyndon Johnson.* New York: Knopf, 1969.

Goldwater, Barry. *The Conscience of a Conservative.* New York: Hillman, 1960.

————. *Why Not Victory?* New York: Hillman, 1962.

Goldwater, Barry M., and Jack Casserly. *Goldwater.* New York: St. Martin, 1988.

Goodwin, Richard N. *Remembering America: A Voice from the Sixties.* New York: Harper and Row, 1988.

Graham, Hugh Davis. *The Civil Rights Era: Origins and Development of National Policy.* New York: Oxford University Press, 1990.

Grantham, Dewey W. *The Life and Death of the Solid South: A Political History.* Lexington: University Press of Kentucky, 1988.

Hamby, Alonzo L. *Liberalism and Its Challengers: FDR to Reagan.* New York: Oxford University Press, 1985.

Hamilton, Charles V. *The Bench and the Ballot: Southern Judges and Black Voters.* New York: Oxford University Press, 1973.

Hardeman, D. B., and Donald C. Bacon. *Rayburn: A Biography.* Austin: Texas Monthly Press, 1987.

Harris, Lou. "How White Feel about Negroes: A Painful Dilemma." *Newsweek*, 21 October 1963, 44–57.

Hawk, Barry E., and John J. Kirby, Jr. "Federal Protection of Negro Voting Rights." *Virginia Law Review* 51 (1961): 1053–1213.

Hoffman, Nicholas von. *Mississippi Notebook.* New York: David White, 1964.

Holt, Len. *The Summer That Didn't End.* New York: Morrow, 1965.

Huitt, Ralph K. "Democratic Party Leadership in the Senate." *American Political Science Review* 55 (1961): 333–344.

Humphrey, Hubert H. *The Education of a·Public Man: My Life in Politics.* New York: Doubleday, 1976.

Johnson, Donald B., comp. *National Party Platforms.* Vol. 2, *1960–1976.* Urbana: University of Illinois Press, 1978.

Johnson, Lyndon Baines. *The Vantage Point: Perspectives of the Presidency, 1963–1969.* New York: Holt, Rinehart, and Winston, 1971.

Johnson, Rebekah Baines. *A Family Album.* Edited by John S. Moursund. New York: McGraw-Hill, 1965.

Kastenmeier, Robert W. "CBS Reports: Filibuster—Birth Struggle of a Law." Transcript of a CBS Network Broadcast, 18 March 1964.

Katzenbach, Nicholas. "Origin of Kennedy's Civil Rights." In *The Kennedy Presidency: Seventeen Intimate Perspectives of John F. Kennedy.* Portraits of American Presidents, ed. Kenneth W. Thompson, vol. 4. Lanham, Md.: University Press of America, 1985.

Kearns, Doris. *Lyndon Johnson and the American Dream.* New York: New American Library, 1976.

Kearns Goodwin, Doris. *The Fitzgeralds and the Kennedys.* New York: Simon and Schuster, 1987.

Kennedy, John F. *Profiles in Courage.* New York: Harper and Row, 1956.

Kessel, John H. *The Goldwater Coalition: Republican Strategies in 1964.* Indianapolis: Bobbs-Merrill, 1968.

Key, V. O., Jr. *Southern Politics, in State and Nation.* New York: Knopf, 1949.

King, Coretta. *My Life with Martin Luther King, Jr.* New York: Holt, Rinehart, and Winston, 1969.

King, Martin Luther, Jr. "Bold Design for a New South." *Nation* 196 (30 March 1963): 259–262.

——. "Equality Now." *Nation* 192 (4 February 1961): 91–95.

——. "Fumbling on the New Frontier." *Nation* 194 (3 March 1962): 190–193.

——. *Stride toward Freedom: The Montgomery Story.* New York: Harper and Brothers, 1958.

——. "Who Is Their God?" *Nation* 195 (13 October 1962): 209–211.

——. *Why We Can't Wait.* New York: Harper and Row, 1968.

Kingdon, John W. *Agendas, Alternatives, and Public Policies.* Boston: Little, Brown, 1984.

Kousser, Morgan. "The Undermining of the First Reconstruction: Lessons for the Second." In *Minority Vote Dilution*, ed. Chandler Davidson, 27–46. Washington, D.C.: Howard University Press, 1984.

Ladd, Everett C., and Charles Hadley. *Transformation of the American Party System.* New York: Norton, 1975.

Lamis, Alexander P. *The Two-Party South.* 2d ed., rev. and enl. New York: Oxford University Press, 1988.

Land, Guy Paul. "John F. Kennedy's Southern Strategy, 1956–1960." *North Carolina Historical Review* 56 (1979): 41–63.

Lawson, Steven F. *Black Ballots: Voting Rights in the South, 1944–1969.* New York: Columbia University Press, 1976.

Lester, Julius. *Look Out, Whitey! Black Power's Gon' Get Your Mama!* New York: Dial, 1968.

Leuchtenburg, William E. *In the Shadow of FDR: From Harry Truman to Ronald Reagan.* rev. ed. Ithaca: Cornell University Press, 1983.

Lewis, Anthony. *Portrait of a Decade: The Second American Revolution.* New York: Random House, 1964.

Lewis, David Levering. *King: A Biography.* Urbana: University of Illinois Press, 1970.

Lichtman, Allen. "The Federal Assault against Voting Discrimination in the Deep South, 1957–1967." *Journal of Negro History* 54 (1969): 346–367.

Light, Paul C. *The President's Agenda: Domestic Policy Choice from Kennedy to Carter, with Notes on Ronald Reagan.* Baltimore: Johns Hopkins University Press, 1982.

Loevy, Robert D. "'To Write It in the Books of Law': President Lyndon B. Johnson and the Civil Rights Act of 1964." In *Lyndon Baines Johnson and the Uses of Power*, eds. Bernard J. Firestone and Robert C. Vogt, 105–127. New York: Greenwood, 1988.

Lomax, Louis E. "The Kennedys Move in on Dixie," *Harper's* 224 (May 1962): 27–33.

Longaker, Richard B. *The Presidency and Individual Liberties.* Ithaca: Cornell University Press, 1961.

Lord, Donald C. *John F. Kennedy: The Politics of Confrontation and Conciliation.* New York: Barron's, 1977.

Lord, Walter. *The Past That Would Not Die.* New York: Harper and Row, 1965.

Lyon, Peter. *Eisenhower: Portrait of the Hero.* Boston: Little, Brown, 1974.

McAdam, Doug. *Political Process and the Development of Black Insurgency, 1930–1970.* Chicago: University of Chicago Press, 1982.

McLemore, Leslie. "The Mississippi Freedom Democratic Party: A Case Study of Grass Roots Politics." Ph.D. diss., University of Massuchusetts, 1971.

MacNeil, Neil. *Dirksen: A Portrait of a Public Man.* New York: World, 1970.

McPherson, Harry. "Johnson and Civil Rights." In *The Kennedy Presidency: Seventeen Intimate Perspectives of John F. Kennedy.* Portraits of American Presidents, ed. Kenneth W. Thompson, vol. 4. Lanham, Md.: University Press of America, 1985.

———. *A Political Education.* Boston: Little, Brown, 1972.

Marshall, Burke. "Congress, Communication, and Civil Rights." In *The Kennedy Presidency: Seventeen Intimate Perspectives of John F. Kennedy.* Portraits of American Presidents, ed. Kenneth W. Thompson, vol. 4. Lanham, Md.: University Press of America, 1985.

———. *Federalism and Civil Rights.* New York: Columbia University Press, 1964.

———. "Federal Protection of Negro Voting Rights." *Law and Contemporary Problems* 27 (1962): 455–467.

Martin, Louis. "Organizing Civil Rights." In *The Kennedy Presidency: Seventeen Intimate Perspectives of John F. Kennedy.* Portraits of American Presidents, ed. Kenneth W. Thompson, vol. 4. Lanham, Md.: University Press of America, 1985.

Martin, Ralph G., and Ed Plant. *Front Runner, Dark Horse.* Garden City, N.Y.: Doubleday, 1960.

Matusow, Allen J. *The Unravelling of America: A History of Liberalism in the 1960's.* New York: Harper and Row, 1984.

Meier, August. "Who Are the 'True Believers'? A Tentative Typology of the Motivations of Civil Rights Activists, 1965." In *Protest, Reform, and Revolt: A Reader in Social Movements,* ed. Joseph R. Gusfield. New York: Wiley, 1970.

Meier, August, and Elliot Rudwick. *CORE: A Study of the Civil Rights Movement.* Urbana: University of Illinois Press, 1975.

Miller, Merle. *Lyndon: An Oral Biography.* New York: Putnam, 1980.

Miroff, Bruce. *Pragmatic Liberalism: The Presidential Politics of John F. Kennedy.* New York: David McKay, 1976.

———. "Presidential Leverage over Social Movements: The Johnson White House and Civil Rights." *Journal of Politics* 43 (1981): 2–23.

Mooney, Booth. *LBJ: An Irreverent Chronicle.* New York: Crowell, 1976.

Morris, Aldon D. *The Origins of the Civil Rights Movement: Black Communities Organizing for Change.* New York: Free Press, 1984.

Moyers, Bill. Letter to Mark Stern, 27 August 1985, Copy in possession of Mark Stern.

Muse, Benjamin. *The American Negro Revolution: From Nonviolence to Black Power.* Indianapolis: Indiana University Press, 1968.

————. *Ten Years of Prelude: The Story of Integration since the Supreme Court's 1954 Decision.* New York: Viking, 1964.

Myrdal, Gunnar. *An American Dilemma.* New York: Harper, 1944.

Navasky, Victor S. *Kennedy Justice.* New York: Atheneum, 1977.

Nixon, Richard M. *Six Crises.* Garden City, N.Y.: Doubleday, 1962.

O'Brien, Lawrence. *No Final Victories: A Life in Politics from John F. Kennedy to Watergate.* Garden City, N.Y.: Doubleday, 1974.

O'Donnell, Kenneth P., David F. Powers, and Joe McCarthy. *Johnny We Hardly Knew Ye: Memories of John Fitzgerald Kennedy.* New York: Pocket Books, 1973.

O'Neill, Tip, and William Novak. *Man of the House: The Life and Political Memoirs of Speaker Tip O'Neill.* New York: Random House, 1987.

Parker, Frank R. *Black Votes Count: Political Empowerment in Mississippi after 1965.* Chapel Hill: University of North Carolina, 1990.

Parmet, Herbert S. *The Presidency of John Fitzgerald Kennedy.* New York: Penguin, 1983.

Phillips, Kevin P. *The Emerging Republican Majority.* Garden City, N.Y.: Anchor, 1970.

Polsby, Nelson W. *Political Innovation in America: The Politics of Policy Initiation.* New Haven: Yale University Press, 1984.

Pomper, Gerald M. "From Confusion to Clarity: Issues and American Voters, 1952–1968." *American Political Science Review* 66 (1972): 415–428.

Powers, Richard Gid. *Secrecy and Power: The Life of J. Edgar Hoover.* New York: Free Press, 1987.

Raines, Howell. *My Soul Is Rested: The Story of the Civil Rights Movement in the Deep South.* New York: Penguin, 1983.

Rauh, Joseph L. Letter to Joyce Tucker, 29 May 1988, Copy in possession of Mark Stern.

Reedy, George E. *Lyndon B. Johnson: A Memoir.* New York: Andrews and McMeel, 1982.

Report of the National Advisory Commission on Civil Disorders. New York: Bantam, 1968.

Riccards, Michael P. "Rare Counsel: Kennedy, Johnson, and the Civil Rights Bill of 1963." *Presidential Studies Quarterly* 11 (1981): 395–398.

Ripley, Randall. *Kennedy and Congress.* Morristown, N.J.: General Learning Press, 1972.

Roosevelt, Eleanor. *On My Own.* New York: Harper and Row, 1958.

Rothschild, Mary A. *A Case of Black and White: Northern Volunteers and the Southern Freedom Summers.* Westport, Conn.: Greenwood, 1982.

"Roundtable of Participants in the Passage of the Civil Rights Act of 1964." Annual Meeting of the American Political Science Association, 1 September 1989. Author's notes.

Runyon, John H., Jennifer Verdini, and Sally S. Runyon, comps. and eds. *Source Book of American Presidential Campaign and Election Statistics, 1948–1968.* New York: Ungar, 1971.

Rusher, William A. *The Rise of the Right.* New York: Morrow, 1984.

Sarratt, Reed. *The Ordeal of Desegregation: The First Decade*. New York: Harper and Row, 1966.

Schattschneider, E. E. *The Semi-Sovereign People: A Realist's View of Democracy*. Hinsdale, Ill.: Dryden, 1975.

Scheele, Henry. *Charlie Halleck: A Political Biography*. New York: Exposition Press, 1966.

Schlesinger, Arthur M., Jr. *Robert Kennedy and His Times*. New York: Ballantine, 1978.

———. *A Thousand Days: John F. Kennedy in the White House*. New York: Fawcett Crest, 1965.

Siegenthaler, John. "Civil Rights in the Trenches." In *The Kennedy Presidency: Seventeen Intimate Perspectives of John F. Kennedy*. Portraits of American Presidents, ed. Kenneth W. Thompson, vol. 4. Lanham, Md.: University Press of America, 1985.

Sigel, Roberta S. "Race and Religion as Factors in the Kennedy Victory in Detroit, 1960." *Journal of Negro Education* 31 (1962): 436–448.

Silver, James W. *Mississippi: The Closed Society*. New York: Harcourt, Brace, and World, 1966.

Sitkoff, Harvard. "Harry Truman and the Election of 1948: The Coming of Age of Civil Rights in American Politics." *Journal of Southern History* 37 (1971): 597–616.

———. *A New Deal for Blacks: The Emergence of Civil Rights as a National Issue, the Depression Decade*. New York: Oxford University Press, 1978.

———. *The Struggle for Black Equality, 1954–1980*. New York: Hill and Wang, 1981.

Solberg, Carl. *Hubert H. Humphrey: A Biography*. New York: Norton, 1984.

Sonenshein, Raphael J. "Can Black Candidates Win Statewide Elections?" *Political Science Quarterly* 105 (1990): 219–242.

Sorenson, Theodore C. *Kennedy*. New York: Bantam, 1966.

———. "The Values of John F. Kennedy: Retrospect and Prospect." In *Six Virginia Papers Presented at the Miller Center Forums, 1984*, ed. Kenneth W. Thompson. Lanham, Md.: University Press of America, 1985.

Southern Regional Council. *The Federal Executive and Civil Rights*. Atlanta: Southern Regional Council, 1961.

"Statistical Summary of School Segregation—Desegregation in the Southern and Border States." Nashville: Southern Education Reporting Service, 1962.

Steinberg, Alfred. *Mrs. R.: The Life of Eleanor Roosevelt*. New York: Putnam, 1958.

———. *Sam Johnson's Boy*. New York: Macmillan, 1968.

Stern, Gerald M. "Judge Harold Cox and the Right to Vote in Clarke County." In *Southern Justice*, ed Leon Friedman, 165–186. New York: Pantheon, 1965.

Stewart, John G. "Independence and Control: The Challenge of Senatorial Party Leadership." Ph.D. diss., University of Chicago, 1968.

———. "Two Strategies of Leadership: Johnson and Mansfield." In *Congres-*

sional Behavior, ed. Nelson W. Polsby, 61–92. New York: Random House, 1971.

Sundquist, James L. *Dynamics of the Party System: Alignment and Realignment of Political Parties in the United States*. rev. ed. Washington, D.C.: Brookings Institution, 1983.

———. *Politics and Policy: The Eisenhower, Kennedy, and Johnson Years*. Washington, D.C.: Brookings Institution, 1968.

Thernstrom, Abigail M. *Whose Votes Count? Affirmative Action and Minority Voting Rights*. Cambridge: Harvard University Press, 1987.

Viorst, Milton. *Fire in the Streets: America in the 1960's*. New York: Touchstone, 1981.

Wagy, Thomas R. "Governor LeRoy Collins of Florida and the Selma Crisis of 1965." *Florida Historical Quarterly* 57 (1979): 403–420.

Walton, Hanes. *Black Political Parties*. New York: Free Press, 1972.

Watters, Pat. *Down to Now: Reflections on the Southern Civil Rights Movement*. New York: Pantheon, 1971.

Watters, Pat, and Reese Cleghorn. *Climbing Jacob's Ladder: The Arrival of Negroes in Southern Politics*. New York: Harcourt, Brace, and World, 1967.

Weiss, Nancy J. *Farewell to the Party of Lincoln: Black Politics in the Age of FDR*. Princeton: Princeton University Press, 1983.

Whalen, Charles, and Barbara Whalen. *The Longest Debate: The Legislative History of the 1964 Civil Rights Act*. Washington, D.C.: Seven Locks, 1985.

Whalen, Richard J. *The Founding Father: The Story of Joseph P. Kennedy*. New York: New American Library, 1964.

White, F. Clifton. *Suite 3505*. New Rochelle, N.Y.: Arlington House, 1967.

White, Theodore H. *The Making of the President, 1960*. New York: New American Library, 1961.

———. *The Making of the President, 1964*. New York: Atheneum, 1965.

White, William S. *The Professional: Lyndon B. Johnson*. Boston: Houghton Mifflin, 1964.

Wicker, Tom. *JFK and LBJ: The Influence of Personality upon Politics*. Baltimore: Penguin, 1962.

Wildavsky, Aaron. "The Goldwater Phenomenon: Purists, Politicians, and the Two-Party System." *Review of Politics* 27 (1965): 386–413.

Wilkins, Roy, and Tom Mathews. *Standing Fast: The Autobiography of Roy Wilkins*. Baltimore: Penguin, 1984.

Wofford, Harris, Jr. *Of Kennedys and Kings: Making Sense of the Sixties*. New York: Farrar, Strauss, Giroux, 1980.

———. "Notre Dame Conference on Civil Rights: A Contribution to the Development of Public Law." *Notre Dame Lawyer* 35 (1960): 328–367.

Woodward, C. Vann. *The Strange Career of Jim Crow*. 2d ed. New York: Oxford University Press, 1966.

Zinn, Howard. "Kennedy the Reluctant Emancipator." *Nation* 195 (1 December 1962): 373–376.

———. *SNCC: The New Abolitionists*. Boston: Beacon, 1964.

Index